THE WAR IN THE YEMEN

by the same author

*

KOREA: 1950–1953

THE ALGERIAN INSURRECTION 1954–62

MALAYA: The Communist-Insurgent War 1948–60

THE GREEK CIVIL WAR 1944–1949

THE INDO-CHINA WAR (1945–54): A Study in Guerilla Warfare

THE RED ARMY OF CHINA

THE ARAB-ISRAELI WAR

THE SINAI CAMPAIGN 1956

THE STORY OF THE FRENCH FOREIGN LEGION

THE RED ARMY

The War in the Yemen

EDGAR O'BALLANCE

ARCHON BOOKS
Hamden, Connecticut
1971

First edition published
in the United States
1971
Archon Books

ISBN 0 208 01038 6
Printed in Great Britain

Preface

I first visited the Yemen in 1948. In those days it was ruled with barbaric despotism by Imam Ahmed, and of all the countries I had travelled in, none gave me such a feeling of being suddenly carried back in time to the Middle Ages. Apart from the firearms and a few battered trucks and cars, the scene must have been unchanged for many centuries, and the description given by John Jourdain, the first Englishman to visit and write about Sana in 1609, was as 'contemporary' in 1948 as it was then. Progress had avoided the Yemen. The gates of the walled cities were locked at sunset every day, remaining closed until dawn. Punishments were primitive and salutary: those who displeased the Imam or his officials were cast into dungeons, without trial and for indefinite periods; hands were cut off for theft. Slavery was part of the accepted pattern of life.

If ever a country was ripe for revolution and political change it was the Yemen; and when in 1962 a group of Yemeni revolutionaries effected a *coup d'état*, assisted by President Nasser, the only surprise was that it had been delayed so long. Since then, a dragging civil war has been in progress, about which many misconceptions have arisen.

The war has served to highlight the inherent suspicions Arab states, statesmen and factions have for each other, since it is after all only part of the larger Middle East struggle for power and domination. The picture that has been brought back to the West is a rather fictitious one of a dethroned Imam sheltering in the mountains with his people braving poison gas, bombs, and Egyptian air raids, glowing with shining ideals and defying the unpopular Nasser with nothing but knives and ancient firearms.

If this account seems a little hard on the Royalists, I should say that I hold no brief for either side, and indeed have criticized both the Yemeni Republicans and the Egyptians in the Yemen equally severely. But the results of my observations and research has not confirmed the somewhat rosy view which the West has taken of the Imam and his cause. Not a great deal is known about the aims and ideals of the various Yemeni personalities involved, but it must be borne in mind that the Royalists have several prominent protagonists who have presented a romanticized picture to Western audiences of the Royalist struggle against Nasser. What has not been sufficiently emphasized is that the Imam was an autocratic ruler seeking to re-impose his domination on his country. It is openly admitted that some countries and political causes, the Royalists among them, employ public relations consultants to burnish their image, and the image of the Royalist cause has been burnished beyond recognition. It is of interest to note that, at the time of writing, Britain still recognizes the Imam as the Head of State in the Yemen.

Hours after the *coup* of 1962, Egyptian troops were being flown into the Yemen to support Colonel as-Sallal, who had emerged as the revolutionary leader; and they remained until December 1967, when after his disastrous defeat by the Israelis in June of that year Nasser was forced to evacuate completely. As soon as Egyptian assistance was given to the Republicans, King Saud of Saudi Arabia sent money and arms to the Royalists, a policy that was continued by his successor, King Faisal, although he had a low opinion of Imam Mohammed al-Badr, the Royalist leader. In the Yemen the UAR and Saudi Arabia fought each other by proxy.

In the spring of 1963, Field Marshal Amer in a smart campaign brought two-thirds of the Yemen under Republican control. Later Royalist pushes and UAR withdrawals reduced this area to about half, which with only slight variations has remained the proportion held by each side ever since. That neither side has been able to defeat the other can be ascribed to the nature of the terrain and the imbalance of arms. Cease-fire and other agreements were blatantly broken by both sides whenever they thought they could obtain some advantage by doing so, while throughout, Nasser manipulated as-Sallal and other Yemeni Republican leaders like puppets, detaining them when they displeased him or were of no further use. He engineered as-Sallal's downfall in November 1967.

The Soviet Union, in its quest for influence and naval bases in the Red Sea to further its new strategy of showing a naval presence in the Middle East and the Persian Gulf, has stepped into the shoes of the departed Egyptians. Soviet arms were rushed to the Republicans, enabling Hassan al-Amri, who emerged as the 'strong man', to hold out in the now famous siege of Sana, when mountain tribesmen concentrated to plunder that city. Forming a militia and arming the citizens, Hassan al-Amri fought them off, thus thwarting the Royalists' last real chance of a victory. After this siege the country again settled down to its former military stalemate.

I hope this account, which at the time of writing is the first comprehensive one to be completed on the Yemen War, will give a glimpse into what recently was, and to some extent still is, probably the last genuinely medieval country and people left in the world today.

Edgar O'Ballance

Acknowledgements

As there is no comprehensive bibliography on the Yemen, or in particular, on the civil war in the Yemen, I have had to rely mainly upon my own practical researches, observations and interviews, both in the Yemen and elsewhere, to gain material and impressions for this book. But I have read with interest, enjoyment and gain, the following works, and I make grateful acknowledgement to the authors, editors or compilers of them.

CLAUDIE FAYEIN, *A French Doctor in the Yemen*, Robert Hale (1957)

THORKILD HANSEN, *Arabia Felix*, Collins (1964)

HANS HELFRITZ, *The Yemen: A Secret Journey*, Allen & Unwin (1958)

DAVID HOLDEN, *Farewell to Arabia*, Faber & Faber (1966)

CARL VON HORN, *Soldiering for Peace*, Cassell (1966)

DAVID HOWARTH, *The Desert King*, Collins (1964)

HAROLD INGRAMS, *The Yemen*, John Murray (1963)

CHARLES JOHNSTON, *The View from Steamer Point*, Collins (1964)

TOM LITTLE, *South Arabia: Arena of Conflict*, Pall Mall (1968)

ERIC MACRO, *Yemen and the Western World since 1571*, C. Hurst, London (1968)

D. VAN DER MEULEN, *Faces in Shem*, John Murray (1961)

WENDELL PHILLIPS, *Qataban and Sheba*, Victor Gollancz (1955)

DANA ADAMS SCHMIDT, *The Yemen: Unknown War*, Bodley Head (1968)

Peter Somerville-Large, *Tribes and Tribulations*, Baylis, London (1967)

Freya Stark, *Dust in the Lion's Paw*, John Murray (1961)

Kennedy Trevaskis, *Shades of Amber: A South Arabian Episode*, Hutchinson (1968)

Manfred W. Wenner, *Modern Yemen*, John Hopkins Press, Baltimore (1967)

Contents

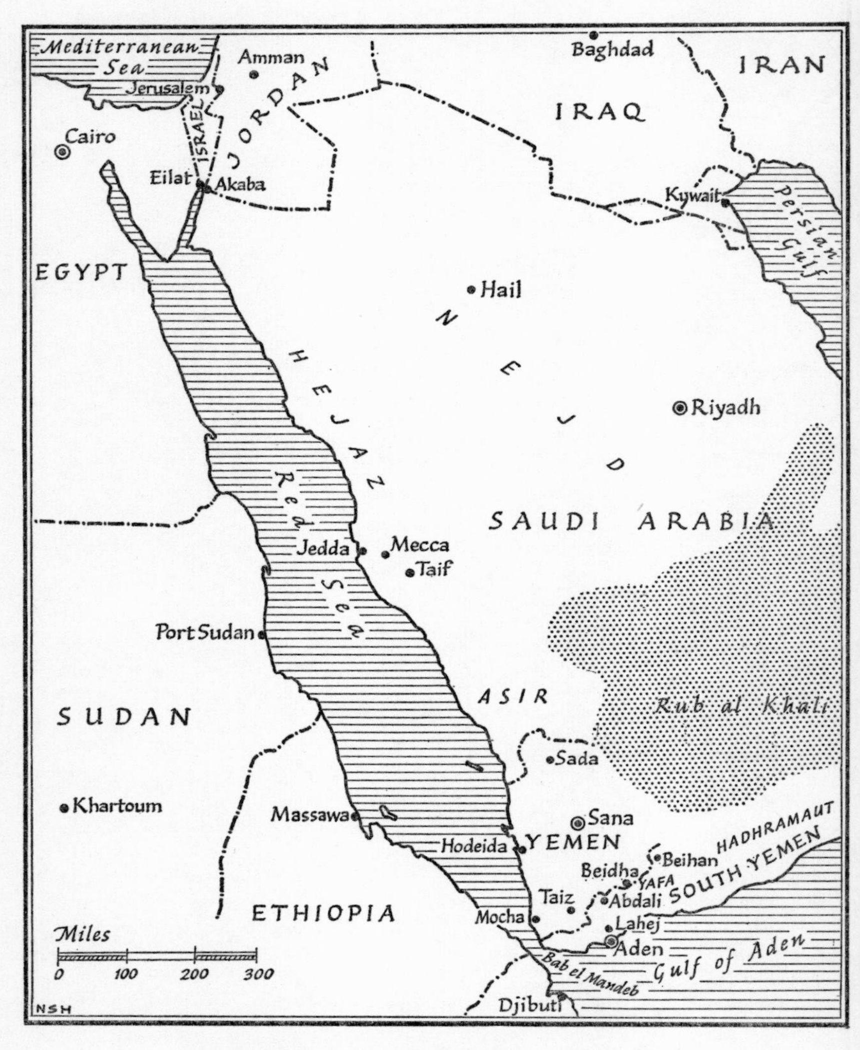

The Middle East showing situation of the Yemen

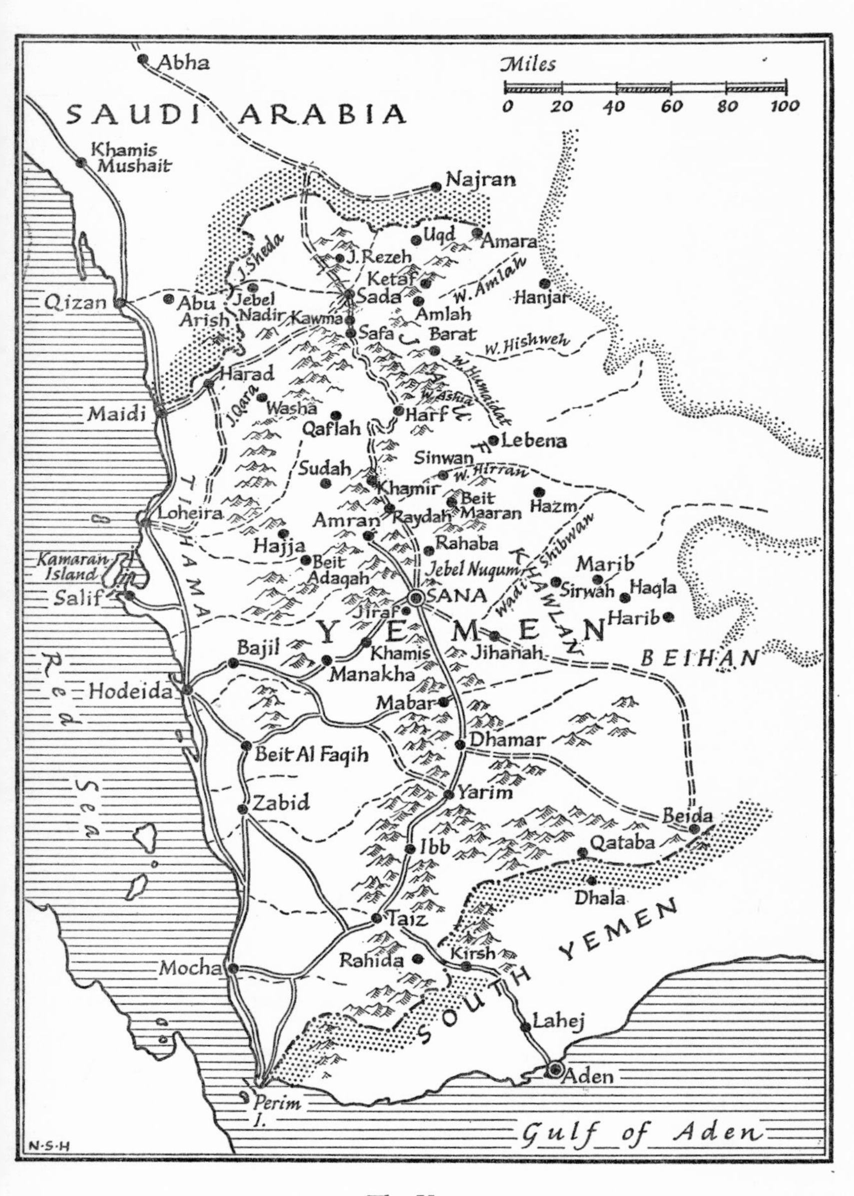
Abha
Miles
0 20 40 60 80 100
SAUDI ARABIA
Khamis Mushait
Najran
Uqd
Amara
J. Sheda
J. Rezeh
Ketaf
W. Amlah
Hanjar
Qizan
Abu Arish
Jebel Nadir
Sada
Amlah
Kawma
Safa
Barat
W. Hishweh
Harad
J. Qara
Washa
W. Humaidat
W. Ashia
Maidi
Qaflah
Harf
Lebena
Sinwan
W. Hirran
Sudah
Khamir
Beit Maaran
Hazm
Loheira
Raydah
Amran
Hajja
Rahaba
Wadi Shibwan
Kamaran Island
Beit Adaqah
Jebel Nuqum
Marib
Salif
Sirwah
Haqla
SANA
Jiraf
Harib
TIHAMA
KHAWLAN
YEMEN
Bajil
Khamis
Jihanah
BEIHAN
Manakha
Red Sea
Hodeida
Mabar
Dhamar
Beit Al Faqih
Yarim
Zabid
Beida
Ibb
Qataba
Dhala
Taiz
SOUTH YEMEN
Rahida
Kirsh
Mocha
Lahej
Aden
Perim I.
Gulf of Aden
N·S·H

The Yemen

CHAPTER ONE

The Yemen

The murder of Imam Yahya in 1948 is a convenient moment at which to stop and take a closer look at the Yemen, its people, government, economics, communications and army. The territory under the Imam's effective control amounted to about 75,000 square miles,[1] near the south-west tip of the Arabian Peninsula. On the west it was bounded by the Red Sea, to the north and the east lay Saudi Arabia, while to the south-east and the south were the (then British) Aden Protectorates. Being about 300 miles wide and 400 miles long, the Yemen can for descriptive purposes be roughly divided into three vertical sections, the coastal plain on the west, the central highlands and the Jauf and the Khawlan regions on the east.

Along the western side, stretching the whole length of the country from north to south, is the coastal plain, known as the Tihama (the ancient Sabaean name for lowland), averaging up to 50 miles in width, and with generally very sparse vegetation, the terrain being mainly sandy and bare. Lying alongside it to the immediate east is a similar strip a further 20 to 40 miles wide, sometimes known as the Upper Tihama, which has some foothills, and rather more fertile valleys. In this account they are collectively referred to as the Tihama, or the coastal plain.

The central region, varying in width from 100 to 200 miles, or even more in the south, is a highland massif, a huge rocky spine, broad at the base and serrated by mountain ranges that rise to over 10,000 feet. The highest mountain in the Yemen, and indeed in the whole of Arabia, is Jebel[2] Shaib, in the south, over

[1] The Yemen is about the size of England and Scotland (without Wales), or the State of either Nebraska or South Dakota. Some authorities insist its area is about 74,000 square miles, but there are disputed regions in the east and north of the country.

[2] Jebel means mountain, or mountain massif.

14,000 feet high. The valleys, or portions of them, are surprisingly fertile. The eastern vertical strip, which is about 100 miles wide, is a plateau which gradually slopes down to the desert sands of the Rub al Khali, the Empty Quarter. It consists of two regions, the northern one known as the Jauf, and the southern as the Khawlan. The vegetation in the valleys gets sparse as one moves eastwards. In the south-east corner in a sector of desert scrub live semi-nomadic tribes. The vast Empty Quarter of shifting sand is a natural defensive barrier, and success in crossing it alive was the exception rather than the rule. It was avoided by all but the most foolhardy.

The climate of the Tihama is hot, rainless and humid near the sea, but in the central highlands the climate is more temperate and the rainfall heavy for Arabia. The Jauf and the Khawlan are much drier and hotter. No rivers or streams contain running water all the year round, but there are many watercourses, especially in the Jauf and the Khawlan, some very wide, that fill briefly during the rainy season. Drinking water is generally obtained from wells. In the winter rainy season, the central highlands are decidedly cool when the sun is not shining, and often very cold at night, depending on one's height above sea level.

Apart from the few semi-nomadic tribes in the south-east, the population of the Yemen (reckoned to be between 4 and 5 million—no one knows for sure as there has never been a census) is a settled one, relying mainly upon agriculture for existence, the valleys producing almost enough for the people to live on. But society is fiercely tribal, and most of the tribes and families have lived in their valleys for generations. In the highlands the people used in the past to supplement their livelihood by extracting toll from passing caravans that used their wells, or by emerging periodically, if they were strong enough, to raid each other or to plunder the towns.

In some places, agricultural activities had softened this fierce tribal way of living, but outside the cities and towns the tribal pattern remained deeply imprinted. About three-quarters of the population lived in the central mountain sector, most of them in its southern part, reaching down to Taiz. The ports, such as they were, had a slightly more cosmopolitan leavening, while the inhabitants of the Tihama plain proper, who relied upon fishing for a living, were darker skinned with more than a trace of negro blood in them. They lived a life more wretched than anywhere else in the Yemen because of the adverse natural conditions. The Upper Tihama was more thickly populated and much more fertile. The port, city and town dwellers were mostly a detribalized mixture: descendants of generations of officials, traders, craftsmen, soldiers, slaves and those who had fled, or been driven, from their tribes. The stock of the inland tribes for centuries had no trace of 'foreign' blood and so they could claim with some authority to be of true Arab descent. This was not true of the cities, towns and ports where darker hues could be seen, and along the coast, also, there were distinct traces of African blood. In the eastern part of the Khawlan, some of the tribes dyed parts of their bodies blue with indigo.

The inhabitants of the mountains looked with contempt on the people of the Tihama, and countrymen everywhere regarded those in cities and towns with envious hostility, their ambition being to have sufficient strength and excuse to attack and plunder them. The cities and towns were entities in themselves, the citizens bound together by the need to protect themselves against unfriendly outsiders. There were great extremes of wealth and poverty, freedom and restraint, in the Yemen, as there were of cruelty and benevolence. Riches and power generated an arrogance towards the materially less fortunate, although the Koranic mandate to give to the poor was observed to some extent. But the cities and towns were crowded with pitiful beggars, who eked out miserable lives on grudging and uncertain charity.

As they were catered for by the Koran, such Yemenis as had been able to afford to do so kept slaves until forced, nominally, to release them by the Turks. Then they merely stayed on as unpaid servants in much the same position as before, as complete release from bondage would have meant merely a beggar's existence in most cases. There was no social stigma attached to being a slave and many rose to positions of responsibility and importance. A few head slaves had become governors of provinces or towns, having found favour with some particular Imam, and indeed the Yemen at times had been ruled by slave dynasties that had risen to power. The Turks had never been able to suppress slavery completely, and it came into the open again when they withdrew. Imam Yahya himself owned a large number of slaves. But slavery was kept to a small proportion by the general poverty of the people, and far more odious was the fact that during Imam Yahya's reign the Yemen was used as a slave route, and to some extent as a slave market and exchange point, for slaves taken in Africa and elsewhere and bound for slave markets in Saudi Arabia. A portion of the toll levied on such traffic, which was still going on in 1948, was paid into the Imam's treasury.

With the exception of the Jews, all the inhabitants of the Yemen were of the Moslem faith, obeying one or other of its two sects which strictly conditioned their way of life and thought. This had not changed since it was imposed upon them about thirteen centuries before. Perhaps in no other place in the world had time stood still for so long with hardly any sign of change or evolution. Nearly half the people, mainly those living in the northern and eastern parts, were Zeidis of the Shia sect, while the remainder were Shafeis, of the Sunni, or Orthodox Moslem, sect. Differences between these two religious divisions were still acute and not helped by the fact that the Zeidi Imam had imposed his temporal authority on the Shafeis, and consolidated his hold by appointing Zeidis to positions of responsibility over them, typical of the domineering Zeidi attitude. Although Zeidis only prayed three times a day, instead of the normal five required of all other Moslems, the Zeidis were more austere and puritanical, considering the Shafeis to be lax. Over the centuries the Zeidis had varying influence and control over the Shafeis, usually dominating them. As a rough rule of thumb, the Shafeis feared and disliked the Zeidis, acquiescing to their demands and frequently bribing them to remain in their good offices or to prevent themselves being plundered. There was also a small community of Ismailis, who had once been a power in the land but had been eclipsed by the Zeidis. There were about 4,000 in all, followers of the Aga Khan, centred around Manakha.

Besides these, there were also large numbers of white, turbaned Seiyids in the Yemen (some authorities alleging as many as 50,000) who claimed descent from the Prophet. Forming an élite class in a theocracy, as in theory they elected the Imams, or at any rate gave the final approval to any Imam who was pro-

elements of reading and writing, but poverty debarred many more, as the Ulema expected to be paid for their educational services. Richer families were able to afford private tutors for their sons, and many achieved a fairly high standard of classical and religious education.

Although Imam Yahya had banned the use of printing presses in his country so that no books or pamphlets, subversive or otherwise, could be produced, he relaxed this restriction to the extent of allowing the publication of a twice-monthly news sheet[1] that circulated chiefly in Sana. Many Imams had a literary bent and some had been quite learned in a donnish way. Yahya must be numbered in their ranks, since it is said that under a *non de plume*, he frequently contributed features and homilies himself to this news sheet. There was no bar on Koranic works and religious treatises being imported into the country, so there was ample reading matter available of a prescribed sort.

According to Moslem custom women in the Yemen were veiled, those of the wealthier and ruling classes being kept in the seclusion of a hareem. Their mission in life was to produce children and to be completely subservient to their husbands, who, if they could afford it, were permitted to have up to the four wives stipulated. Most of the women worked very hard indeed[2] either in the home where, for example, all water had to be drawn from a well, probably some distance away, or in the fields if they lived in the countryside. It was a man's world and education was not for women. Even the most wealthy were completely illiterate. Their opinion or counsel on serious matters was never sought, nor were they permitted to appear in public unless so shrouded that the shape of their bodies was not discernible.

The Yemen was a theocracy autocratically governed by the Imam, who administered his country according to the laws expounded in the Koran and his own personal whims. He kept his throne and extended his authority by playing off one faction and tribe against another, by hostages, bribery and fear, and by instigating or encouraging a counter to any potentially

[1] Known as 'Al-Imam'.

[2] The economically-minded Imam Yahya put the ladies of his hareem to work on making uniforms for his soldiers.

... appointed the more trust- ... relatives and systematically stripped authority from other ambitious families.

Any dissidence against the Imam's authority (and there were many who considered that they or their families had a better right to the throne than Yahya) met with a death penalty and in addition a crippling fine was levied on the family or tribe. Personal fortunes were often summarily confiscated on mere suspicion of disloyalty, perhaps for nothing more than an incautious utterance. Beheading in public was the customary method of execution and the decapitated heads were publicly displayed so that all could see and heed the lesson. Political suspects were kept in prison, in appalling conditions, in fetters, chains or handcuffs, without trial for as long as the Imam thought fit. The dungeons at Sana, Hajja, a northern fortress, and at other provincial capitals, became notorious and dreaded places of confinement. The conditions and practices within these prisons, not excluding torture, would be difficult for a twentieth-century mind to credit.

Mr. Van der Meulen,[1] who was in Sana in 1931 for three months as a Dutch diplomatic representative, and spoke Arabic

[1] *Faces in Shem.*

fluently, wrote of the 'barbaric cruelty, the fear that hung like a pall over everyone, and the utter degradation of the poor and the wretched'. He became a friend of Dr. Petrie, a Scottish doctor who was then working at Sana, and said that in his professional capacity Dr. Petrie had been inside the Imam's prisons, where he had found, shackled, sons of the Imam himself, as well as ... aristocracy and other important Yemenis.

Medical care was something completely unknown to the majority of Yemenis. The Turkish occupation forces had their own military hospitals for their soldiers and officials, but their doctors did not minister to civilians, and when they withdrew they took all these medical facilities with them, leaving merely a small Italian hospital that had been established at Hodeida in 1912. Yahya had accepted European doctors, and two other small elementary hospitals had been set up, one at Sana and the other at Taiz, but the doctors had been more or less compelled to attend to the ruling and wealthier classes, rather than those in direct need. In any case, except for the few European doctors, the Iraqi, Syrian, Egyptian and Moslem ones worked primarily for money, and those who could not pay did not receive medical attention. The three hospitals were chronically short of trained staff, drugs and medicines. The Italian doctors of the 1930's and later the French ones of the 1940's, had nearly all left, slipping away one by one and not returning, owing to unrealistic restrictions and the lack of medical facilities. A Scottish religious medical mission had gone to Sana in 1937, but left in 1943, owing to the appalling working conditions. However, one or two European doctors still remained despite adverse circumstances, but they had to give priority attention to the Imam, his family and friends. A few Egyptian doctors were employed to look after the Seiyid government officials and the soldiers.

Peculiar to the Yemen was the national habit of chewing 'qat', the leaves of a small narcotic bush grown in the country areas. Practically the whole population, especially in the cities and towns, seemed to spend every afternoon, when all business ceased, chewing qat and relaxing. The qat habit, which is reputed to produce a sense of lazy well-being, was bad both for the health of the people and for the economy of the country.

The literacy rate was, for Arabia, fairly high in the cities and towns although lower in the countryside. The Turks had established a few secular schools but these had been repressed when they departed. This meant that there were only two 'high schools' in the country, a situation which led to profound ignorance on the part of most people as to what was happening outside the Yemen. The responsibility for education rested upon the Ulema, who usually taught children in their mosques. The curriculum was Koranic and stilted. Large numbers learnt the

Imam Yahya relied heavily upon the hostage system. It is believed that at the time of his death he held about 4,000 of them, mostly his own relatives, sons of provincial governors, Seiyid families and tribal sheikhs, even representatives from the smaller and semi-nomadic Bedu tribes, who were seized as a surety for the good and loyal behaviour of their parents. Some hostages had been kidnapped from rulers in the Aden Protectorate in order to exert pressure on them. If any of the parents proved to be disloyal or were suspected of plotting against the Imam, the hostage was executed and often tortured into the bargain. It was a system that had been going on in the Yemen for centuries, to one degree or another. It proved to be fairly effective under these barbaric, primitive conditions, and it enabled Imam Yahya to keep his hand firmly on the helm of state. Several authorities assert that Imam Yahya was a benevolent ruler, much loved by his people, but the available evidence hardly seems to support this.

Imam Yahya, like other Imams before him, had developed his own intelligence service so he could know what was happening in all parts of his kingdom and nip in the bud any plot, or revolt. His intelligence service was not the only one in a land without newspapers[1] or radio station. Each provincial governor, Seiyid, tribal sheikh or important government official, had his own secret service to give him information of political shifts and changes, so that he could protect himself and at the same time find out what was going on elsewhere. These intelligence operations naturally varied considerably in scope, efficiency and size, but the Yemen was a land where one power-seeker was forever spying on another power-seeker.

[1] Except the news sheet mentioned. The radio station at Hodeida did not broadcast to the people, being used only for government communication purposes. It was not until 1950 that a radio station was installed at Sana, and began broadcasting.

Although, in 1944, the Imam had divided his kingdom up into four, and then, a few months later, into six, regions,[1] and appointed a governor to each, these governors had very limited freedom of action, as in his single-minded determination to centralize control in his own hands the Imam insisted on being consulted on every detail, no matter how trivial. Yahya did not trust anyone with power, with the possible exception of his son, Crown Prince Ahmed, and took all decisions himself. This meant that the business of government was painfully slow. All requests were written down formally on a piece of paper and handed to the Imam, who, after glancing at them, wrote his decision on the back, or above the script. In his prime it was said that he dealt with up to 300 such requests daily; but in the latter years of his life, when he was a sick man, it could have only been a fraction of that number. The devious process (riddled with bribery and evasiveness) by which requests reached the Imam and were returned from him, made things that much slower. Ministers of State, who were either his relations or friends, were similarly unable to make any move without his prior permission. In foreign affairs the Imam was advised by Ragheb Bey, an old Turkish ex-diplomat[2] whom he trusted and who had been in his service since 1919, but he too had absolutely no freedom of action.

The skeletal civil service was run first by the Turks employed by Yahya, and then by Iraqis, Palestinians and men from other Middle East countries, but no matter how skilful, competent or trusted, they remained powerless to make departmental or individual decisions. When the Imam was ill, engaged on other business, or pleasure bent, the government machine practically stopped as no official, even a regional governor, dared create a precedent by acting without the

[1] These were based on Sana, Taiz, Hodeida, Ibb, Sada and Hajja.

[2] Mohammed Ragheb Bey, who also served his successor, died in Sana in 1960, when nearly eighty years of age. He was a famous character, known outside the Yemen because it was his duty to interview and keep an eye on all foreigners visiting the country. Several Westerners, who have written accounts of their contacts with this old gentleman, report him as having been a courteous, but cautious and evasive old fox. He had served in Paris and Rome as a Turkish diplomat before 1914, and had found himself in the Yemen during World War I, after which he entered, and remained in, the Imam's service. One of his daughters married Crown Prince Ahmed.

Imam's direct authority. This usually consisted of some sentences scribbled on a piece of paper that passed through so many grubby hands before it reached its destination that the message was sometimes very nearly indecipherable. No state records were kept.

For the ordinary people the laws of the land were simple and clear, and punishments for infringement often barbaric. For theft, a hand could be chopped off[1] and perhaps nailed up in a public place as a visual warning, and for a second conviction the other hand too might be amputated, thus reducing the unfortunate individual to a life of beggary. For slander, the tongue could be cut out. Sometimes a foot was chopped off for a religious or civil offence, while the practice of affixing fetters around the ankles for a period of time for misdemeanours, or until a debt was paid off, or merely for incurring higher displeasure, was commonplace. People accepted their lot philosophically and went hobbling about their daily tasks.

Murder was often a matter between the families concerned. The Imam, or his qadis, the appointed judges, were only brought in when it was a question of unsatisfactory compensation, and the murderer's life could be declared forfeit, depending upon a variety of factors that might seem illogical to a Western mind. The murdered man's relations could demand the death penalty in all cases, but this prejudiced compensation, and sometimes the Imam or his qadis would intercede and urge them to be merciful.

Alcoholic drink, music and dancing were considered foreign and ungodly evils and forbidden, but it is more than likely that these evils were occasionally sampled by a few younger members of the richer classes in the strict privacy of their own houses. The Jews were a discreet source of forbidden alcohol, since they were allowed to make it for themselves in their own ghettos.[2] The radio had invariably made its appearance in many houses, despite official disapproval, but it was not allowed to be played in any public place.

[1] Ironically, the Minister of Health was responsible for executions and judicial amputations.

[2] I was once shown a large pile of empty spirit bottles, mainly South African brandy as far as I could make out, in a disused house in Sana, which was pointed out by a Republican guide as evidence of the decadence of the Imam's regime.

The basic foreign policy of Imam Yahya had been one of isolation, with only the briefest possible contact with other countries. Reluctantly, he joined both the Arab League and the United Nations, but refused to allow resident foreign diplomats in the Yemen, although from time to time diplomatic missions and representatives visited him or his Ministers by invitation or arrangement, and some of the European or Middle Eastern traders at Hodeida acted as unofficial contacts with foreign countries. Yahya did send a small delegation to the UN, but at the time of his death he had only one ambassador abroad, in Cairo.

Arabs and other Moslems from Middle East countries, and even Turks, seemed to be able to find employment in the Yemen without undue difficulty, although most were put off because the pay and conditions were poor and salaries usually in arrears. Turkish, Iraqi, Indian, Syrian and Palestinian personnel had at various times been employed by Yahya in the civil service, the army, and as technicians. He seemed to fear that foreign influence and contacts would upset the established and traditional way of life in the Yemen (in which, of course, he had such a deeply vested interest) but at the same time he appreciated their skills.

There had always been a general bar against the entry into the Yemen of Europeans and Westerners, traditionally on the score that they were heathens and idolaters, but this ban was sometimes briefly, and surprisingly, lifted by various Imams. Over the years many Westerners had set foot in Hodeida, mainly in the course of trade, and some of them had lived there for long periods, but not many had been permitted to penetrate inland. In recent centuries a few managed to do so, but we don't know what their purpose was, how they fared, or whether they returned safely. A handful of written accounts has come down to us, so we know of the experiences of some of them: the Englishman John Jourdain, who reached Sana in 1609, a Danish-financed party of six in the mid-eighteenth century, and one or two others in the nineteenth century. In the fifty years before 1948, a fair number of Europeans reached Sana, saw other parts of the Yemen away from the coast, and returned to write about their experiences. While not exactly welcoming travellers, the Yemen was not quite such a closed country to Westerners as popular imagination would have it, and in the two decades following World War I, scores of people went there briefly as doctors, technicians, traders, concession-hunters, arms-dealers and the like. Many were not anxious to advertise the fact that they had slipped into the Yemen at all.

The Imam's policy on allowing his subjects to leave the country was an obtuse one, with one law for the poor and another for the rich. He certainly could not prevent hundreds of poor Yemenis emigrating to find work every year as sailors, traders and labourers as they had been doing long before he came into power. Small, expatriate colonies of them had grown up not only in Aden, Somalia, the Sudan and Saudi Arabia, but also in Baghdad, Port Said, Cairo and such faraway ports as Marseilles and Cardiff. There has for a long time been a small Yemeni colony in London's dockland. These Yemenis sent money home to their families, and although there was no bar to their return, most preferred to live under milder and safer political regimes. The few who did return kept their mouths shut about what they had seen in the outside world, and behaved with discretion. Occasionally in the Yemen I came across a Yemeni who spoke English or French, with a coarse, dockland accent.

In Turkish days there had been the opportunity for wealthier families to send their sons to be educated in Constantinople or wherever else they fancied, but such was the insular atmosphere that few took advantage of this freedom. When he assumed control, Imam Yahya clamped down on this, and for some years no young Yemeni was allowed to leave the country to be educated abroad at all. In fact, for a while, the only valid excuse for leaving the Yemen was that of requiring urgent specialist medical attention. Yahya realized what an unsettling influence young Yemenis educated abroad might have on the way of life and thought in his country.

But eventually he was persuaded to modify this stern rule and in the early 1930's he allowed the first group of specially selected young Yemeni men go to Iraq for further education, mostly at the Military Academy. The suspicious behaviour of those who returned, made Imam Yahya turn away from Iraq and instead favour Egypt, where he approved of the religious education given at the Al Azhar Islamic University in Cairo.

Eventually there arose a small band of Yemenis who had been trained abroad, mostly as military officers and engineers[1] but also a few who had received a classical university education. On returning home these foreign-educated Yemenis, extremely restricted in the way they employed their abilities, wisely kept their thoughts and opinions to themselves. Most fell back languidly into the old medieval pattern of life.

Agriculturally the Yemen was self-sufficient, but that was about all that could be said for it, since the economy of the country was run on extremely haphazard lines. Overmuch is made by some writers of the fertility of the Yemen.[2] It was true that the fertile valleys and small plains were intensely cultivated, the best soil being terraced and irrigated and the yields fairly high for Arabia as a whole, but it could not be compared with output in agricultural areas anywhere else in the world. And of course, the cultivated part was only a tiny percentage of the whole, compared with the vast tracts of barren mountain mass and desert. Enough food was produced to feed the population adequately, given an even distribution, but much was exported and in the less rich agricultural sectors the people barely had enough to eat. Again, agricultural methods were extremely primitive and wasteful, exemplified by the crude ox-drawn ploughs still used to till the land.

The main crops were millet, maize, oats and sorghum, and there were ample fruits of many kinds. The main export was coffee, which grew best at altitudes of between 4,000 and 5,000 feet above sea level, and of which over 20,000 tons were shipped overseas annually. Other exports included qat, hides and cotton, and in return the Yemen mainly imported consumer goods like cloth, petrol and small items of machinery. There were no factories in the kingdom, only scattered cottage industries: soap-making, saddle-making and the manufacture of such items as shoes, daggers, jewellery and domestic utensils, most of them relying heavily on Jewish craftsmanship. Although electric and motor power had come to the Yemen and been reluctantly

[1] There do not seem to have been any Yemenis trained as doctors during Imam Yahya's regime.

[2] The 'lost' province of Asir to the north was far more fertile than any part of the Yemen, being the only place in Arabia to have running streams all the year round.

accepted by the Imam, their potential was barely touched, except to light a few Royal Palaces, pump water from private wells and provide transport for the Imam and his officials.

There was no national budget, the whole revenue of the state being regarded as the private income of the ruler; although part of it was expected to be reserved for religious purposes, having been donated to the Imam, or levied by him, in his spiritual capacity. Money was raised by customs duties, tithes, fines, a head tax, confiscation of private fortunes and property, arbitrary taxation based on the amount the tribe or individual would pay without actively rebelling, and the profits of the state-run postal, telegraph and transport services. All government employees were looked upon as the Imam's personal servants, and he was expected to pay them himself from his income. Imam Yahya was careful in money matters and had acquired a reputation of being a miser. Rumours circulated that his treasury was extremely rich, which may not have been altogether true. The Imam himself probably did not know how much money he possessed, since no accounts were kept. He certainly squeezed his subjects as hard as he could and paid out as little as possible, the salaries of his officials and servants being usually well in arrears.

There was no banking system in the Yemen, and indeed no bank, not even a foreign one. All financial transactions were carried out in cash, the monetary unit being the Maria Theresa thaler, or dollar. The actual coin was a silver replica of the old Austrian Maria Theresa thaler with the date 1780[1] also faithfully reproduced. It was a coin which for some inexplicable reason had gained widespread popularity, not only in the Yemen, but in other parts of Arabia too, and indeed is still much favoured. Its popularity is additionally puzzling as Moslems are forbidden to reproduce the likeness of any living form of man or animal, and keep their womenfolk well hidden from other male eyes. The coins were latterly minted at Sana and Taiz, although previously quantities had been minted in Europe. Merchants had to keep sackfuls of these silver coins for their business transactions, while Government servants, for example, often had to go to the Treasury with a camel or a mule to collect

[1] A die with the date 1751 was also used.

their wages in bulk. British gold sovereigns also circulated and were accepted, if to a lesser extent.

Lack of good, or even adequate, communications retarded development in the Yemen, and of the few roads worthy of the name, most had been made passable by the Turks for military purposes. The Turks had introduced and used a few motor vehicles, but took them when they left, so that none remained except a handful at Hodeida, owned by foreign traders. When he visited the Imam in 1923, Lieutenant-Colonel Jacob took a Ford car to Sana and gave it to the Imam, who after initial hesitation accepted and rode in it, and other cars later on, although generally preferring to be driven about his capital in a ramshackle old horse-drawn carriage. As soon as it was seen that the Imam had approved of this foreign invention,[1] princes and rich merchants began to acquire them, and provincial governors and officials who had to travel long distances from city to city began to appreciate their value. Gradually a sort of nationalized transport concern developed, operated at a profit by the Imam, to carry passengers and goods. To enable this to function, the villagers living beside the main roads were made responsible for keeping their section passable and were fined heavily for any neglect, but, despite this, motoring in the Yemen remained an exciting and unpredictable hazard.

Elsewhere there existed only age-old tracks along which passed camel trains, mules and donkeys. The terrain of parts of the central mountain massif had only to be seen from the air, or in an aerial photograph, for one to realize that large areas were literally impassable, even to people on foot, the trace of the paths being channelled inexorably by the sharp, jagged ridges and huge outcrops of rock. Provincial cities, such as Sada, Hajja, Marib, Ibb and Manakha, were situated at the junction of tracks and so were in commanding positions.

The Imam would not allow any railways to be constructed in

[1] The other 'foreign' invention thoroughly approved of was the rifle. I once listened to a Zeidi Seiyid discoursing on foreign evils that were corrupting Yemeni youth, such as the radio, insisting that no good could possibly come of anything 'foreign'. When asked about the rifle, he was surprised at the question, being fully convinced it had been invented by a Moslem (from Iraq, he thought) inspired by Allah. When the maker's trade mark on the Mauser rifle one of his followers was carrying was pointed out to him, he thought it was a Moslem good luck symbol.

his country, and had rejected the British project to build one from Aden to Sana. The Turks had favoured a railway from Hodeida to Sana, and the French had become interested in the idea. In 1908 they laid a five-mile stretch at Hodeida, where they were carrying out some harbour improvements. It functioned with a couple of engines and a few carriages, but when the port was shelled by the Italians in 1912[1] nothing further was done, and, probably as the result of sabotage to the Hejaz Railway in the desert during World War I, the Turks turned to motor transport whenever possible instead of relying on the vulnerable railway track.

A single telegraph line had been laid by the Turks between the main cities and frontier posts, which was still maintained and used by the Yemenis, enabling the Imam to have direct contact with his provincial governors and military detachments. The line could be used by civilians, but the Imam made a heavy charge, which together with his postal charges, helped to swell his revenues. Yahya had constantly refused to allow a national, or even local, telephone system to be installed in his country, although World War I field telephones were used in his palaces, by soldiers on guard at the city gates at Sana and Taiz, and in some other places by the army. A small radio station had been established at Hodeida under the Turks in 1912, and this was taken over by Yemenis in 1925, when the Imam entered that city and employed French technicians to run it. The French also offered to install radio stations at Sana and Taiz, and the Imam toyed with the idea. Contracts were placed and some crates of equipment arrived, but the Imam changed his mind, so the equipment lay rusting and unused. The telegraph remained Yahya's only instant communication means over long distances until after World War II, when small radio stations were established at Sana, Taiz and Sada. But these, as I've said, were used only for official intercommunication, and not for broadcasting to the Yemeni people.

The first half dozen aircraft were taken to the Yemen in 1926 by the Italians. The Imam showed an interest, a few rough landing strips were levelled near the main cities and a small flying school was opened. The aircraft were used to ferry high

[1] The Italians also shelled Mocha and Sheikh Said the same year.

officials and personages from one place to another, and all went well until a plane crashed, killing a Royal prince. The aircraft were then grounded and left to deteriorate on airfields, and the Imam's interest in flying was not revived until 1946, when he was persuaded to buy a few aeroplanes from Egypt and Sweden, and to hire foreign pilots to fly them. An elementary workshop was set up at Taiz, and the main landing strips that had fallen into disuse were again made serviceable, others being constructed at Sada, Hajja, Yarim and other provincial cities. The Imam later bought three Dakotas, and by 1950 a somewhat irregular air service was developing between Sana, Taiz and Hodeida, from Aden, and from African and Arab airports.

The small trading ships of several nations called at Yemeni ports, mainly Hodeida[1] which had been improved by both French and Italian concerns during the early years of this century, although its facilities had declined since the Turks left. Coral reefs made the harbour dangerous, and ships had to stand off shore and be unloaded by lighter. Added to this, Hodeida had no good wells and the drinking water had to be brought to the city by a 'sweet water' canal. The port of Mocha had run right down and been allowed to silt up, because the fresh water springs had failed, but there were several other small ports, such as Salif, Loheira and Maidi, each of which carried on a certain amount of mercantile trade. The Imam privately owned a fleet of about a dozen coastal ships which traded between Aden, Suez, Jedda and Djibuti, and he periodically put an embargo on the overland Aden to the Yemen trade routes for his personal gain.

In military matters Yemeni thinking, strategy and tactics reflected to some extent the general Arab principles of warfare. It was based on a sudden dawn attack on the enemy's sleeping town or encampment, taking him by surprise and killing as many as possible of his number before he roused himself to defence. If this was successfully accomplished, the surviving defenders would slip away and the day would be won by the attackers. On the other hand, if surprise was not complete or the defenders were able to fight back strongly, the attackers would withdraw to lick their wounds. Prolonged fighting was not the

[1] The population of Hodeida was probably about 35,000.

Arab way of warfare and there are remarkably few instances of lengthy, hard-fought, pitched battles in their history. In the deserts the Arab commander would rely upon a massive, surprise charge on camels or horses to overwhelm and scatter the enemy in one blow, since, once committed to battle he would lose control over his men, who ran away if unsuccessful, and if victorious, turned aside to loot and kill. Although many Yemenis, tribesmen and townsmen alike, were armed and considered themselves to be warriors and their chiefs to be military leaders, they had little idea of strategy, tactics, discipline or control in battle, and their vaunted military ability and potential amounted to little more than mob tactics.

When the Turks left, Imam Yahya realized that he must quickly form a small regular army to deter external aggression, extend his authority over the whole country and crush any revolts or dissidence, and he decided that this should be backed by a small conscript militia. Latterly the Turkish occupation forces had consisted of about 3,000 Turkish soldiers and about 6,000 Yemeni auxiliaries, scattered in garrisons at strategic points. About 300 Turkish officers and soldiers had agreed to stay on, at least for a while, to help create a small regular army, based on the Turkish-trained auxiliaries and increased as more Yemenis were recruited or conscripted. It was centred on Sana, where it occupied the former Turkish barracks and accommodation and was used in several pacification campaigns, but small detachments were kept at vital communication centres and frontier posts. The Turks left behind quantities of obsolete military arms and equipment and a few old field guns, which were sufficient to give this small new army superiority over the least well-armed and organized tribesmen. Over the years there had been a small infiltrations of arms into the Yemen from various sources, including the Italians in the 1920's and the Germans in the 1930's.[1] In fact, the Yemen had been a very profitable area for the small-time illegal arms smuggler.

An Iraqi Military Mission eventually took over from the Turks, and at one stage the regular army and the militia were each commanded by an Iraqi colonel, but the Mission did not seem to make a great success of raising the level of efficiency and

[1] One known arms deal was with Germany in 1937, when that country supplied 50,000 old Mauser rifles.

training of the Yemeni soldiers. The army was mainly composed of small infantry units, but there were also detachments of cavalry, and small groups mounted on camels to patrol the desert frontier regions. The military façade was completed by three military bands,[1] which were in ample evidence on all possible occasions. The best and most efficient element of the regular army was the Palace Guard, about 3,000 strong, whose main task was to protect the Imam, and this stayed the whole time in barracks just outside Sana. Other units rotated round the garrisons and frontier posts. The provincial governors were entitled to detachments of the regular army to act as body-guards and to make a show of force when necessary, but these were pared down by Yahya, who did not trust anyone else with a large number of soldiers. This meant that the majority of the regular army spent most of its time at Sana under his immediate eye.

The Palace Guard was reviewed weekly at Sana by the Imam. To fascinated Western eyes, it was more of a comic opera than a military occasion, with hordes of soldiers parading rather haphazardly in a multiplicity of uniforms, or just ordinary working garb. Indicative of the state of the Yemeni regular forces, most of the men were bare-footed, and the officers leading them, sometimes bare-footed like their soldiers, rode on horses, mules or donkeys, or walked with the men. All marched proudly, and were given enthusiastic applause by the watching citizens who thought it was a marvellous show of strength. A wide variety of arms were on parade, ranging from a few modern rifles and machine guns, which had pride of place, to very ancient muskets. Some soldiers had no firearms at all and had to be content with spears, swords or jambias. Two or three old Turkish field guns were usually in evidence, and the Imam made his appearance in his rickety old horse-drawn carriage.

Despite the apparent unattractiveness of military life, the regular army, which may have varied between 15,000 and 20,000 men, consisted of at least three-quarters volunteers, with not more than one-quarter having to be raised by conscription.

[1] The instruments were a mixture of Turkish and German ones, and the tunes, played by ear, were a discordant medley of those heard on European military parades, both the sounds and the sight appearing quite incongruous in the medieval, Arab setting.

Military service had become almost traditional in some families, but pay was very low, and always in arrears, so the best men were not attracted. The soldier joined for life and was burdened with many irksome duties, often of a non-military nature. The only way to obtain his discharge if he wished to leave, apart from losing a limb or through acute illness, was either to buy a 'substitute', which families did if ever they came into any money or suddenly prospered, or else to feign madness. Most did not want to leave the army, although it was a miserable existence, and the men were usually much too poor even to marry, because the only alternative was to become a beggar on the streets. Even their scanty pay was not all their own to buy food with. They had to purchase their own ammunition from the crafty Imam, who periodically ordered them to discharge two or three rounds on ceremonial occasions so that they would have to buy more from his armoury.[1] Physically the soldiers were not impressive. Most of them were short of stature, as were all Yemenis compared with the Wahabis or other Arabs, and many had deformities or other blemishes.

The army seemed to be the exception to the general ban on music, singing and dancing. Apart from the military bands, which played loud, jarring parodies of Western military tunes, the soldiers had developed a war-song or chant, known as the 'zamel', which was sung frequently by them as a kind of morale raiser and togetherness symbol. The soldiers also had their own military dances which they performed on ceremonial occasions, or to while away the boredom of barrack and camp life. Another military habit was that of sentries at night continually calling out to each other, and periodically indulging in songs or shouted choruses. The theory was that it gave the soldiers confidence and warned any potential enemy that they were awake and alert and that a surprise attack would be useless.

The whole army chewed qat constantly, and soldiers had been known to sell their arms, ammunition or uniforms to buy the drug, and even to treat with the enemy to obtain the means to do so. Generally, the Yemeni regular army can be summed up

[1] At first the Imam had a small armoury, run by an Austrian, which was capable merely of casting bullets and filling cartridges, but in 1926 the Italians established a small factory that was able to produce cartridges and carry out minor repairs of firearms.

as having poor pay, poor arms, poor equipment, poor uniforms and poor training, and as the leadership was also very indifferent it inevitably followed that morale was usually poor as well.

There was not a great deal of prestige attached to the status of an army officer in Yahya's day. Most Yemeni officers were Zeidis, carefully selected by the Imam, or recommended by the Ulema who chose intelligent boys from the 'middle class', which is to say the sons of lesser chiefs, landowners, or others still lower on the social scale. They were not usually from the Royal family or from the powerful Seiyid families, partly because the profession did not attract, but mainly because the Imam feared they might be tempted to use military knowledge and influence to further claims to the Imamate. Few knew very much about their job. Only a tiny handful went to Egypt for military training, and the remainder had to pick up what they could at the small military academy that was opened at Sana in the 1930's, and run first by the Iraqis and then by a mixed collection of foreign Arab officers.

Even in 1948, there still remained quite a number of 'foreign' Moslem officers in the Yemeni army, and indeed the regular soldiers and the militia were still commanded by Iraqi colonels. The mixture of Moslem officers from a variety of armies introduced a confused pattern of tactics, training and procedure. Yahya had continued to employ Arab soldiers of fortune, both to give a professional leavening to his army and as a counterbalance to any groups of Yemeni officers who might tend to gang up or combine for disloyal purposes. He shrewdly mixed up his officers, frequently and without warning reshuffling them, and posting or transferring individuals to the far corners of his kingdom.

In addition to the regular army there was the militia, which had developed from the Imam's original plan to give military training to a quarter of all males in the Yemen. He had hoped to introduce national conscription on the Turkish model, which he admired, and to decree that Yemeni male adults could be called up for six months' service. He had some difficulty in getting this scheme under way, because of opposition from the tribes, but it gradually gained momentum. The conscripts, of whom there were perhaps 15,000 to 20,000 assembled at a time, were housed in old Turkish barracks outside Sana, and given elementary training by foreign, Moslem officers. Uniforms were non-existent, and there were not enough arms to go round. Theoretically they could be recalled to service if necessary, but this does not seem to have ever happened, perhaps because their military value was so low. Militiamen could buy a substitute, and there arose a small class of poor people who might well be called 'professional militiamen', as their services were continually in demand.

The Imam did not want a strong, efficient, regular army which might turn against him, and despite the value of such an army, he seems deliberately to have kept his forces in a comparatively poor condition. Yahya relied heavily upon local tribes with their small proportion of semi-trained 'militiamen' whenever he needed extra force to impose his will on some section or other of his people. He meant the 'militia' elements in the tribes largely to counter-balance each other on the power scales, with the regular army to give the controlling tilt. He also felt that if he relied too much upon his regular army there might be danger either of it disintegrating because of diverse tribal loyalties under stress within it, or of it falling under dissident control.[1]

The Yemeni army was in many ways a general-purpose force, as it was not only expected to fulfil normal military tasks, such as quelling revolts, guarding the Imam, and keeping the peace, but had many other jobs to do as well, like tax-collecting, police duties, customs work, providing government messengers, or drivers for the state transport concern, tasks which might normally be considered to belong more properly to local government or administrative departments. When the Jews left Sana, for example, the soldiers had to take on the task of sewerage disposal and street-cleaning.

[1] A great admirer of Turkish methods, Imam Yahya adopted one when dealing with minor dissidence. He sent a large detachment of his soldiers into the critical area, which by Arab and Islamic custom had to be fed and housed by the local people. He then left them there, eating their heads off, until the Sheikh promised to be good, begging the Imam to withdraw his soldiers before his tribe was reduced to absolute poverty.

CHAPTER TWO

Imam Ahmed

MAIN EVENTS

1944 Free Yemenis emerge in Aden.
1948 (February) Imam Yahya assassinated at Sana.
Abdullah al-Wazir attempts to seize the throne.
Crown Prince Ahmed seizes the Imamate.
(March) Sana pillaged.
(May) Imam Ahmed moves his seat to Taiz.
1949 Governor of Aden visits Imam Ahmed.
1950 Anglo-Yemeni Conference in London.
1954 Governor of Aden visits Imam Ahmed.
1955 (April) Attempt to dethrone Imam Ahmed.
1956 (April) Treaty of Jedda, between Egypt, Saudi Arabia and the Yemen.
(November) The first shipment of Soviet arms arrives.
1957 Imam Ahmed's Press Conference.
1958 (March) The Yemen joins the United Arab States.
1959 (February) Inauguration of the Federation of South Arabia.
(April) Imam Ahmed to Rome for medical treatment (returned in October 1959).
1961 (December) United Arab States dissolved.
1962 (September) Imam Ahmed dies in bed.

Imam Yahya resisted modernization and change as it would have undermined his absolute power, but he had not been able to prevent a measure of political enlightenment reaching into the Yemen. Such young Yemenis as had been abroad for their education had seen the world changing, and had come into contact with revolutionary ideas. They saw that no country was more in need of enlightenment than their own. The radio now becoming commonplace in the homes of the governing and wealthier classes propagated liberal thoughts of which to speak openly in the Yemen was to invite either decapitation or an indefinite spell in prison. Also, foreign Moslems who had come to the country, especially the Iraqis and Egyptians, often arrived with an underlying political purpose, and expounded revolutionary ideas to those they thought to be discontented and susceptible to them. Particularly in the armed forces was there opportunity to spread dissension, and advantage taken of it.

Inevitably such a situation threw up active political malcontents, a number of whom, having expediently left the Yemen, congregated in Aden, where there was a Yemeni labour force of about 48,000.[1] In that city a subversive political organization known as the 'Free Yemenis' came into being, probably in the latter part of 1944. The chief founder-members were Ahmed Mohammed Numan[2] and Abdul Rahman Iryani, and also prominent was Mohammed Mahmoud as-Zubeiri.

Ahmed Numan had absorbed revolutionary ideals when he went to Cairo in 1937 to study at the Al Azhar Islamic University. He returned to the Yemen in 1941 to be given an educational post at Taiz, where he became tutor to Prince Mohammed al-Badr, the son of Crown Prince Ahmed. But his enlightened ideas did not appeal to the Imam, and Numan thought it best to leave the country, early in 1944, for his own safety. Abdul Rahman Iryani was a qadi, or judge, whose liberal ideas and views also displeased Imam Yahya, and he too quickly decamped to avoid being imprisoned. Mohammed as-Zubeiri was another qadi whose differences of opinion with Crown Prince Ahmed led to his arrival in Aden in the same year as Numan.

At first the Free Yemenis were cautious, merely advocating modest and harmless reforms in the Yemen, but gradually their voice became louder and more forthright, attracting to their programme Yemenis of a like mind. This subversive organization caused concern in the Yemen, and Imam Yahya sent Crown Prince Ahmed to Aden to discuss matters with its leaders in April 1946. His task was either to persuade them to return home where they could be dealt with in the traditional Yemeni

[1] According to the 1955 census.

[2] Not to be confused with his son, Mohammed Ahmed Numan, also a politician, whom I shall call Mohammed Numan.

manner, or, by threats or bribes, to stop them from continuing to publicise their adverse opinions.

Crown Prince Ahmed promised that if the Free Yemenis would stop putting out propaganda against the country's form of government, the Imam would employ foreign technicians to set up industries and exploit mineral wealth, and also start a secular education programme. Ahmed also indicated that the Imam would be prepared to open up the country a little and enter into proper diplomatic relations with all other Arab countries. He remained in Aden for six weeks, but his offers and threats came to nothing and he had to return home empty-handed. Shortly after he left, the Free Yemenis began to print in Aden a newspaper known as the 'Voice of the Yemen', in which they spotlighted the many shortcomings of their country. They were, however, careful not to attack the Imamate direct.

The Imam's sons were jealous of one another, and in November 1946 Prince Ibrahim defected and went to Aden to join the recently formed Grand Yemeni Association, which at about the same time merged with the Free Yemenis. This gave them considerably more prestige, and the organization gained confidence and strength until by September of the following year it was openly and loudly calling for revolution in the Yemen, and the substitution of a republic for the Imamate.

Despite dreadful penalties if caught, there was no shortage of plotters against Imam Yahya within the Yemen, one of whom finally brought about his assassination.

On 17th February 1948 the Imam was machine-gunned to death, together with his Prime Minister, while travelling in a car a few miles outside Sana. He was then probably about eighty. The plot was organized by Abdullah al-Wazir, the former general who had originally helped Yahya to pacify his country, but had fallen out of favour because the Imam suspected he had ambitions to seize the Imamate for himself. He had in fact been removed from the Governorship of Hodeida, and his family had been systematically stripped of all responsible positions. Abdullah al-Wazir watched the assassination through binoculars from his tall house in Sana.[1]

[1] On 17th January 1948 there had been an unsuccessful assassination attempt on Imam Yahya, when the plotters had put out the story of his 'death' before it had been verified, and the Ulema at Sana had proclaimed

Once the deed was done, Abdullah al-Wazir assumed command of the Sana garrison, closed the city gates, and imprisoned many of Yahya's relatives who had been lured to the capital. In the scuffles three of the Imam's sons were killed or died later of wounds. The next day, the Ulema of Sana proclaimed Abdullah al-Wazir to be the Imam. The news of the assassination was suppressed, it merely being given out that Imam Yahya had died.

On hearing the news of Imam Yahya's death, the leaders of the Free Yemenis in Aden immediately tried to leave for Sana by air. They were prevented from doing this by the British authorities who did not wish to become involved at all in Yemeni affairs, so they had to make their way back by land. It was three days before Prince Ibrahim reached Sana, and was appointed Prime Minister. Other Free Yemenis arrived in Sana at about the same time, but began to squabble amongst themselves. Yet others were directed to make their way to various provincial cities to rouse them to Abdullah al-Wazir's support. Abdullah al-Wazir stated that he would instigate reforms and appoint a legislative council. He called upon the cities and tribes to support him, but most held back, becoming suspicious when all details of Yahya's death were kept back and no one was allowed to see the body.

There followed a period of general hesitation and fence-sitting, during which Abdullah al-Wazir appealed to the Arab League for recognition. The Arab League was also suspicious about the circumstances of Yahya's death, but agreed to send a commission to examine the situation. Two of its members arrived at Sana on the 22nd. The rest of the commission was detained in Riyadh by King Ibn Saud, who had his own misgivings about the events of 17th February. In the meantime Abdullah al-Wazir was rapidly running short of money. He had failed to secure the treasury in his first *coup*, and it was now held by a section of the regular army which had become hostile to him when it realized that Yahya had been murdered. The

Abdullah al-Wazir as Imam. The Free Yemenis in Aden eagerly took up the story and broadcast the 'news' over their radio and in their newspaper. Abdullah al-Wazir was arrested, but was able to satisfy Yahya that he was not involved and that the Free Yemenis were simply using his name to cause dissension, and so was released.

Sana garrison was demanding not only arrears of pay but a bonus for its continued support. Many who might have stepped forward to acknowledge him as Imam, had their palms been crossed with a suitable amount of silver, hesitated to declare themselves. The tribes, similarly expecting largesse for their new loyalty, became restless when they were not given anything. And finally the Free Yemenis who had reached Sana were bitterly divided and of no help to him. He had only been in contact with them to further his own ambitious purpose, and they were beginning to suspect he had been merely using them and had no more intention of liberalizing the Yemen than Yahya.

Crown Prince Ahmed, who was the Governor of the Taiz region, now comes into the picture. Like other members of the Hamid ud-Din family he had been summoned to Sana on false pretences. He had started out, but when part way there had suddenly become suspicious and returned to Taiz,[1] where he heard of his father's death and the proclamation of Abdullah al-Wazir as Imam. Ahmed then went north to Hajja, where he had once been Governor and still had a reputation as the victorious commander in some of the earlier scuffles against tribes on the Asir border, to try and raise the Bakil federation to support his own claim to the Imamate.

Prince Hassan, a brother of Crown Prince Ahmed and Governor of the Sada region, also had not responded to the invitation to Sana. When he heard of his father's death and the proclamation of Abdullah al-Wazir, he declared for Ahmed and set about raising the Hashid federation warriors on his behalf. By promising them a week's pillaging in Sana if they seized that city for him, Prince Hassan persuaded several thousand Hashid tribesmen to march south with him, and lay siege to the capital. The citizens, fearing their fate at the hands of these wild attackers, held out as stoutly as they could. At first most of the regular army and the militia stood aside, but gradually most of the militia went over and joined the besiegers. The siege dragged on for four days and was finished with a traditional dawn rush on 13th March, when the tribesmen and militia forced their way into the city. Abdullah al-Wazir and some of

[1] Some reports indicate that by turning back he avoided an ambush that had been set for him by the Wazir family.

his supporters managed to hold out for another five days in a fort at the base of Jebel Nuqum, before being captured.

To the west, Crown Prince Ahmed was moving southwards towards Taiz at the head of several thousand Bakil tribesmen when he heard the good news from Sana. Immediately he sent the tribesmen home again, as he had no intention of allowing them to pillage Taiz which he intended to live in himself, and made quickly for Sana, which he entered the next day, the 14th. A bare four weeks after his father's assassination he was able to proclaim himself Imam. After a week's murder, destruction and plunder, in which 5,000 or more people lost their lives, the hubbub in Sana died down and the Hashid tribesmen were persuaded to return home, leaving Ahmed in control of the situation. Ahmed stayed in Sana for a few weeks only, before moving his capital to Taiz. Having allowed his supporters to sack Sana he had good reason not to trust the citizens, and despite several later requests to move the capital back again, as Sana lost much trade and prestige by this decision, Ahmed never relented. He seemed to blame the citizens for his father's murder, and it was said that he never set foot in Sana again in his lifetime. He spent most of his time either at his palace at Sala, about four miles from Taiz, or at another residence at Wadi Dhali, which was perched on a huge rocky outcrop near Hodeida.

Having secured his position, Imam Ahmed turned to wreak vengeance on those who had attempted to deprive him of it, and his cruelty was excessive even for the Yemen where cruelty was taken as a matter of course. Abdullah al-Wazir was publicly beheaded at Hajja, as were about thirty others who had supported and helped him,[1] many more were imprisoned, and there were well-founded rumours of torture. His liberal-minded brother, Prince Ibrahim, who had espoused the cause of the Free Yemenis, 'died' in prison. The Free Yemenis had, in general, a distinct lack of success. The leaders of it detailed to rally the provincial cities all arrived too late or not at all. Ahmed Numan, destined for Dhamar, was captured and sent to Hajja fortress prison, as was Abdul Rahman Iryani. Mohammed as-Zubeiri, who had been a member of Abdullah al-Wazir's

[1] Including a Yemeni army officer who had been one of those originally sent to Iraq as a cadet for training.

delegation that had gone to meet the Arab League commission in Saudi Arabia, was imprisoned by King Ibn Saud for three years, after which he made his way to Cairo.

Ahmed instituted other purges to ensure the security of his position, but, shrewdly, he rewarded as well. His brother Prince Hassan, who had turned the tables for him, was made Prime Minister[1] and Governor of the important Sana region. Ahmed also forgave his son, Mohammed al-Badr, who when captured at Sana, had been forced to take an oath of an allegiance to Abdullah al-Wazir to save his own life.

Like his father, Imam Ahmed suspected foreign influence and the motives of individual foreigners, and there was little relaxation of restrictions for them under his regime. Their movements remained prescribed and closely supervised, but he did appreciate their value and attempted to employ a few more technicians, doctors and engineers. He allowed a tiny degree of modernization to creep in by permitting wider use of electricity for lighting in palaces, government buildings and private houses and for pumping water from wells in the cities. He also permitted greater use of motor vehicles and encouraged the newly-established radio stations to develop. He had a scientific and engineering turn of mind and would engage in long discussions with foreign experts on subjects that interested him, showing far more knowledge on such matters than he is usually credited with. However, other than relaxing the ban on the use of radio sets, no major modern innovations were introduced during his reign, which like that of his father, was highly personal and centralized. In short, the Yemen stayed technically as backward as before, although more young Yemenis were allowed to go to Egypt and other Arab countries to be trained and educated.

Soon after he was installed in 1949, Imam Ahmed sent his brother, Prince Abdullah, whom he had appointed his Foreign Minister and who was slightly more pro-British than most Yemenis, to Britain to ask for technical advisers and doctors. He also asked for the appointment of a British Minister to Sana and suggested meetings to arrange a settlement over the border

[1] Prince Hassan's prestige was so high that it was rumoured he supported Ahmed only on condition that he should be Crown Prince and rule after him.

problems, but the non-committal answers he received did not please Imam Ahmed. That year, in November, the Governor of Aden[1] visited him at Taiz, but the meeting was not a very satisfactory one. Ahmed wanted British armoured cars but was refused them, as it was feared they might be used against Protectorate rulers or tribesmen. A few British doctors and technicians were sent to the Yemen, but could not be persuaded to stay long.

Basically antagonistic to the British in any case, Imam Ahmed now felt they were deliberately harbouring and encouraging the Free Yemenis in Aden for a nefarious purpose, probably scheming to form a Shafi federation which would encroach on his territory and alienate from him the Shafi tribes in the Yemen. Ahmed was also alarmed because Britain now openly claimed an area of 112,000 square miles in the two Protectorates, so he felt he must hit back, and accordingly did his best to stir up dissension along the Protectorate borders. The Ruler of Dhala State, who had fled to the Yemen after incurring British displeasure for his barbarous and disloyal behaviour, with the Imam's encouragement invaded his former domain with about 600 armed tribesmen, and had to be ejected by Government Guards, the armed levies under the control of the British Political Officers. There was also trouble in Beihan State, which provoked RAF reprisal bombing of Harib fort, just over the Yemeni frontier.

Anxious about this deteriorating situation and the new Imam's unfriendly attitude, Britain arranged an Anglo-Yemeni conference which was held in London in 1950. It was agreed that diplomatic representatives would be exchanged and a frontier commission set up, and after this things quietened down for a short while. The frontier commission never materialized, and although diplomatic representatives were exchanged at the end of 1951, the Imam did not receive the British chargé d'affaires for several weeks. Trouble soon broke out again. In April 1952, the Ruler of Lahej fled to the Yemen, and Britain gave recognition to another in his stead. Despite a visit by the Governor of Aden[2] to the Imam at Taiz in October 1954, Ahmed became more hostile and anti-British, especially when

[1] Sir Reginald Champion.
[2] Sir Tom Hickinbotham.

Britain began to consider the creation of a federation of South Arabian states.

Imam Ahmed was also plagued by trouble at home[1] as the Arab League, prompted by Yemeni revolutionary exiles, was singling out his country for propaganda attacks. A small group of people, several of whom had either been educated abroad or had visited other countries, were agitating privately against Ahmed's continued political oppression and his policy of hampering technical progress. They were ashamed of the ignorance of the people and the backwardness of the state generally, and would have liked to have seen at least moderate reforms initiated. A few discontented idealists openly defected, slipping away quietly to Aden to join the Free Yemenis. Included in this number was the Governor of the Sana region, Prince Hassan, who had played the vital part in helping Ahmed gain the Imamate.

In August 1952 King Farouk was expelled from Egypt, and the success and idealism of the new Egyptian revolutionary regime, led before long by Gamel Abdul Nasser, was a source of inspiration to many in Arab countries, the Yemen not excepted. Soon Radio Cairo was booming out rousing revolutionary themes which reached past the Imam directly to his people and gave the Yemeni plotters and would-be revolutionaries fresh hope and encouragement. In a bid to stop such treasonable communication, the Imam ordered the confiscation of all radios in public places. Many remained in private houses though, and he was unable to stop the surge of Arab nationalism seeping through into his own country.

Such was the way things worked in the Yemen that, from his prison at Hajja, Ahmed Numan of the Free Yemenis was able to maintain a regular correspondence with Imam Ahmed. Numan urged Ahmed to appoint as Crown Prince, his son Mohammed al-Badr, who was Numan's former pupil and enlightened for a member of the ruling class. In February 1955, the Imam released Ahmed Numan from Hajja prison and gave him an educational appointment. Abdul Rahman Iryani had been released the previous year.

In April 1955 there was a minor revolt in the Tihama, and

[1] In February 1950, he imprisoned his brother, Prince Ismail, the Minister for Education, for plotting to seize the Imamate.

a body of about 600 soldiers, under a Yemeni officer who had been one of the original Iraqi-trained cadets, was sent to deal with it. On returning to Taiz this officer was persuaded by Prince Abdullah, the Foreign Minister and a brother of Ahmed, to surround the royal palace, seize Imam Ahmed and hold him in detention. Ahmed was forced to sign a document surrendering his executive powers to Prince Abdullah, but he refused to give up the Imamate. Despite this, Abdullah proclaimed himself Imam, but recognition and support were not forthcoming. Everyone waited for more positive signs of success. There had been many bungled attempts to oust an Imam in the past, with fatal consequences to those who had stepped forward to declare themselves too quickly and too thoughtlessly in support of a would-be usurper.

At this stage Prince Mohammed al-Badr, Governor of Hodeida, whom Ahmed Numan had recommended should be appointed Crown Prince, and with whom Numan was once again in close contact, went north to Hajja where he rallied some 8,000 Bakil tribesmen. By bribes and promises he persuaded them to follow him to Taiz to rescue his father. The news that such a large body was advancing on the city caused considerable alarm. Everyone remembered what had happened in Sana so recently. The determination of the military detachment supporting Prince Abdullah wavered under the strain, and during this period of intense uncertainty Imam Ahmed was able to turn the tables and emerge the victor. The most commonly told account was that he seized a machine gun from one of his guards and mowed down all his captors in sight, but the truth is that he bribed the soldiers guarding him with sackfuls of silver thalers to be loyal to him and not to Prince Abdullah.[1]

Imam Ahmed's vengeance was summary. He decapitated Prince Abdullah, the Yemeni army officer, and several others, including another brother, Prince Abbas, who had been released from detention but was involved in this plot. Scores of others were imprisoned. He dismissed Prince Hassan,[2] who had supported his bid for the Imamate in 1948, from his post as

[1] Later he arrested all the soldiers involved in his detention and 'fined' them the amount of money he had given them as bribes. Like his father, Imam Ahmed was no spendthrift.

[2] Prince Hassan's flirtation with the Free Yemenis had been brief. Imam

Prime Minister (although he had been in Cairo at the time), and appointed him head of the Yemeni Delegation to the UN. The Wazir family, suspected of being implicated in the affair, had all its property confiscated and several members of the family arrested. They were released the following year and the family pardoned, although the property was not returned until 1960. The Wazir family was too powerful and influential to antagonize for long.

For his part in rescuing his father, Mohammed al-Badr was named Crown Prince. Al-Badr was an unusual character to be appointed to such a position, or indeed to inspire the confidence of his father, since he was something of a reformer and seemed to be slightly influenced by Nasserism. He had travelled abroad and was under no illusions about the backward state of his country or about what should be done to improve it. As Governor of Hodeida, he had come more into contact with foreigners and foreign ideas than his contemporaries, and a number of earnest young reformers were attracted to him, amongst whom inevitably were some less well-motivated schemers. Despite this and Imam Ahmed's continued suspicion of foreigners, and even the fact that Mohammed al-Badr had once sworn allegiance to Abdullah al-Wazir, in his abortive attempt to seize the Imamate in 1948, Crown Prince Mohammed al-Badr gained his father's approval. As Ahmed's health began to fail he was given an increasingly active part in governing the country, and was appointed to the posts of Foreign Minister, Defence Minister and Commander-in-Chief of the Armed Forces. Imam Ahmed had slightly modified his father's policy of placing Zeidis in positions of responsibility to the exclusion of all others, and the Crown Prince continued this relaxation, appointing some Shafis to governmental posts in Shafi territory.

In the tussle for power between Imam Ahmed and Prince Abdullah, the Free Yemenis came out openly in favour of Prince Mohammed al-Badr's action, and Mohammed as-Zubeiri, who was in Cairo, broadcast over the Voice of the Arabs network urging everyone to support al-Badr's efforts to try and rescue his father. Far from being pleased at this support

Ahmed had forgiven him, allowed him to return and appointed him Prime Minister.

from the Free Yemenis, Imam Ahmed was annoyed, and Ahmed Numan had to leave the country very quickly to escape imprisonment. He had not been impressed by Numan's recommendation that he should appoint Mohammed al-Badr, the Crown Prince guessing shrewdly that the Free Yemenis merely wanted to use Mohammed al-Badr as a tool for their own ends. The Imam had appointed Mohammed al-Badr partly because he appreciated his efforts against Prince Abdullah, but as much perhaps to divide support for Prince Hassan, his brother, who was extremely popular in many quarters, and whom he had sent out of the country. Numan joined as-Zubeiri in Cairo, where together they revived the newspaper, the 'Voice of the Yemen' and made radio broadcasts calling loudly for revolution.

Imam Ahmed jealously saw other Arab states, such as Saudi Arabia, strike it rich in oil, and wanting to do the same had made an agreement (in 1953) with a West German firm which allowed it to search for oil in the Yemen, and to produce and market salt. Little came of it, since the concern disliked the close supervision of, and restrictions on, its personnel, so the Imam cancelled this agreement in 1955, and instead gave an American group permission to prospect for oil. Similar unreasonable restrictions produced the same negative results, much to the Imam's annoyance. These mineral surveys confirmed deposits of iron ore in the north, a thin strata of coal near Sana, and limestone suitable for making cement, but little else.

British diplomatic and economic pressures had prevented the Western Powers from selling arms to the Yemen, and as the Imam badly needed modern armaments, Nasser, in Egypt, had seen his chance. In May 1947, an Egyptian-Yemeni friendship pact had been signed and diplomatic representatives exchanged, but relations had remained distant and cold between the two countries. In April 1956, Nasser organized a meeting at Jedda, between King Saud[1] of Saudi Arabia, Imam Ahmed and himself, at which Nasser persuaded the oil-rich King Saud to give the Imam money (believed to have been about £5 million) to buy arms from Communist sources. This agreement, which also catered for a unified military command structure between the three countries concerned, became known as the Jedda Pact.

[1] The old King, Ibn Saud, had died in November 1953, to be succeeded by his eldest surviving son.

Crown Prince Mohammed al-Badr, who had previously visited Nasser and had been completely captivated by his charm, went off on a tour of Iron Curtain capitals, establishing diplomatic relations with both the Soviet Union[1] and Communist China, and concluding certain arms agreements. A Soviet mission arrived in the Yemen in January 1957, and a Soviet Legation was opened at Taiz. This was followed later in the year by a Chinese mission and a Chinese Legation also at Taiz. Groups of Chinese workers began to arrive, Yemeni students were sent to Czechoslovakia and other Iron Curtain countries to be trained as engineers and doctors, and cadets and officers were sent to Egypt for training. America had seen this arms deal coming and had belatedly given two trainer aircraft to the Imam in 1955, but it was modern arms he wanted.

Crown Prince al-Badr was able to obtain Soviet arms, and the first shipment was landed at Salif in November 1956. Consisting of small arms, mortars, grenades and ammunition, the first deliveries were mainly taken into use by the regular army[2] which desperately required them, but some were distributed to tribes on the borders of the Aden Protectorate and a few actually smuggled to dissident tribesmen within the Protectorate itself. To ensure that these arms were not used against Yemenis, the Imam's policy was to take a hostage from a tribe in the Protectorate for every ten rifles issued.

Larger and more sophisticated weapons, such as T-34 tanks, SU-100's, field guns and anti-aircraft guns, followed,[3] in over half-a-dozen shipments up to August 1957. Most of them were left on airfields or in parks to rust away in neglect, not so much because no one knew how to handle or maintain them, as a fifty-strong Soviet training-team had arrived to teach the Yemenis how to use and look after them, but because the Imam forbade the weapons to be touched. It might have seemed as though they were attractive items he had coveted in a jackdaw-

[1] The rather meaningless treaty with the USSR of 1928 had been renewed in October 1955, and a trade agreement had been signed in March 1956.

[2] There had been a mutiny in October 1956, because of arrears of pay and because some units had been sent to the frontiers at short notice.

[3] These amounted to 30 T-34 tanks and SU-100's, 70 armoured carriers and trucks, 100 field and anti-aircraft guns, and 20 aircraft.

like fashion, and now that he had them he merely wanted to look at them, but the truth was that he had suddenly realized what a dangerous potential they had if they got into disloyal hands and his policy of neglect was a deliberate one. The same thing happened to the 20 YAK aircraft that were received. About half-a-dozen were flown in to airfields in Sana and Taiz, and simply left there. One later took off, piloted by a novice Yemeni, to crash ignominously a few moments later. The remainder came in crates by sea, which were dumped on the Hodeida airfield and left unopened.

In August 1957, the flow of arms stopped as suddenly as it had started, partly because the Imam blandly refused to pay any money for them or give concessions instead, partly because the Russians objected to them being left to rust away, and partly again because the Soviet Union failed to gain any influence in the Yemen, with civilians or with the Yemeni army, which had been one of its main objectives. It was thought the Russians would have liked to prospect for uranium, then scarce in the Soviet Union, and also to look for oil, but the Imam would not allow this.

Although he watched the Soviet arms rusting away with a cynical smile, the Imam was not so impractical about other benefits that might be obtained from foreign countries, and he placed the Crown Prince in charge of what could be called a 'foreign aid to the Yemen' programme. Al-Badr was expected to wheedle as much foreign economic and technical assistance as he could. He persuaded the Soviet Union to construct port facilities at Hodeida and to build a hospital there, and also to enlarge and improve the airfield at Sana. The Chinese were talked into making a motorable road from Hodeida to Sana, and by the end of 1958, there were over 500 Soviet and 1,000 Chinese technicians and workers in the Yemen.

Apparently payment of any kind was never in the Imam's mind, and much later (in January 1962) when the 143-mile Sana-Hodeida road was completed and opened with ceremony, he bluntly told the Chinese that he would not pay them a single Maria Theresa thaler for it, and that they could take it away with them if they wished. At the same time he made sure the Chinese workers had no opportunity of sabotaging the road by quickly shipping them out of the country. A similar procedure occurred (in June 1962) when the Hodeida hospital and the new Hodeida port on which some 300 Soviet technicians had worked for three years, were completed. The Soviet Union was faced with a blunt refusal by the Imam to pay for them.

Crown Prince al-Badr tried to play the West off against the East, but without much success. Few western countries were inclined to do anything for the Yemen, most of them repelled by the conditions their personnel would have to work under. The best he could do was to persuade the United States to equip a small hospital, provide a few doctors, drain a small area of marsh and construct a small irrigation system. The year 1958 was one of famine, but the Imam refused to accept a large consignment of American wheat. One or two other small projects were timidly embarked upon by Western countries, such as the establishment of a tannery, a cement factory and a tobacco concern, but few were completed. Britain was not interested in doing anything at all for the Yemen until its border problems were settled. The Swedish pilots who had been flying the Imam's private fleet of three Dakotas and three other aircraft were replaced by Moslem Yugoslavs, and then by Russians.

In January 1957, a most unusual event occurred. The Imam unexpectedly invited a party of ten British and American journalists into the Yemen, something that had never happened before. In fact, journalists of any nation were strictly discouraged from entering the country, and the few that slipped through were especially heavily supervised and restricted. The reason for this press invitation was for the Imam to give international publicity to his claims to parts of the Aden Protectorate. He also wanted to show, somehow, that the British were scheming against him, since he believed that in some inexplicable way they had thwarted oil exploration in his country and so had deprived him of riches such as his neighbour, King Saud, enjoyed. The failure of the Anglo-French attack on Egypt in November 1956, had caused many Arab leaders to revise their former views on Western strength and determination, and it probably gave Ahmed a feeling of confidence.

The Press visit included a carefully stage-managed frontier incident at Qataba, overlooking the border of Dhala State, which provoked armed British retaliation, including RAF action. The correspondents had a grandstand view of a battle that lasted several hours, in which much ammunition was expended on both sides at the cost of only three or four casualties. The pressmen visited Sana where they were able to interview several prominent Yemeni officials,[1] and they also had an interview with Imam Ahmed at his palace at Wadi Dhali, near Hodeida, where he gave the first and only press conference of his life. Then the Yemen firmly closed its doors again to publicity, leaving many to wonder what had prompted the Imam to take such an uncharacteristic step. He had most probably hoped it would have repercussions in his favour, arousing world opinion against Britain, but he was disappointed, as it only aroused curiosity, revealed feudal backwardness and brought floods of requests for further facilities.

By this time the Imam had a marked anti-British complex, and he encouraged dissidence as much as he could within the Protectorate and along the border. There were, for example, over seventy 'incidents' in Dhala State in February. In January 1957, the Yemeni representative at the UN claimed that the whole of the Aden Protectorate was an 'integral part of the Yemen'. The British Political Officer was besieged in a fort by armed tribesmen led by the deposed Ruler of Dhala, and British troops had to be brought in to restore order. The heat was then turned on Beihan State, which was invaded by Yemenis with Soviet weapons who were not driven out until September.

Crown Prince Mohammed al-Badr visited Britain in November (1957). On his return to the Yemen there were fresh disturbances along the Protectorate frontier, some involving the use of artillery and mortar fire. The Governor of Aden[2] twice went to the Yemen, in November 1959 and again in January 1960, to try and reach a settlement, but without much success. Clearly in an expansionist mood, Imam Ahmed was also engaged in imposing his authority on the semi-nomadic tribes on the fringe of the Rub al Khali, the Empty Quarter, which had never really been governed by anyone before, and in doing so he created further hostility with King Saud who also claimed jurisdiction over them.

[1] A Council of Ministers had been established in 1955, but it had no authority, its members functioning in a purely advisory capacity, and then only when asked to do so by the Imam.

[2] Sir William Luce.

In February 1958, Nasser had announced the formation of the United Arab Republic, of Egypt and Syria, and in March the same year, the Imam shrewdly jumped on the bandwagon by joining it on a federal basis, in what became known as the United Arab States. This was a cynical and empty, but cleverly calculated gesture on his part. He ceded nothing and co-operated not one little bit, remaining completely independent and aloof. On the other hand he gained a tremendous advantage as this move curbed the vitriolic tongue of the 'Voice of the Arabs' which now was forced to say friendly things about him and his regime. It also caused Nasser to silence Mohammed as-Zubeiri who had been making broadcasts from Cairo on behalf of the Free Yemenis, calling for revolution in the Yemen. King Saud had sent an unsuccessful emissary to Imam Ahmed to try and dissuade him from joining Nasser's UAR, but relations between the two monarchs were not too cordial. No doubt the Imam still thought of his lost province of Asir, and he rightly suspected that some of the tribes in the eastern part of his country were being incited to revolt by Saudi Arabian bribes.

In January 1959, pamphlets were discovered that indicated the existence of a subversive Yemeni Officers' Movement. Many Yemeni officers, especially the younger ones who had graduated from the small Military Academy at Sana, now run by Egyptians, had appreciated how the Egyptian Young Officers' organization functioned, and had noted its successes. Several of them now were imprisoned, a few were dismissed from the service and some others transferred to widely-dispersed garrisons. The angry Imam deported the Egyptian staff of his Military Academy, and also carried out a minor purge of other foreigners working in the Yemen, especially Egyptians.

During 1959, an economic pact was made with the United States, who promised to construct a road from Mocha through Taiz to Sana; and a US Legation, with a chargé d'affaires, was established at Taiz. This was another famine year, and this time the Imam accepted some 15,000 tons of American wheat. This arrangement was made as a counter-balance to the Soviet and Chinese presence in his country, and the Imam remained displeased that a rich country like America would not give him much more economic aid.

For some years Ahmed had been in bad health, and in April (1959) he suddenly left the country and went off to Rome for medical treatment. This move was unpopular with Zeidi and conservative elements, since, once appointed, the Imam was by tradition not supposed to leave the Yemen. No one really expected Ahmed to return, or indeed to live very long; an opinion shared by the Crown Prince who began to put his own liberal ideas into practice. But Mohammed al-Badr was neither a firm nor successful ruler. He gave weekly talks at the main mosques at Sana and Taiz, outlining the reforms he wanted to make and calling upon expatriate Yemenis to return home to put their skills, money and experience to the benefit of their country and its future. He removed several of the old dyed-in-the-wool governors, qadis and officials who obstructed or displeased him, and appointed more liberal-minded ones in their places. He also nominated a new Advisory Council. These liberal moves made him unpopular with the Ulema and brought down stern condemnation and criticism from those with vested interests. Additionally they provided much greater scope for people to scheme and plot for their own purposes, which were not always in accordance with Mohammed al-Badr's shining ideals. Imam Ahmed's method of governing was undoubtedly harsh and barbaric in the extreme, but it was effective, and he had managed to keep his domain under some sort of control, whereas Mohammed al-Badr's innovations and relaxation of controls were more deeply disturbing.

The Crown Prince was greatly impressed by Nasser's personality and thought all things Egyptian were marvellous. Accordingly, he adopted many Egyptian ideas and imported Egyptian personnel to put them into operation. A small UAR Military Mission arrived and was encouraged to train the Yemeni army to use the Soviet weapons that hadn't rusted to bits, and Egyptian instructional establishments were set up at Hodeida and Sana. Also, Egyptians were re-appointed to staff the Sana Military Academy.

Mohammed al-Badr had continual trouble with the Yemeni army, and thinking that low pay and arrears were the main source of trouble, promised a pay rise and immediate cash payments, but these funds were embezzled and the money never reached the soldiers. He also promised free medical treatment for the soldiers, who had previously had to pay for this service. On several occasions Yemeni troops ran amok in both Taiz and Hodeida, compelling the Crown Prince to take severe punitive action. He beheaded over a dozen officers, imprisoned others and ordered wholesale punishments. Some Egyptian officers were given positions of responsibility within the Yemeni army, not unusual in itself as Imam Ahmed had continued to employ a number of Moslem foreigners. The Crown Prince also contrived arbitrary promotions, another source of discontent.

An army mutiny in Sana so alarmed him that he called in several thousand tribesmen from both the Hashid and Bakil federations, who encamped outside the city. Their presence undoubtedly brought the Sana garrison to its senses, but caused consternation among the citizens, who had vivid memories of what had happened in 1948, especially as the tribesmen seemed to be reluctant to return to their homes. Eventually Mohammed al-Badr had to bribe them heavily to persuade them to leave, using for the purpose certain funds earmarked for religious purposes, which brought him into fresh conflict with the Ulema. The Crown Prince called off the dissident campaign against the British-protected Federation of South Arabia, which had been inaugurated in February 1959, and sent a telegram to Aden, signifying willingness to discuss a frontier settlement.

Without warning, in August (1959) Imam Ahmed returned refreshed, to find his son's stewardship had not been a great success and that his country was seething with discontent. He quickly put matters right with cruelty and firmness; heads fell, hands and feet were cut off, and many people were thrown into dungeons, some chained up like wild animals. He expelled large numbers of foreigners and thinned out the Egyptian Military Mission, although he allowed it to remain. He closed down an airforce training-centre the Egyptians had started up with Mohammed al-Badr's approval. Radio Sana stopped broadcasting liberal speeches and no more was heard about reforms. His unsatisfactory governorship brought Mohammed al-Badr a period of disfavour during which he was sent off on a health cure, but there was a reconciliation in October, when he was appointed acting Prime Minister and Minister of the Interior, in addition to the posts he already held of Foreign

Minister and Minister of Defence. Imam Ahmed despite the results of his medical treatment was really in failing health. Forced to delegate many of his responsibilities, it seems he had little choice other than to give them to his son, Mohammed al-Badr, as he did not trust any of his other sons[1] or relatives. The one really popular contender for the throne who might have governed well for him, was his brother, Prince Hassan, whom he had banished to the UN. Whatever the Imam's private reasons, Mohammed al-Badr remained the heir apparent, and was sent off on another visit to Moscow.

In September 1961, Syria broke away from Nasser's UAR, and this brought about a slightly changed attitude towards the Yemen, a much harder and more critical line emerging from Egypt. Imam Ahmed had never liked the advanced views of either the young Nasserites or the Syrian Baathists, considering them to be disruptive to established order and Islamic society. In August, the Imam refused to receive an Arab League Mission that was touring member countries to discuss details of an Arab armed force for Kuwait. He declined to contribute to this project on the grounds that his army was occupied along the border with the British-protected Federation of South Arabia. He also disliked the increasing flow of adverse comments emanating from Radio Cairo, so he wrote a poem criticizing Nasser, his methods of government and propaganda, which in early December was broadcast from Radio Sana and also published in an Aden periodical. Like his father, Ahmed had a literary turn of mind. Nasser's response was to make a radio speech on the 23rd of that month attacking the Imam, and then on the 31st he formally dissolved the United Arab States, which had largely been a fiction anyway.

Mohammed as-Zubeiri was re-introduced as the leader of the Free Yemenis in Cairo, and Abdul Rahman Baidani became their spokesman, broadcasting about their aims and intentions. Nasser also gave support to the Free Yemenis operating from Aden. He switched from the moderate South Arabian League, composed largely of middle-class elements, to the newly emer-

[1] At least two of Imam Ahmed's sons were in prison, reputedly shackled to a wall, and Ahmed had ordered the execution of three of his own brothers, Abdullah, Ibrahim and Abbas—so it was not a particularly happy, trustful family.

gent People's Socialist Party[1] and strongly encouraged it to work for revolution inside the Yemen, as well as to free the south from British rule.

In the meantime, Imam Ahmed was having difficulty in getting back the money the Crown Prince had paid out in bribes to the northern tribesmen, and his methods caused discontent and revolt. A large part of the Yemeni army had to be sent hurriedly to Hashid country to quell dissidence. In April 1960, there was a Bakil rising which had to be crushed, and in June there was a revolt amongst tribes in the Khawlan region, when they refused to hand over hostages that were demanded. In the latter case, Imam Ahmed was compelled to compromise for a while.

There was no doubt that in addition to all this, the 'Voice of the Arabs' radio programme, beamed from Cairo, attracted Arabs everywhere in the Yemen; partly because Nasser's propaganda machine was both skilful and experienced, and partly because there was no competitive alternative. Egyptians working in the country as military instructors, school teachers and doctors, all subtly and insiduously aided the spread of Nasser's views. Under the Crown Prince's urging, Imam Ahmed had allowed some Egyptian school teachers into the Yemen to start a few secular schools and to give advanced education to sons of richer families, and their number had been increased during the Imam's absence in Italy. All this had a profound effect on young, restless, impressionable minds in the Yemen.

Manifestations of unrest began to appear. In January 1960 more subversive pamphlets relating to a Young Officers' Movement were discovered in Taiz, which resulted in that city being placed under martial law for a while, and in June there were bomb incidents in both Taiz and Ibb. There was another rash of explosions in Taiz in November, when many people were detained, and several similar incidents in both Sana and Taiz in 1961. In May 1962, the Imam ordered two villages to be razed for harbouring 'nationalists', and in August, demonstrations in some of the secular schools against alleged approval by the Imam of the American bases in Saudi Arabia, led to a

[1] Which became the Front for the Liberation of the Occupied South Yemen, FLOSY, in 1966.

public protest march in Sana—something unheard of so far in the Yemen. Soldiers opened fire, killing several demonstrators, and as a warning a few were executed, many imprisoned and the secular schools closed. The fact that such a demonstration had taken place at all in a country where penalties were so drastic, indicated the presence of a yet unassessed, uneasily stirring nationalism that was straining against repression. In early September, there were 'student riots' at the two schools of further education, one at Sana and the other at Taiz, which had been established and staffed by Egyptians. The Imam's picture was trampled underfoot and pictures of Nasser displayed instead.

On 18th September, after several days' illness, Imam Ahmed died in his bed. A most hated and feared ruler, who had survived many assassination attempts, probably seven in the last twelve months of his life, he was in his early seventies.[1] He had been involved in a motor accident in January 1961, in which he was badly hurt, and the last known attempt on his life occurred at Hodeida hospital in March of that year, when several bullets had entered his body. Crown Prince Mohammed al-Badr proclaimed himself Imam, and had his father's body flown to Sana for burial.

[1] Estimates of Imam Ahmed's age vary from about sixty-six to seventy-four years. Like his father, he probably did not know exactly himself. The experts all disagree, which adds weight to this opinion.

CHAPTER THREE

Revolution

MAIN EVENTS

1962	
September 26th	Imam Mohammed al-Badr bombarded in his Sana palace by rebel tanks.
27th	Death of Imam reported. Republican *coup d'état* announced by Colonel as-Sallal.
28th	UAR troops arrive at Sana and Taiz by air.
	Soviet Union recognizes the new Republican regime.
29th	UAR ships with military supplies arrive at Hodeida.
30th	Abdul Rahman Baidani arrives from Cairo to become Deputy Premier.
October 2nd–8th	Saudi Arabian pilots with aircraft defect to UAR.
5th	Prince Hassan assumes title of Imam, and sets up Government-in-Exile in Saudi Arabia.
7th	Republicans change the Yemeni national flag.
9th	(probable) Imam Mohammed al-Badr arrives at Najran.
	Statement issued by Government-in-Exile that he is alive.
10th	Royalists take Marib.
13th	Radio Mecca announce that Mohammed al-Badr is alive and is willing to accept Prince Hassan as Imam.
15th	Radio Amman announce that Mohammed al-Badr has sent a message to King Hussein of Jordan.
	Republican Government abolishes slavery.
16th	Baidani announce the formation of the Popular Union.
	Republicans ask the Yemenis in Aden not to return home yet.

17th	Radio Mecca announce that Prince Hassan is willing to support Mohammed al-Badr as Imam.
31st	Provisional Republican constitution published.
November 10th	Imam's press conference.

Although signs of active discontent bordering upon revolt were obvious, no special significance was attached to them. The Yemen had been plagued with violent troubles for so long that they had almost come to be accepted as the normal way of life. Dissidence, revolts and squabbles by rival claimants for the Imamate were to be anticipated, and it was accepted that they should periodically be quelled with harsh punitive measures. Cheap transistor radios imported from Aden enabled Egyptian-sponsored propaganda to reach the people of the Yemen, and the 'Voice of the Arabs' had been conditioning their minds for revolt for several months. On 26th April (1962), for example, an announcer called for a rising against Imam Ahmed, and on 12th May a suggested Republican constitution was broadcast. And on the very day of Ahmed's death, coincidentally,[1] another exhortation to rebel against the Imam came over the air.

After burying his father's body with due ceremony at Sana, Mohammed al-Badr formally assumed the Imamate. He made an initial speech pledging to institute long overdue reforms which would give citizens new rights, abolished the hostage system, allowing the hostages to return to their homes,[2] and released many political prisoners. He assumed the office of Prime Minister, and began to appoint a forty-man Advisory Council, of which, he hoped, half would eventually be elected from centres with a population of over 5,000. His foreign policy was to offer friendship to all countries that would reciprocate it, but he did not want to enter into any formal alliances. Imam Mohammed al-Badr wished to become one of the world's neutrals.

Most countries sent him condolences on the death of his

[1] Mohammed al-Badr announced on 19th September that his father had died the day before, after several days' illness. Presumably he had delayed making this announcement until he had completed preparations and security arrangements for his own proclamation.

[2] There were about one hundred and fifty hostages, according to Dana Adams Schmidt.

father and recognized Mohammed al-Badr as the new ruler of the Yemen, although Nasser's recognition did not arrive until the 23rd. This time there was no violent attempt by a pretender to snatch the Imamate. The one possible strong contender was his uncle, Prince Hassan, extremely popular in Zeidi circles, who had been sent to the UN by Imam Ahmed, and when, on 23rd September, Prince Hassan sent a message of loyalty to Mohammed al-Badr, acknowledging him as Imam, all seemed set for a peaceful accession. But although the rest of the world seemed to accept Mohammed al-Badr as the new Imam of the Yemen, and hoped he would introduce a new era of enlightenment, the Free Yemenis no longer gave him their support. Having become completely alienated from the Imamate, they were working single-mindedly to establish a republic. Abdul Rahman Baidani, in charge of the Free Yemeni broadcasts from Cairo, heaped abuse on the new Imam and agitated for revolution.

Several groups of plotters aiming to overthrow the Imam had been working to this end for some time past, both inside the country and abroad. A principal of one such powerful faction was Colonel Abdullah as-Sallal, who, as a senior army officer and long-time confidant of Mohammed al-Badr, was able to make contacts and preparations without exciting suspicion. He had been appointed Chief of Staff by the new Imam immediately after his accession, and he had obtained permission to bring some of the neglected armoured vehicles from Hodeida to Sana.

The UAR Ambassador to the Yemen was involved in, or at least had a comprehensive knowledge of, some of the plots, as did the Egyptian Military Mission, whose personnel had secretly helped as-Sallal to put some of the Soviet armoured vehicles into running order. In fact it is believed that the Sallal faction of intriguers had been making plans to kill the old Imam, Ahmed, and had prepared to make the assassination attempt at the end of September. Imam Ahmed had thwarted them by dying in bed, and as the new Imam moved his seat to Sana, fresh murder preparations had to be made. One cannot be sure at that stage exactly what Sallal's plans were, but it is usually accepted that he hoped to kill the Imam, raise support for the absent, but very popular, Prince Hassan, and then take advantage of the situation to seize power himself.

There was at least one Young Officers' Movement, based on the Egyptian model, that schemed to form a governing military junta. In addition, there was a known Hashid subversive group, and a completely separate Bakil one, both tribal groups having been completely alienated by Imam Ahmed's actions, and each presumably with a different candidate to back. As has been seen, Imam Ahmed was unloved by his family, and there were a number of Royal Princes actively working to de-throne him. How many such disloyal factions actually existed, their strength, potential capabilities and determination, and the extent of their knowledge of, or liaison with, each other, must remain a matter of speculation.

During the day of 26th September, a small armoured column of six T-34 tanks and four other armoured vehicles, trundled along the road from Hodeida to Sana, arriving in the capital late at night—about 2300 hours according to most reports. Imam Mohammed al-Badr had been holding an evening meeting at his palace at Sana, which was attended, amongst others, by Colonel as-Sallal, Abdul Rahman Iryani and another prominent politician, Mohammed Ali Othman. About 2300 hours the meeting ended, and as-Sallal hastily asked to be excused, apparently much to the Imam's surprise as he seems to have asked as-Sallal to stay on to discuss problems with him. As soon as as-Sallal had left, the sounds of the armoured column entering Sana were heard in the palace, but they did not cause any alarm as permission for their arrival had formally been given. But at about 2330 hours, the tanks opened fire on the palace, a four-storey building that had been constructed as a Turkish military hospital. Known as the Bashir Palace, it had been Mohammed al-Badr's Sana residence for some years. About the same time, rebel troops of the Yemeni regular army seized the Sana radio station and the airfield.

Firing at the Bashir Palace continued spasmodically for several hours, though only at the top two stories since the streets were so narrow that the tanks could not approach it but had to fire over the tops of other buildings. During this bombardment three Palace Guards were killed and the remainder deserted their posts, as did the other officials and servants, leaving the Imam practically alone with his womenfolk.

As-Sallal broadcast that the Imam had been killed in the

bombardment of the palace. He declared a Republic, and called upon the army to rally to him, which after some initial hesitation the majority of the Sana garrison did. The only clash in which life was lost was when a detachment of rebel troops moved to take over an ammunition depot in the city, from which nothing could normally be issued without direct permission from the Imam. The defenders resisted and in the struggle that followed, over one hundred soldiers were killed. Owing to the preparatory work carried out by the Young Officers' Movement and other military revolutionaries, the main part of the garrison openly declared for as-Sallal, and those regular soldiers in Sana who did not do so immediately, remained passive, watching and waiting, as did the militia in barracks and camps outside the city.

By dawn the capital was in rebel hands, and after a further radio broadcast by as-Sallal explaining the abolition of the Imamate and the emergence of the Yemeni Arab Republic, the streets soon became filled with cheering citizens, and the remainder of the army and the militia openly threw in their lot with him. Early in the day the Royal Palace in Sana, deserted by all except women, was ransacked by soldiers and citizens. The palace women, together with other female relations of the Hamid ud-Din family, were rounded up and detained in a large house in the city.[1] In Taiz and Hodeida, on hearing the news of the revolution, Young Officers' Movements and military revolutionaries carried the garrisons with them, and encouraged by rousing propaganda on Radio Sana, the inhabitants of the three main cities were soon joyfully espousing the new cause of the Republic. In other places the response was slower and more cautious, but the Republicans had made vital initial gains.

What actually happened just before, and immediately after, the bombardment of the Bashir Palace is still not absolutely clear. The only sure fact is that as-Sallal emerged as the dominant figure of the Revolution, with authority and a following. It is generally assumed that as-Sallal was the key personality throughout, that he had been plotting for years

[1] They amounted to about a hundred in all, and after being kept in detention for about a year, they were exchanged for Republican prisoners held by the Royalists. They included Mohammed al-Badr's two wives and two daughters.

and that it was his unswerving ambition and revolutionary zeal that were responsible for the *coup* and the other diverse groups of discontents simply rallied to him when opportunity suddenly presented itself. Certainly, as-Sallal himself has not said anything that gives any indication to the contrary, although others have suggested they also played leading parts and that as-Sallal was not the solitary giant.[1]

However, in some manner as-Sallal became the successful leader of the revolt against the Imamate, which had been organized and planned with Nasser's knowledge and more than a little Egyptian aid and encouragement. As-Sallal was then about forty-five years old. A Zeidi, he had been one of the original batch of Yemeni cadets sent to Iraq for military training. He was no doubt selected because of his family background (his father being a blacksmith[2] and not a Seiyid), and because he belonged to no powerful tribe or faction, which lessened the risk of disloyalty. Iraq in the 1930's, backward though it may have been, was a revelation to him, and he saw quite clearly how backward the Yemen was and how many things urgently needed putting right.

Returning to the Yemen, as-Sallal was commissioned into the army and earnestly applied himself to the profession, something more than slightly unusual for a Yemeni officer in those days, and this brought him into contact with the (then) Iraqi Military Mission in Sana, which was trying to train the Yemeni armed forces. Revolutionary traits soon showed through and it was not long before as-Sallal was imprisoned on suspicion of being implicated in subversive activities, although after eight months he was released and reinstated in the army as a lieutenant. When Ahmed made good his accession to the Imamate after the murder of the old Imam, Yahya, he sent as-Sallal to the Hajja fortress prison because he believed him

[1] An interesting account given by Dana Adams Schmidt is that the *coup* was precipitated, and that the lieutenant who has brought the armour from Hodeida shelled the palace on his own accord. He then sent a vehicle for as-Sallal, who had retired to bed and knew nothing about the bombardment, asking him to participate in the revolution. As-Sallal is alleged to have replied, 'Yes, if I become President', and this condition was agreed to. The lieutenant was sent to the Khawlan region where he was killed a few weeks later.

[2] Latterly as-Sallal has insisted that his father was a farmer.

to have been in some way involved in the intrigue against him. According to some reports, as-Sallal spent part of his time chained to a wall, with fetters on his ankles. While in Hajja prison he came into contact with other political revolutionaries who were detained with him, and he listened to their arguments and plans. He also became an admirer of Nasser, and was profoundly influenced by his ideas and successes. It is often alleged that as-Sallal spent this period studying famous revolutionary works, but this may be doubted as he was essentially a practical man rather than a thinker.

In 1955, as-Sallal was released from Hajja prison due to the intervention of Crown Prince Mohammed al-Badr, who thought he was a genuine reformer who merely wanted to do the best he could for his country. As-Sallal was given back his commission, promoted and placed in charge of Hodeida harbour which was soon to be enlarged and improved by the Russians. Well-established in the Crown Prince's confidence, he came into contact with many of the Egyptians Mohammed al-Badr brought to the Yemen during his father's absence in Rome in 1959, and with them and others who became Free Yemenis he made secret liaisons. About this period he reached the conclusion that the Imamate had to give way to a republic, and he coldly and calculatingly used his friendship with the Crown Prince to further this ultimate aim.

At the official opening of the new Soviet-built and Soviet-equipped hospital at Hodeida in March 1961, an attempt was made to kill Imam Ahmed, in which the Imam was wounded. One of the would-be assassins briefly took refuge in the Harbour Master's office, which brought as-Sallal under suspicion. Imam Ahmed dismissed him from his post, but a sympathetic Mohammed al-Badr made him commander of his personal bodyguard, which was, of course, part of the Yemeni regular army. As-Sallal later admitted being involved in this particular attempt on the Imam's life, and he may have been involved in others too.

Shortly afterwards the Crown Prince put as-Sallal in charge of the Sana airfield. There followed another spell as Harbour Master at Hodeida, after which he was appointed commandant of the small Yemeni Military Academy, at Sana, now again staffed by Egyptians. These different posts gave as-Sallal ample opportunity to contact revolutionaries, gain support from army officers, recruit more Free Yemenis and enlist the technical help of the Egyptians. As soon as he became Imam, Mohammed al-Badr made him his army Chief of Staff, where he was better placed than ever to effect a violent overthrow of the Imamate.

Once the *coup* had been accomplished, Colonel as-Sallal announced the formation of the Government of the new Yemeni Arab Republic, a Revolutionary Council and a Presidential Council. He named himself Premier and Commander-in-Chief of the armed forces, and appointed Abdul Rahman Baidani to be Deputy Premier. Other personalities who became Ministers and who later play prominent parts in this account include Mohsin al-Aini, Foreign Affairs, Brigadier Hamoud al-Jaifi, Armed Forces, Ahmed Numan, Abdul Rahman Iryani, Mohammed as-Zubeiri and Hassan al-Amri. Most were army officers or Free Yemenis who had been active in trade union movements in Aden and elsewhere, and a few were intellectuals who had been educated abroad. Some were in the Yemen; others were in exile, and these hurried back to their native country as quickly as they could. Mohsin al-Aini, for example, had been sent to study in Cairo as a youth and had also visited France, and when he returned to Aden he became deeply involved in trade union activities. Deported from Aden by the British, he went to Cairo again, to work with the Egyptian-sponsored Free Yemenis. At the time of the revolution he was in the Yemen, having returned secretly just after Imam Ahmed's death.

There was great enthusiasm among all the various groups of Yemeni exiles, and many began to flock homewards to the new Republic. In fact so many returned that the Government did not know what to do with them all. They simply added to the existing unemployment problem, which quickly became acute. On 16th October, an appeal was broadcast to Yemenis in Aden asking them to postpone their return for a short while.

The Revolutionary Council, a sort of Inner Cabinet and the initial controlling body of the revolutionary regime, consisted of six officers, headed by as-Sallal.

The new Premier announced that his aim was to build a socialist republic on the Egyptian model, and his manifesto stated that the regime was to be based on social justice for all, the abolition of tribal differences, encouragement to Yemenis abroad to return home, and opportunities for the Yemeni people to run their own country. His foreign policy was to promote Arab unity, to consolidate the Arab League and to give support to the UN Charter. Friendly relations would be established with all countries recognizing the new regime, and there were vague and undefined remarks about resistance to imperialism and foreign intervention;[1] as-Sallal also announced that international agreements made by the former Government would be respected, and mentioned the 1934 Treaty of Sana. The army was to be reorganized and modernized.

The first country to recognize the new regime, on 28th September, was the Soviet Union, and in a message Premier Khrushchev said that any act of aggression against the Yemen would be considered an act of aggression against the USSR. Egypt followed, on the 29th, and by mid-December over thirty countries had recognized the as-Sallal Government. These did not include Britain, America, Saudi Arabia, Jordan or Morocco. Since Jordan withheld recognition in early October the small Jordanian Military Mission that had been in Sana since June was expelled.

Immediately after the *coup*, the frontiers were closed and a ban put on all air flights, including the—by this time almost regular—services from Aden and Cairo to Hodeida, Taiz and Sana; and for a few days the only news from the Yemen came over Radio Sana. Then there was a sudden relaxation of restrictions, and foreign journalists were invited to come and view for themselves the sad state of the country, and see what had to be accomplished. Many journalists, including a few British ones, seized the opportunity of visiting and reporting on a hitherto forbidden land, and by mid-October had crowded into Sana, Taiz and Hodeida, which three cities they reported to be firmly under Republican control. The Yemen was no longer a tightly-closed country that shunned all forms of publicity, and was largely unknown and misjudged because of this.

On assuming power, as-Sallal, in true Yemeni tradition, ordered a number of executions[2] that included at least 15 male

[1] On 14th November 1962, as-Sallal even announced his intention of forming a 'Republic of the Arabian Peninsula'.

[2] Including the former Director of Prisons.

members of the Imam's family as well as several others with anti-Republican sympathies. Many more were imprisoned. On 8th October, he announced that he had shot 23 people and put 20 others in prison, but this was certainly a gross understatement. The property and wealth of many powerful Seiyid families was confiscated, and the Royal Princes were sentenced to death in their absence. The Imam's estates, comprising about one-third of the best land in the country, were confiscated as well. A price of about 5,000 Marie Theresa thalers was put on the heads of all the Imam's male relatives.

A first show-piece trial was staged in November. Two old men, one a former Governor of Sana, and the other a former Chief of Staff, were sentenced to death. In a much publicized act of mercy, for world consumption, as-Sallal commuted the sentences to imprisonment. He claimed he had released thousands of prisoners from the five main prisons, some of whom 'had not seen the sun for years'. On 15th October, he announced the abolition of slavery, something which really existed in the Yemen,[1] and many manumitted slaves were promptly put out on to the streets to swell the increasing numbers of beggars and unemployed, two problems that were severely embarrassing the new Government.

Already, on 30th September, Abdul Rahman Baidani had arrived from Cairo to take up the appointment of Deputy Premier. He was the exception rather than the rule in the Government, being a Shafi Moslem when most of the Yemeni revolutionaries were Zeidis. Also, he was an intellectual of the diplomatic type, instead of either a trade union worker or a rough and ready practical revolutionary. Born in Cairo of Yemeni parents and educated there, Baidani was looked upon as being more an Egyptian in thought and habit than a Yemeni, and was suspected and disliked for that reason. In 1955 he had come into contact with Crown Prince Mohammed al-Badr who later persuaded the Imam to send him as Yemeni Minister to Bonn, where he obtained a doctorate in political economy. Returning to the Yemen in 1959, when Mohammed al-Badr was briefly in charge, he fled to Egypt as soon as the Imam came back from his health cure. Although affable in public towards

[1] This stung Saudi Arabia into finally abolishing slavery on 28th November 1962.

him, as-Sallal personally disliked Baidani, and soon the two men were privately at loggerheads. They were opposites in many respects. Considerable Egyptian pressure must have been brought to bear on the Premier to force him to accept Baidani as his Deputy, but Nasser wanted a reliable pro-Egyptian near the seat of power to act as a check against any independent nationalistic acts or attitudes.

In mid-October, a UAR Mission visited Sana to assess the situation, and this was followed a few days later by Field Marshal Abdul Hakim Amer, Nasser's right-hand man. A larger Cabinet was formed, personalities were reshuffled and new, unknown names came into the limelight. A few people who had been active in Aden, but were now regarded as being too narrowly nationalistic, were dropped, and only those who looked to Nasser for political inspiration and would work with Baidani, were chosen. This was all forced on as-Sallal, who could not govern for a single day without UAR support.

Colonel as-Sallal became President, Premier and Commander-in-Chief,[1] and Abdul Rahman Baidani was appointed Vice-President, Deputy Premier, Deputy Commander-in-Chief and Foreign Minister. Brigadier Abdullah Jizailan took over the Armed Forces from Hamoud al-Jaifi, and Mohsin al-Aini was sent off to the UN as head of a delegation which was seeking to claim the Yemeni seat. Ahmed Numan, the only other Shafi in the Government apart from Baidani, was appointed Yemeni Representative at the Arab League in Cairo. On 31st October, a provisional constitution was published, which was intended to remain in force for five years after which there was to be an election. On 16th November, Abdul Rahman Baidani announced the formation of the Popular Union, which was to be the only political party permitted in the country. Closely modelled on Nasser's Arab Socialist Union, its declared aim was to enable the people to govern themselves.

On 15th February 1963, as-Sallal announced that power was not to be entrusted to a single individual but to a Presidential Council, which would be composed of 'officers of the revolution', heads of various tribes, businessmen and economic experts. He also announced elections to a Tribal House of

[1] The Colonel promoted himself Field Marshal on 13th December 1962.

Representatives. This was to consist of between 160–80 sheikhs, of whom 60 per cent were to be elected and the remainder nominated; but little came of it. As-Sallal took care to improve his public relations with the world at large, but kept as much power in his own hands as possible.

A National Defence Council was appointed to look after defence matters, and steps were taken to form a Revolutionary National Guard in which it was hoped to enrol thousands of young men and instil in them the ideals of defending the revolution. But no one seemed to have any clear, practical idea of how this should be accomplished. Many unemployed Yemenis and recent exiles were pressed into this new force, which vaguely came under military command and took on a loose military form. This Revolutionary National Guard took the place of the old ramshackle militia that had largely disintegrated after the *coup*, when the conscripted tribesmen, seeing there would be little or no opportunity to plunder Sana, had faded away to their mountain homes.

Abdul Rahman Baidani, as a political economist, realized the need to establish a sound economy if the Republic was to survive and prosper, and so he tried to launch a two-year plan, and called upon foreign investment and help in this. He wanted, for example, to improve the harbour facilities at Hodeida, so that that port could replace Aden as the main trade entry of the country, but the complete lack of any statistical data was a severe handicap in this as in other plans. An economic agreement was made with the Soviet Union in December, when about 400 Soviet engineers, technicians and experts in agriculture and water supply, arrived to study the possibilities of developing industry and the radio services and initiating banking facilities. Also, that month, East Germany was persuaded to supply a number of tractors.

A National Bank, eventually known as the Yemeni Reconstruction and Development Bank, was established at Sana, and it was later stated that about eight million thalers[1] were found in the Imam's Treasury, although no accounts of any sort had ever been kept. Currency reform was tackled, and the Marie Theresa thaler which had been in circulation for almost

[1] Perhaps £3 million, or $7 million.

180 years was gradually withdrawn, from December, and replaced by another silver coin, the 'bakha', the first Yemeni currency ever issued. The new Republican Government had wanted to circulate paper money, but considered the problem of resistance from illiterate tribesmen to be insurmountable. Paper money was gradually brought into circulation in 1964 and was used concurrently with the bakhas.

As-Sallal and his fellow revolutionaries would have liked to have made a clean start in many other ways. He would have liked to modify the month-long Ramadan fast when no food can be eaten in daylight, something which took a heavy toll of productivity and temper, but as he sought the support of the Ulema and the fanatically Moslem Zeidi tribes, he dared not tamper with anything religious or traditional. But modern symbolism was not overlooked, and in keeping with new revolutionary ideas, the national flag was changed on 7th October from being red with a white scimitar and five white stripes, to one made up of three horizontal stripes, black, white and red, with a green star on the centre white stripe.

Meanwhile, as soon as the death of Imam Mohammed al-Badr had been announced by the Republicans on the radio, Prince Hassan, the late Imam's uncle and Yemeni Representative at the UN, claimed legal succession to the Imamate, stating that the revolt was only supported by a small group of army officers and that he expected the people and the tribes to rally to him. The Prince left New York and flew by way of London and Khartoum to Jedda, in Saudi Arabia, where he was joined by such members of the Hamid ud-Din family who had escaped. They acknowledged him as Imam, and on 5th October, he set up a Government-in-Exile. A Royal exception was Prince Kassem, a cousin of Mohammed al-Badr, who gave his allegiance to the Republicans. The Yemeni Legations in Washington, London, Bonn and Amman supported Prince Hassan, while those at Cairo, Rabat and Rome opted for the Republicans.

The conflicting reports of the death of Imam Mohammed al-Badr that had been hastily put out by the Republican Government were bound to cause suspicion and doubt. Foreign journalists who had been allowed into the Yemen in the hope of harnessing world opinion for the Republican cause, looked for proof of death. They wanted real evidence or witnesses to interview, but neither were forthcoming. The first statement had alleged that the Imam had been crushed to death under the ruins of the Bashir Palace, but when journalists saw that the palace was not in total ruin, but that only the top two floors had been wrecked, they were not satisfied. Then the Republican Government stated that Mohammed al-Badr had been shot, and even produced a soldier who was alleged to have fired the fatal bullet, but his story did not stand up to cross-examination.

The absence of a body was particularly suspicious in a land where it was customary to exhibit the head and body of people executed so that the object lesson would be plain for all to see. As no one could be found who had actually seen the Imam's body, rumours that Mohammed al-Badr had escaped and was alive began to circulate and multiply. On 9th October the Government-in-Exile issued a statement saying that this was indeed the truth, and that he had been in touch with them, but this was ridiculed by the Republicans, who issued a counter-story that the Imam had died of wounds. On the 15th it was announced over Radio Amman that Mohammed al-Badr had sent a message to King Hussein telling of his escape, and this was discounted by them too.

Rumours that Mohammed al-Badr was alive persisted, but Republican denials continued until suddenly, on 10th November, near Jebel Nadir, just inside the north-west corner of the Yemen, the Imam appeared, and held a press conference. A swashbuckling figure of a brigand king, with crossed bandoliers glittering with rifle bullets, he held forth to the sixteen journalists who had assembled, and his words were reported around the world. Faced with this *fait accompli*, the Republicans could no longer persevere with their contradictions. Their public relations exercise had badly misfired and turned out to be a shabby and embarrassing failure.

CHAPTER FOUR

The Imam Fights Back

MAIN EVENTS

1962	
November 4th	First UAR aerial attack on Najran, in Saudi Arabia.
	Military alliance between Saudi Arabia and Jordan.
9th	UAR troops reinforce Sada.
10th	Imam's press conference.
	First UAR naval and air attack on Qizan, in Saudi Arabia.
	Joint Defence Pact between UAR and the Yemen.
10th and 11th	Jordanian pilots and aircraft defect to UAR.
December 19th	America recognizes the Republican regime.
20th	UN seat given to the Yemeni Republican Government.
1963	
February 15th	As-Sallal announces that power will rest with Presidential Council.
16th–March 7th	—The Ramadan Offensive by Republicans.
16th	British Legation at Taiz closed.
18th	Abdul Rahman Baidani dropped from the Sallal Cabinet.
25th	Marib re-taken by Republicans.
March 7th	Harib, the last town in the Yemen, taken by the Republicans.

At his first dramatic press conference to American, British and Jordanian journalists near Jebel Nadir, Imam Mohammed al-Badr claimed that his supporters were in possession of the greater part of the Yemen, and that only Sana, Taiz and Hodeida were in Republican hands. He said he had an army of tribesmen under his personal command to the west of Sada, that his uncle, Prince Hassan, had another army to the east of

Sana, and that there was yet another near Harib, in the south-east. Together they totalled some 20,000 men, all of whom were about to march to crush the Republicans, and put the Imam back on his throne in Sana within three weeks. His claims were inaccurate and his boasts over-optimistic, but they stirred the imagination of the world and dismayed the Republicans. The conference had been arranged by King Hussein of Jordan, and was an effective demonstration of the fact that the Imam was alive and fighting back.

At this press conference the Imam gave an account of his escape. He said that at about 2300 hours on 26th September, after a late meeting at his Bashir Palace, he had been going to his quarters for the night when a soldier of the Palace Guard had pushed a sub-machine gun in his back and pressed the trigger. The gun misfired, and the soldier was arrested. Then news was brought to him that tanks were approaching the city, which did not alarm him as they were expected. Moments later sounds of the armoured vehicles moving towards the palace were heard, and shortly afterwards the tanks began to bombard the building. During this bombardment the Palace Guard disappeared. In the small hours of the morning the guns began to knock to pieces the third floor of the building. After listening to as-Sallal's broadcast announcing his death, Mohammed al-Badr saw the situation was hopeless, and as the rebel encirclement of the palace was not complete, he was able to slip away through the back door with five guards, all that remained with him. He claimed he had sent away the women of his household before he left, but this was not borne out by later evidence (as-Sallal was able to produce most of them for Western journalists to see in Sana). Once in the alleyways of the capital, the Imam was recognized by a woman who took him into her house and exchanged his conspicuously rich robes for a common soldier's tunic. That evening when it was dark, the Imam and his small escort scrambled over the city wall to make their way northwards.

The Imam claimed that his march northwards, beginning in such a small way, had become a triumphant one with tribes eagerly rallying to him at every step, and that it had ended at Sada with hundreds of loyal warriors mustered under his colours, but this was far from the truth. At that date Mohammed al-Badr had not dared to attempt to enter Sada, which was held by a small detachment of the Yemeni army loyal to the Republic. At first the Imam had been continuously cold-shouldered by the tribal sheikhs, especially those of the Hashid federation. But when he received cash from Saudi Arabia with which to bribe them, and the arrogant behaviour of the UAR occupation army had created widespread resentment, some of them at least reluctantly agreed openly to support him, not against the Republican Government as such but in his fight against the 'foreign invaders'. The prospect of pillaging Sana again or sacking either Taiz or Hodeida, however remote, must have been foremost in their thoughts and have been a compelling inducement to offer loyalty to the Imam instead of as-Sallal.

The reason for this lack of support from the quarter from which it might have been most expected, and indeed had been given before in Imamic emergencies, dated back to 1959, when as Crown Prince, Mohammed al-Badr had been left in charge of the country in his father's absence. It will be remembered that he had been alarmed by the mutiny in the army and the general unrest of the citizens of Sana, and had called upon the Hashid federation to help him. Several thousand tribesmen had duly arrived to camp outside the city, and their presence had certainly awed the soldiery and citizenry into docility, but Mohammed al-Badr had had to bribe them handsomely to go home again afterwards. A depleted treasury had awaited Imam Ahmed on his return from Rome, and the infuriated Ruler had ruthlessly and savagely set about recovering the money paid out.

Among other things, he had resorted to treachery, enticing the Hashid paramount sheikh and his son to a meeting under a promise of safe conduct, only to seize and behead them as soon as they arrived. He also imprisoned Abdullah bin Hussein al Ahmer, another son, who was nominated by the federation to become paramount sheikh when his father was killed, but the Imam feared a drastic Hashid rising if he continued to keep him in detention, and had been forced to release him early in 1961. The Bakil federation, which Mohammed al-Badr also had to buy off, had not been treated much better, and consequently both major tribal federations of the north and east, as well as many other tribes who might normally, by bribes and promises of loot, be persuaded to rally to an Imam in trouble, were alienated and stood coldly aloof.

Furthermore, the abolition of the hostage system, which removed a barbaric but effective Imamic influence, was taken as a sign of weakness. Without its restraints, each tribe became a law unto itself in its mountain fastness, able to ignore inconvenient Imamic requests now the Imam was no longer in a position to decapitate or torture a sheikh's son, previously held as a hostage for just such a refusal. While the righteousness of the Imam's cause was not openly questioned, since he was still their spiritual head, material incentives were necessary to persuade the Zeidi tribes to help him recover his temporal domain and powers. Clearly, had the Imam possessed the loyalty and fierce backing of the Zeidi mountain tribes which he claimed, he would have been able to persuade them to march on Sana straight away, before the UAR garrison was reinforced, when there would probably have been no difficulty in sacking the city and beheading all revolutionaries who fell into his hands.

What actually happened was that after escaping from Sana, Mohammed al-Badr made his way to Hajja, where he had previously been successful in rousing the tribes to help him, only to find that its garrison had declared for the Republicans. Unable to expect hospitality from the Bakil federation at this stage, he turned, with only a very small following, and made his way over the border to Qizan, in Saudi Arabia. He then moved on to Najran, where the Royal Princes were rallying to his uncle, Prince Hassan. The Prince, back from New York, went to see King Saud, of Saudi Arabia, at Riyadh. His meeting must have been a fairly satisfactory one, for he then returned to Najran, which became a focal rallying point for Royalists, despatched several of the Royal Princes back into Zeidi territory to rouse the tribes, and began to prepare generally the forthcoming struggle against the Republicans.

Arriving on 8th or 9th October, a full fortnight after the *coup*, Mohammed al-Badr was perhaps less well received than has ever been admitted. A tough problem faced the Royalists. Prince Hassan was the popular leader whose personality had attracted many Royal Princes, but Mohammed al-Badr was legally the Imam. There must have been considerable argument and discussion in the Royalist camp, and perhaps disagreement. On the 12th, Mohammed Ahmed al-Shami, who had been the Yemeni diplomatic representative in London, had quickly joined the Royalists, and was now Foreign Minister in the Government-in-Exile, was sent off to New York to compete for the Yemeni UN seat against Mohsin al-Aini, who was already there. Mohammed al-Shami was a strong supporter of Prince Hassan.

The next day, the 13th, it was announced over Radio Mecca that Mohammed al-Badr was alive, and had agreed to accept the validity of Prince Hassan's claim to the Imamate. However, on the 17th, again over Radio Mecca, it was announced that Prince Hassan had renounced his claim and now recognized Mohammed al-Badr as the Imam. What actually happened in those few days is not known, but it may be that although Mohammed al-Badr was now acknowledged as the Imam, no doubt to give a strong political appeal to the Royalist cause and to demonstrate unity, the Royal Princes were to retain much individual discretion and power. Once he was assured of his position, Imam Mohammed al-Badr reshuffled the Royalist Government-in-Exile, and Prince Hassan became the Premier. Cabinet members were named (mostly Royal Princes) but in practice this amounted to little, since they were scattered across the Yemen and were barely in touch with the Imam or his Premier.

The Imam set up his headquarters in some caves near Jebel Qara, in the mountains in north-west Yemen about forty miles south-west of Sada. He remained here until forced to move by a UAR offensive in August 1964. Prince Hassan made his headquarters near Amlah, about twenty miles to the east of Sada, also in caves. The many caves in the rocky sides of the valleys provided convenient living accommodation as well as air-raid shelters for the Royalist groups operating in the mountains.

The Royal Princes who played prominent parts in the early days of the war were Prince Abdullah Hussein, who went to the Jauf, Prince Mohammed Ismail, who went into Bakil country, Prince Abdullah Hassan, who was sent to the Khawlan region, and Prince Hassan Hassan,[1] who went to the Marib

[1] The names of the several Royal Princes are often very similar and confusing, so this simplified form is adopted, to distinguish, for example, Prince Hassan (Hassan bin Yahya) from Prince Hassan (Hassan bin Hassan).

area. The one commoner prominent in the Royalist cause was Ahmed al-Sayaghi who had been nominated as Minister of the Interior, and who moved in to seize Harib fort in the Imam's name. Ahmed al-Sayaghi had been imprisoned at Hajja for having contact with the Free Yemenis, and had remained in exile in Lahej since his release in 1953. He refused a Government post offered to him by Mohammed al-Badr when he became Imam, but after the *coup* came out openly on his side. Najran, over the border in Saudi Arabia, became the political and military rally-point of the Royalists, and Prince Mohammed Hussein was put in charge of those who went there to support the Imam. He also set up camps and organized supplies. For a while Najran became the real link, and indeed for a long time was the only medium of contact between the Imam and his Premier. Poor communication between the Imam and his field commanders was a big drawback to the Royalists.

There can be little doubt about UAR involvement in the Republican *coup* in the Yemen, since on 28th September, the very day after its announcement, Egyptian troops landed by aircraft at both Sana and Taiz. UAR paratroops promptly formed the personal bodyguard of as-Sallal, partly because as-Sallal did not trust his fellow Yemenis, but mostly because Nasser did not want this pro-Egyptian leader to be removed from the scene by other ambitious revolutionaries, who might not have been so well-disposed towards him. On the 29th the first of several UAR ships carrying troops, tanks, guns, vehicles and military stores, docked at Hodeida. These ships must have been loaded some time before, and were most probably at sea while the *coup* was taking place. By the beginning of October there were at least 3,000 UAR soldiers encamped outside the three main cities of the Yemen, with armoured vehicles in conspicuous evidence and scores of aircraft flying noisily overhead.

The Republicans had barely enough military force to impose their authority on the three main cities, let alone defend themselves against tribal attacks in mass, and the new Government was only sustained by the presence of UAR bayonets. Without these it would not have lasted many days, since there were other factions ambitious to take over the mantle of power discarded by the fleeing Imam. To justify the presence of foreign troops on Yemeni soil, false reports were put out to the world that Saudi Arabian and Jordanian forces were entering the country and that there was fighting against them in the border areas in the north, east and south-east. The Republicans alleged that tribesmen from the State of Beihan were invading the Yemen, which was also false, although a clandestine route was being established from the Federation of South Arabia through Beihan into what later became Royalist-held territory. In fact, there were no Saudi Arabian or Jordanian troops on Yemeni soil, nor were any attacks made by them.

Within days of the *coup* the UAR forces took on the characteristics of an army of occupation, despite their claims that they were simply there to defend the revolution. More Egyptian formations and units continued to arrive, until by mid-November it was estimated that there were over 8,000 UAR soldiers within the Yemen, supported by large numbers of tanks, guns and aircraft. As a result, the Republicans were able to control Sana, Taiz and Hodeida, the triangle of territory between those cities, and a large proportion of the coastal strip; but that was about all except for the few isolated inland garrisons that had to be supplied by air. Throughout the rest of the Yemen there did not seem to be any central authority, and for some weeks tribal anarchy reigned. Released hostages had returned, so there were no more restraints upon the wilder tribes, who, if strong or bold enough, moved out against their neighbours to pay off old scores or simply to engage in banditry. The Royal Princes had a hard task to rally them to the Imam's banner.

Although the allegiance of the Yemeni regular army had been sharply divided by the *coup*, the majority of the officers had been persuaded beforehand to accept Republican loyalties. This meant that only a few outlying or isolated detachments declared for the Royalists. Some elements of the army just disintegrated, and many soldiers deserted to their homes. It was largely a matter of where the Yemeni soldiers happened to be at the time that governed the side they opted for and the conditioning of their officers, although it was estimated that there were about 200 Cairo-trained Yemeni officers in the army. As-Sallal ordered a large pay rise for his troops to ensure their loyalty, and this was given at once.

A very much enlarged UAR Military Mission got to work re-organizing the Yemeni army, which at this stage may have numbered less than 7,000 men. Egyptians were brought in as staff officers and placed in command of units, but only a limited quantity of arms was doled out. Little real progress was made in training. The soldiers were neither respected nor completely trusted by the UAR staff, who regarded Yemeni military ability as negligible. In the first flush of the revolt many Yemeni officers stopped wearing badges of rank, some, in particular, who felt they might be suspected of too great loyalty and subservience to the old regime, or of an anti-Republican past. But as the Egyptians gained a grip, this Yemeni army very slowly blossomed out into a pale copy of the UAR one, with an officer corps complete with prestige and status, differential pay rates, badges of rank and discipline. As-Sallal's personal bodyguard remained completely Egyptian, and soon rose to a strength of about 3,000 paratroops.

As a monarchy, Jordan was hostile to the new Republican regime, and at this period King Hussein was antagonistic towards Nasser because of UAR propaganda directed against his country. When Prince Hassan first arrived at Jedda from New York, King Hussein sent an emissary to him to express friendship and sympathy, and was instrumental in transporting journalists to the Imam's dramatic press conference. Some material aid was sent to the Royalists—not a great deal as Jordan had little to spare—and a few Jordanian army officers[1] were lent to advise and help train Royalist volunteers in camps that were being established near the Yemeni border. Pakistan also sympathized with the Royalists and very discreetly sent a little material aid, which mostly consisted of old British rifles.

The Saudi Arabian Cabinet held divided views on the new Republican regime, but since the monarchy was hostile to the UAR, it regarded the as-Sallal Government coldly, and the Saudi Arabian Legation at Taiz was closed on 1st October. King Saud began to send sums of money, arms, ammunition and instructors to the small groups of Yemeni Royalists congregating with his approval in camps around Qizan, Najran, and other points along the northern border with the Yemen.

[1] In November 1962, King Hussein admitted that about sixty of his Jordanian officers were helping the Royalists.

Once it was known that Imam Mohammed al-Badr was alive the volume of these increased. Nasser meanwhile was at the height of one of his Saudi Arabian hate-campaigns, and by means of his 'Voice of the Arabs' radio station in Cairo, was trying to reach past King Saud and stir up discontent within Saudi Arabia, on occasions with some success.

On 2nd October, barely a week after the *coup* in the Yemen, a Saudi Arabian aircraft destined for Najran with military stores on board, landed in Egypt instead, and its three Saudi Arabian pilots defected to Nasser. Between the 3rd and the 8th, three more Saudi Arabian aircraft flew to the UAR, which led King Saud to ground his whole air force for weeks while his pilots were re-screened. The defection of the pilots and the loss of the aircraft were probably the final indignities which prompted the Saudi family to make the weak and vacillating King Saud hand over actual power to his brother, Prince Faisal, who became Premier and took over the Government of the country. The Yemen was the traditional enemy of the Wahabis, of Saudi Arabia, and there were differing views on the amount of support, if any, that should be given to the Royalists. Although he was not himself well disposed to the Imam and the Hamid ud-Din family, Prince Faisal decided that the aid begun by King Saud should be continued. He reformed the Saudi Arabian Cabinet, and six ministers who had suggested that the Sallal regime should be recognized were dropped.

In riposte, UAR aircraft began to attack small Saudi Arabian towns and villages near the Yemeni frontier, at one stage with such regularity that it was thought to be a prelude to open war—no doubt a great temptation while the Saudi Arabian air force was grounded as unreliable. When speaking about Saudi Arabia, as-Sallal refused to recognize what he called 'artificial boundaries' and asked a prominent Saudi Arabian refugee to form a Government-in-Exile. This never materialized, but the Yemeni Republican Government boastfully announced that if its territory was attacked from the air, its own air force would bomb both Saudi Arabia and Jordan, and it warned the population of those two countries to keep away from airfields, government buildings, camps and radio installations. The Yemeni Government did not have any aircraft but the UAR did, and so it was evidently acting on Nasser's behalf.

One of the first assaults by UAR aircraft on Saudi Arabian territory took place on 4th November, when five small villages near Najran were bombed. The inhabitants decamped, but little material damage was done. On the 10th, Qizan and other small coastal habitations were bombarded by UAR naval craft, with hardly any real effect. The attacks then slackened off, and on the 14th Prince Faisal told a press conference that the UAR had stopped bombing Saudi Arabia, but the situation frightened him into buying an expensive ground-to-air defensive missile system, and more aircraft from Britain.

On 4th November, it was announced that there was to be a military alliance between Saudi Arabia and Jordan, and that a Joint Defence Council was to be formed. Nothing ever came of this, except for a few military liaison visits between the two kingdoms. This move was countered on the 10th by a Joint Five-Year Defence Pact between the UAR and the Yemen, in which there was far more substance. It really replaced the vague Jedda Pact of 1956, which the UAR had invoked as the legal vindication for sending an expeditionary force into the Yemen. A Supreme Council for military policy and a War Council for military planning were to be set up, and Egypt also granted the Yemen a loan of £E1 million. All this in practice gave Nasser the overall say in running the war. On the same day, the 10th, the chief of the Jordanian air force defected to Cairo, stating that a squadron of his command, based near Taif in Saudi Arabia, had been ordered to carry out offensive operations against Republican troops in north Yemen. The following day two more Jordanian pilots deserted to Egypt, and all three were granted commissions in the UAR air force.

At first mainly in deference to Saudi Arabia in which it had a very large oil stake, America refused to recognize the as-Sallal regime. In an attempt to prevent hostilities breaking out between Arab countries, US aircraft flew sorties over Jedda and Riyadh, during the period of acute tension and a US warship was despatched to show a presence in Jedda. At a meeting on 10th November between Abdul Rahman Baidani, the Vice-President of the Yemen, and the US chargé d'affaires, Baidani stated that Yemeni (meaning obviously UAR) aircraft would only bomb airfields and bases in Saudi Arabia and Jordan if the Yemen was attacked first. In return it was decided that all American aircraft would be withdrawn from Saudi Arabia, or adopt a neutral attitude, should either Saudi Arabia or Jordan attack the Yemen. This seemed to pave the way for better relations but American recognition still did not follow. As-Sallal asked the Americans to continue work on the road from Taiz to Sana, which had run into labour difficulties as a result of the American attitude and this they agreed to do. The 313-mile road was then about one-third completed.

Republican relations with Britain were not good either, because of friction along the Federation border and because of Britain's refusal to recognize the new regime. It was alleged that the British were allowing troops and aid for the Royalists to cross the frontier freely. On 15th October, it was put out that Britain had permitted Federal Army troops from Beihan to give transport, arms and ammunition to Royalist sympathizers to use in the Marib sector, and in this allegation there was a certain amount of truth. UAR aircraft attacked a small town in Beihan State on 22nd October, and the following day British troops were sent there to forestall an anticipated attack. On 9th November, as-Sallal openly accused Britain of plotting against the Republic, but later he paid compensation for the air attacks on Beihan territory.

It was not until 28th November that the UAR made its first pronouncement of its intention in the Yemen, declaring that its aim was to combat the danger of foreign invasion. An interesting side-light was later revealed in the *Last Will of Abdul Hakim Amer*[1] which was published widely after his 'suicide'. He wrote, 'We did not bother to study the local, Arab and international implications of intervention or the political or military questions involved. After years of experience we realized that the Yemen war is a war between tribes and that we entered it without knowing the nature of the land, their traditions and ideas.'

Nasser believed that a swift, savage campaign would break all opposition and carry the revolution beyond the borders of the Yemen into Saudi Arabia, but there were doubts in the Republican Government as to whether this was the right kind

[1] Dated 7th September 1967.

of course. The leading opponent of this policy was Ahmed Numan, and he was supported to a lesser degree by Abdul Rahman Iryani and Mohammed as-Zubeiri. Ahmed Numan advocated conciliation and benevolence towards the suspicious tribes, and the making of a series of agreements with local sheikhs to wean them one by one from the Imam's side, and so gradually extend the influence of the Republican Government. He noted that Britain had achieved considerable success by similar methods in the Federation of South Arabia. It is questionable how successful this policy would have been. The Republicans might have been able to give evidence of having a wise, understanding government that would contrast favourably with the bad ones of the Imamic era. But Nasser's strategy prevailed and was put into practice with dog-like devotion by as-Sallal who relied entirely upon UAR troops to maintain his government and his own position in power.

At first the UAR commanders were able to gain the co-operation of some of the tribes to a degree, but the sheikhs did not relish old ties being reimposed, and very soon they could no longer be relied upon. They tended to change sides continually, and as allies in the field they constantly let down both the Egyptians and the Royalists, as the war dragged on. The tribes encircling Sana stood aloof, perhaps hoping for a later opportunity to descend and sack the city if they did not suddenly become committed to supporting the Republicans. Sackfuls of thalers went in bribes that had little lasting effect because the sheikhs continually asked for more. When Royalist money began to make its appearance in late October, some of the tribes on the fringe areas accepted it and temporarily turned their coats. As-Sallal had to pour out more thalers to persuade them to turn back again. Some tribes thought they were on to a good thing and switched sides for financial considerations whenever the opportunity offered.

A combination of bombing, UAR military presence and bribes brought about complete submission of the people living in the triangle between Sana, Taiz and Hodeida, and on its borders, but the Republican Government's writ did not run much outside this area. President as-Sallal re-introduced a system of hostages in a slightly different form, forcing or encouraging as many tribal sheikhs as he could to send their sons to school in Sana. Despite the cash motive, the brutality of UAR actions tended to lead the tribes, one by one, to turn against the Republican Government. The malpractices of the Imamate began to be forgotten and the Imam, so generally feared and detested in the past, began slowly to gain popularity, as he posed as the resistance leader for all Yemenis determined to rid the country of foreign invaders. It was a good rallying platform, and initially Mohammed al-Badr made full use of it. It is doubtful whether any other Imam in history had ever been so popular with certain sections of the population, ruling as they all had with force, fear, threats and hostages. Imam Mohammed al-Badr had none of these aids to total power and had to rely solely upon subtle methods of persuasion, personal leadership, cash and diplomatic and political skill.

With great strain to the economy of the UAR, Nasser had to increase his Expeditionary Force much more than he had anticipated, to stop the infant Republican Government from being toppled. Egyptian troops now settled in the Republican-held part of the country and caused considerable tension by their actions, attitude and overbearing presence. The Egyptian soldiers were themselves unhappy at being suddenly moved into such an inhospitable land for an indefinite period, and they looked down with contempt on the inhabitants. Most of them, the officers as well, were originally under the impression they were only to remain in the country for a few weeks to help train the Yemeni army, and they had expected to be welcomed with open arms. When, on the contrary, they were met with hostility or indifference, they became sullen and arrogant towards the Yemenis.

Although the as-Sallal Government relied completely upon the UAR Expeditionary Force to maintain its position it was not entirely a puppet one. As-Sallal, whatever his faults, was a nationalist, even if a very pro-Egyptian one. He had appointed several ministers and officials from among Yemenis educated abroad, and they had rushed home to reap the benefits of the revolution and to claim the jobs they thought their education warranted. There was much intriguing and jostling for position. Financial arrangements were not yet regularized and salaries were often unpaid; such silver coin as was available being earmarked in the first place for bribes or payment to

Republican soldiers. For a similar reason there was a split within the Republican Government itself, between top officials and army officers. The military officers were paid their salaries promptly and regularly, while the civilians had to wait.

The UAR took over the defence responsibilities of the Republic, but left other civilian matters, so long as they did not interfere with the overall defence plan, to as-Sallal. Because, as of old, the people insisted on their right of direct approach to their ruler, and now demanded to confront as-Sallal in person with their troubles and problems, it meant that, in the early days of his power, he was hopelessly overworked, while as a rule his ministers did not have enough to do. In the past, no matter how despotic they were, the Imams had always, in theory, been accessible to even their lowliest subjects, though in practice this façade usually meant a very long wait, much patience, and frequent failure. But the tradition was inbred, and although it severely handicapped him, as-Sallal did not dare dispense with it altogether.

During the early months there was more jostling for position than real fighting between the Republican forces and the Royalists. With comparatively small numbers the Egyptians did not attempt to force their way into the mountainous areas against opposition, but seeped outwards as far as they could, using air support and air supply for their isolated detachments. There were a number of small initial skirmishes, but these indicated that the Royalists formed no dire military threat to the Republican Government. UAR aerial attacks and fire power generally forced the tribesmen to keep their distance. This made as-Sallal confident that before long, with continued UAR military assistance, he would be able forcibly to occupy the whole country. Perhaps after all, he reasoned, Nasser was right in believing that a swift campaign would break all opposition.

The small garrison at Harad, on the northern edge of the coastal plain and on a main route south to Sana, early went over to the Royalists, coming under the influence of Prince Mohammed Ismail. On the other side of the country, on 10th October, local tribesmen led by Prince Hassan Hassan overwhelmed the Republican detachment holding Marib. UAR aircraft bombed both places, and then turned their attention to other areas where there was anti-Republican activity, like Sada which was precariously held by a small Republican garrison. A strong Egyptian armoured column, covered by aircraft, forced its way northwards from Sana and succeeded in reaching Sada by 9th November, but the city remained ringed by hostile tribesmen who were only kept at bay by the liberal use of bombs and bullets.

To make good the boast that Sada was in Royalist hands, Prince Hassan, the Premier, managed to rouse some of the adjacent Hashid federation tribesmen to move against the city. There was a clash on the night of the 12th (only two days after the Imam's famous press conference), another on the 23rd, and yet another on the 28th, in each of which casualties were suffered by defenders and attackers alike. Greatly exaggerated claims were made by both, but Sada remained in Republican hands, with a garrison holding out in the city itself and another one securely ensconced on an overlooking hill, while the hostile tribesmen perched on the heights that partially surrounded the city. The UAR took hostages from the Hashid federation tribes in this region to keep them docile.

In the Jauf, Prince Abdullah Hussein seized Hazm, a large village at an important track junction in the Wadi Humaidat. He then mustered tribesmen to move with him westwards into the Wadi Hirran, which contained, at Sinwan, a Republican-held fort reinforced by UAR guns and vehicles. In attacks in mid-November, he ambushed a UAR convoy, seized some arms and vehicles, and then overran Sinwan, killing or capturing its inhabitants. Under Prince Abdullah Hussein's urging, the tribesmen unsuccessfully attacked the small town of Barat, also in Wadi Humaidat but farther to the north.

The Royalists had some success in the Sana-Marib corridor, and after Prince Hassan Hassan had taken Marib,[1] he pushed westwards along it towards Sana (briefly overrunning the tiny town of Sirwah), only to be pushed out again by the Republicans who occupied two strong hill positions overlooking the town. In an effort to relieve the pressure on Sirwah, the UAR dropped four small groups of paratroops, but they all fell wide of the target and most of them were killed by the Royalists. As the Prince could not persuade his followers to mount an

[1] At Marib the Royalists captured three UAR helicopters, with Soviet crews, which had landed thinking the city was still in Republican hands.

attack in the face of UAR bombing and defensive fire power, the Republicans maintained their positions blocking the Sana-Marib corridor.

To the south-east, there was desultory fighting around Harib Fort, which was occupied for the Royalists by Ahmed al-Sayaghi. He tried to extend his influence in the region but unsuccessfully because it was swarming with Shafeis, who tended to have Republican sympathies. Ahmed al-Sayaghi was a man of energy and ideas, and he organized a long-range raiding group to extend Royalist domination, but this was not a success because the tribesmen had little idea of how to put it into practice. By mid-December, the skirmishing throughout the Yemen died down, a lull which lasted until early February (1963). This was mostly because the winter rains caused the valleys to mist up for most of the day, something which restricted military activity on both sides.

The main achievement of the Royalists had been that their cause had been put firmly on the world map by the colourful and enthusiastic reports of journalists who had been invited to visit them in the mountains and at their training camps. World imagination was caught by a King fighting for his throne against the ogre, Nasser, and living a simple life in mountain caves amongst his followers who, with only knives and ancient muskets, were defying the modern might of the UAR Expeditionary Force. The Royalist public relations effort, which was really at this stage the Saudi Arabian one, received much attention and sympathy. This in turn boosted Royalist morale and encouraged an aggressive, anti-UAR spirit that was starting to sweep through the mountains of the Yemen. Under Prince Mohammed Hussein's direction, numerous small Royalist camps began to mushroom just beyond the Yemeni northern border, especially in the vicinity of Najran, where Saudi Arabian and Jordanian officers were helping to organize and train those flocking to the Royalist standard. Other Arab and European mercenaries were to arrive later on.

Although there was a lull in the ground skirmishing, UAR aircraft remained active whenever weather conditions permitted, and on occasions bombed Saudi Arabian territory. Najran was bombed on 30th December, and again two days later. On 3rd January (1963), the alarmed Saudi Arabian Government ordered general mobilization and cancelled army leave, although in practice this meant little. The following day it stated that its aid to the Royalists would be increased. Three squadrons of Saudi Arabian jets were sent to airfields near the Yemeni border, and anti-aircraft guns were moved to the region of Najran. By this time the Saudi Arabian air force was considered to be reliable once more.

Meanwhile, on 27th November, President Kennedy of America confirmed that he had written to as-Sallal, Nasser, Prince Faisal and King Hussein of Jordan, offering his good offices to bring about a peaceful settlement. He suggested a phased evacuation of UAR troops from the Yemen, the ending of Saudi Arabian and Jordanian aid to the Royalists, and the withdrawal of Saudi Arabian soldiers from the border areas. On 9th December, as-Sallal publicly welcomed one part of the offer only: that to help prevent Saudi Arabian and Jordanian aggression against the Yemen. Nasser assured President Kennedy that UAR intervention was not designed to pull down the Saudi Arabian and Jordanian thrones but to protect the young Yemeni Republic, and said he was willing to withdraw his troops just as soon as Saudi Arabian and Jordanian aid ceased. King Hussein countered with a proposal that a UN team should investigate the Yemen situation. On 8th January (1963), a letter of support was sent from President Kennedy to Prince Faisal, which was interpreted as a warning to Nasser not to attack Saudi Arabia. Later that month, Prince Faisal said the Yemeni question should be settled by pan-Arab arbitration.

On 14th December, as-Sallal threatened to close down the foreign diplomatic missions in the Yemen of all the countries that did not recognize his Government, and on the 18th, at a press conference, Abdul Rahman Baidani said that after negotiation, America had agreed to recognize the Republican Government. This it did the following day.[1] The American Ambassador to Saudi Arabia was to be responsible for the Yemen, but he was to have a diplomatic representative at Taiz to report to him. Britain still withheld recognition, and the British Legation at Taiz was closed on 16th February 1963.

[1] The same day, 19th December 1962, both Australia and Canada recognized the Yemeni Republican Government.

Both the Republicans and the Royalists had a representative at the UN, each claiming the Yemeni seat. The matter was put to the vote in the General Assembly on 20th December, the day after American recognition, and the decision was taken to opt for the Republican regime.[1] Mohsin al-Aini occupied the seat and commenced lobbying his cause, which meant among other things making repeated complaints of alleged British support for the Royalists. Mohsin al-Aini had been dropped from the first Sallal Cabinet because his Baathist[2] sympathies offended Nasser, and he had been sent out of the country to New York as the UN Representative, where he remained until 1966. Just before, on 27th November, the Royalists had asked the UN to supervise a plebiscite of the tribes, and although the Republican delegate welcomed the idea, the United States disapproved, considering it impracticable, so no further action was taken.

On 29th January 1963 a small Republican force, about 120 strong, moved into Beihan State, killing a Federal soldier in the process. During the next few days this detachment doubled in size, and, reinforced with mortars and machine guns, remained about one mile from Harib Fort, in what was, to the Yemenis, disputed territory. After being shelled by British artillery the Yemenis withdrew on 26th February. Throughout, Royalist forces remained in possession of Harib Fort. By early February there were already stirrings of activity. On the 2nd there had been a clash between Republicans and Royalists in the Jauf, and there was another on the 7th. On the 12th and 13th, UAR aircraft again bombed Najran.

Royalist strategy was vague and confused, impelled only by a general desire to close in on Sana from all sides, and to liquidate all other Republican-held garrisons in the process. The idea of Ahmed al-Sayaghi, who had left Harib Fort to confer with the Imam, Prince Hassan the Premier, and others, was to gain sufficient tribal support to make a mass assault on Sana, bypassing and ignoring all other Republican-held points to do so. In practice the strategy would depend entirely upon the princely field commanders and their success in persuading tribesmen to march with them.

[1] By 73 votes to 4, with 23 abstentions.

[2] The Syrian Baathist Party was disliked by Nasser because it objected to his claim to the leadership of Arab Socialism.

Sana tended to dominate strategic thinking, and all eyes turned in that direction. Each of the commanders pushed as far forward as he could. It was hoped to surround and cut it off entirely, and some progress was made in this when, in early February, Prince Abdullah Hassan laid a successful ambush that caught a UAR armoured column near Raydah, about twenty miles north of Sana. His attack inflicted heavy losses on personnel, arms and vehicles, and effectively closed the road to Sada. The road east from Sana to Marib was also blocked, and armed tribesmen with mortars moved close enough to the capital to make the UAR command move its MiG and Ilyushin aircraft from the Rahaba airfield, about twelve miles north of Sana. The UAR Dakotas still remained at the other, smaller, airfield at Jiraf which was much closer to the capital. The road southwards from Sana to Dhamar and Taiz was still not passable to the Republican forces, which left open only the road out westwards from Sana to Hodeida. Royalist attempts to close this by ambush were unsuccessful, but even so, with Sana all but besieged, the prospect of an all-out assault by Royalist tribesmen seemed likely and impending. Royalist hopes ran high in February, although by this time, Field-Marshal Amer had already arrived from Egypt to take command of the opposing forces.

The strengths of the UAR Expeditionary Force were never published, and owing to dispersal and rotation were hard to assess accurately, but by the beginning of 1963 there were probably some 15,000 Egyptian troops in the Yemen, with ample tanks and guns, and supported by over 200 aircraft which operated from a number of airfields and airstrips. Although the roads radiating out from Sana (which had a garrison of over 7,000 UAR troops) were generally blocked, with the possible exception of the one leading to Hodeida, the Republicans remained in strong possession of the Sana-Hodeida-Taiz triangle, and the coastal strip. In addition, there were isolated Republican garrisons, supplied by air, at such places as Safa, Harf, Barat, Khamir, Raydah, and Amran along the Sada-Sana mountain ridge, Sirwah to the east, and Mabar, Dhamar, Yarim and Ibb to the south, while along the Sana-Hodeida road, garrisons at such places as Khamis and Manakha, the Ismaili centre, kept the route open. Field-Marshal Amer planned to stop the Royalists creeping towards Sana, to open the roads leading from the capital, to seize all the major towns in the country, and generally to increase the territory under Republican control. He arrived in the Yemen in late January 1963 and remained until early March, during which time he personally conducted a series of operations which, as they coincided with the month-long Ramadan fast, became known as the Ramadan Offensive.

First of all he asked for the number of UAR troops to be brought up to 20,000, and the first reinforcements arrived early in February. On the 16th, with a strong armoured column, he pressed northwards along the mountain ridge towards Sada. Prince Mohammed Hussein, who had about 1,500 Yemenis in training in camps near Najran, was ordered to take them to block the Egyptians. They were completely unsuccessful, being poorly-trained and were brushed aside and scattered. On the 18th Field-Marshal Amer was in Sada, and his aircraft, tanks and guns had driven back into the shelter of the mountains all the Royalist tribesmen who had attempted to oppose him.

A similar strong, armoured thrust was next pushed out eastwards along the Sana-Marib Corridor, tumbling back the Royalists who vainly tried to stand up to a rain of bombs and bullets. Marib was taken on the 25th by Amer, who next turned his attention to clearing the road southwards from Sana through Dhamar, Yarim and Ibb. This was done within days. He then made for Harib, now the only town of any size still held by the Royalists, and this fell to the Egyptians on 7th March, the garrison decamping into Beihan as the Republicans approached. In a short three-week offensive, the Field-Marshal had seized every single town of any size in the country, cleared all the main routes, and pressed the Royalists back into the mountains. Additionally, his control of Harib meant the cutting-off of what had developed into a main Royalist supply route up through Beihan. The Ramadan Offensive had been a huge success. Over half the country was under effective Republican authority, many more tribes had been brought within its writ, and as a result, many others had second thoughts about backing the Imam.

This short, sharp offensive tended to overshadow the growing discontent within the Yemen about the excessive Egyptian interference in Yemen affairs, and criticism had become centred on the person of Abdul Rahman Baidani, the Vice-President and Deputy Premier. Baidani left suddenly for Cairo on 20th January, and did not return. For a while nothing was said officially, and it was not until 18th February, by which time Amer's offensive was in full swing, that as-Sallal re-shuffled his Cabinet and formally dropped Baidani from it, depriving him of all his posts and titles. On the 21st, Abdul Rahman Baidani spoke out from Cairo, admitting he had differences of opinion with as-Sallal, but denying rumours that the UAR had been asked to send him back to the Yemen to face treason charges. Clearly Baidani had been sacrificed by Nasser for the sake of expediency.

CHAPTER FIVE

UN Intervention

MAIN EVENTS

1962	
December 20th	UN Seat given to the Republicans.
1963	
April 15th	Disengagement Agreement announced.
June 11th	UNYOM authorized by the Security Council.
June 13th	Advance party of UNYOM arrives in the Yemen.
August 20th	General von Horn resigns as UNYOM commander.
September 10th	Lieut.-General P. S. Gyani appointed UNYOM commander.
November 4th	Signor Spinelli appointed Head of UNYOM.
1964	
September 4th	UNYOM terminated.

The short and unhappy account of United Nations intervention in the Yemen can be told in a single chapter. Poorly supported, and subjected to many conflicting pressures, it was a dismal failure, generating misunderstanding and hostility rather than an atmosphere conducive to peace. The UN Mission itself was beset by internal bickering, and was regarded with deep suspicion by all directly involved in the war.

President Kennedy had already made attempts to mediate by writing to the war leaders, and he now wanted to bring the United Nations into the picture. As a peace-keeping organization anxious to increase its waning prestige, the UN itself was not averse to this, but the UAR, Saudi Arabia, the Republicans and the Royalists were none of them interested in UN mediation unless on their own terms, to which none of the others would agree. It was not until March 1963, that the UN was able to participate in Yemeni affairs, mainly under American urging, after two representatives had shuttled to and fro between Nasser, as-Sallal and Prince Faisal in attempts to obtain simultaneous assurances from them about conditions for a cease-fire. Dr. Ralph Bunche, the UN Under-Secretary for Special Political Affairs, and Mr. Ellsworth R. Bunker, a former US Ambassador to India, were the two representatives, but such were the prejudices of the situation that Bunche was not permitted to enter Saudi Arabia, and Bunker was not allowed into the Yemen, during the negotiations.

Dr. Bunche visited the Yemen in March 1963, after being kept back for a few days so that Field Marshal Amer could capture Marib, and thus show that all cities and towns were in Republican hands. His visit lasted from the 1st to the 4th, during which time he had discussions with both as-Sallal and the Field Marshal. He visited Sana and the new Republican showpiece, Marib, and then went on to Aden where he held a press conference announcing that as-Sallal had asked for technical aid and UN assistance so that the Yemen could establish peaceful relations with its neighbours. Bunche then went to Cairo, where he had talks with Nasser and tried to persuade him to withdraw UAR troops from the Yemen if the Royalists agreed to stop their war against the Republican Government.

During these months of March and April, Mr. Bunker paid at least three visits to Saudi Arabia to talk with Prince Faisal, and also went to Cairo to discuss the war with Nasser. The talks and visits by these two men eventually resulted in an announcement over Radio Cairo on 13th April that an agreement to end the war in the Yemen had been reached between the UAR, Saudi Arabia and the Yemen Republic. No details were released, nor were the Royalists mentioned. The high cost to Egypt of maintaining an Expeditionary Force in the Yemen in a situation that seemed likely to be prolonged indefinitely, and the Saudi Arabian Government's fear that, if provoked too far, the UAR might launch a full-scale war against them, were almost certainly responsible for the nature and timing of this statement.

On the 15th, Radio Mecca announced that Saudi Arabia had accepted what became known as the Disengagement Agreement, provided that there was no interference in Yemeni internal affairs, and that the Yemeni people were allowed the right of self-determination. More backstairs negotiation followed, and it was not until the 29th (of April) that U Thant, the UN Secretary-General, was able to broadcast the conditions of this Disengagement Agreement. These were, briefly, that Saudi Arabia would terminate all aid to the Royalists and prohibit the use of its territory to them, while the UAR would begin a phased withdrawal of its troops from the Yemen without taking any punitive actions against the Royalists. A demilitarized zone was to be established, extending twenty kilometres on either side of the northern Yemeni border.

The main clause, so U Thant announced with pride, was that UN Observers were to be stationed in this demilitarized zone to check that this agreement was honoured. They would ensure that neither side tried to introduce troops or arms into the zone, and would make sure of the repatriation of UAR forces and the cessation of Royalist activities in Saudi Arabia. At last the UN had gained a foothold in the Yemeni struggle. The very next day, U Thant ordered Major-General Carl von Horn, Chief of Staff of the UN Truce Supervision Organization in Palestine, to visit the UAR, Saudi Arabia and the Yemen to discuss the implementation of the UN part of the agreement.

The Disengagement Agreement failed for the simple reason that the Royalists had not been consulted. For this reason, Imam Mohammed al-Badr refused to accept it and would not issue orders to tribesmen loyal to him to cease fighting. He no doubt strongly suspected that there were designs afoot to eliminate him, and he had no intention of being usurped. Radio Cairo had repeatedly said that he was unacceptable, that he should leave Arabia completely, and go into exile. Prince Faisal, who was not personally impressed by the Imam, had also been urging him to retire to Europe.

A distinct lack of mutual trust between the UAR and Saudi Arabia made them suspect that the other was not carrying out its part of the bargain, and mutual recriminations were soon being bandied about. Although a contingent of some 2,000 Egyptian troops returned home from the Yemen on 4th May, the Saudi Arabian Government alleged that reinforcements had taken their place and that the UAR Expeditionary Force was larger than before. The UAR countered by alleging that Saudi Arabia was continuing to give aid to the Royalists. Both allegations were true. The Disengagement Agreement was an empty letter that had changed nothing, except to allow the UN into the Yemen.

On 27th May, U Thant reported to the Security Council that UN Observers were urgently needed in the Yemen, and that he would send an advance party within a few days. He said that the mission was to consist of about two hundred Observers, and was to stay in the Yemen for four months. It was, additionally, to have a military unit with small arms, vehicles, air and ground crews for eight aircraft, a staff, and other supporting services. The cost for the four-month period was later estimated at $807,500, with an additional $102,400 for each subsequent month that the mission's tour was extended. U Thant said that the UAR would contribute half the cost for a two-month period, and that Saudi Arabia had agreed to accept a 'proportionate share' of the financial obligation.

The Soviet Union was not in favour of the UN mission to the Yemen, and requested a meeting of the Security Council, its view being that such peace-keeping tasks should be uniquely authorized and financed by the Council. At a vote taken on 11th June, the Security Council formally authorized the UN Yemen Observation Mission, UNYOM, by ten votes to nil, with the Soviet Union abstaining. UNYOM was now on a regular footing, and General von Horn was nominated to command it. The advance party arrived in the Yemen on 13th June and was deployed to Sana, Hodeida, Sada, Najran and Qizan. Only six Observers arrived with the first detachments which were based initially at Hodeida and Sana. UNYOM at this stage consisted of a small Canadian air unit and a Yugoslav reconnaissance unit. Personnel for the staff and supporting services were from Australia, Austria, New Zealand, Norway, Sweden and the USA, and most of these were drawn from the UN forces deployed in the Middle East and the Congo.

Everywhere in the Yemen and Saudi Arabia, UNYOM met with lack of co-operation and hostility. In the Yemen, it was dangerous for the personnel to move out of Sana into the ountryside. Limited facilities were grudgingly given, and many handicaps were deliberately put in the way of the Mission. Its members, for example, were not allowed to go near the Rahaba airfield, about twelve miles north of Sana, which the Soviet

Union was extending and improving. At first UNYOM was forbidden by the UN to have any contact with the Royalists at all, and it was not until August (1963) that this embargo was rescinded. Nothing being achieved during the first four months of UNYOM's existence, a two-month extension was reluctantly granted. In his first report, published on 4th September, U Thant admitted that no progress had been made towards effecting the implementation of the Disengagement Agreement, and he said that in some respects neither the UAR nor Saudi Arabia had fulfilled the conditions. But both had agreed to finance UNYOM's expenses for another two months.

Meanwhile there had been friction between General von Horn and U Thant. The Mission was operating on a shoe-string amid hostile circumstances and had anticipated personnel, vehicles and equipment that were not forthcoming. On 20th August, General von Horn resigned, for 'urgent reasons largely personal in nature', and this was accepted by U Thant. If General von Horn had hoped the tendering of his resignation would have been sufficient to jerk the UN into improving the conditions of the UNYOM, he was disappointed. U Thant was glad to see him go, and when on the 25th General von Horn withdrew his resignation, U Thant would not accept it. General von Horn had to go, which he did with a bad grace.

On 4th September, General von Horn said that U Thant had refused to send him enough aircraft and funds, and without this aid UNYOM could not carry out its task satisfactorily. U Thant's reply was that he had not been in a position to comply with von Horn's requests, as the Mission had to operate within the financial resources made available to it by the UAR and Saudi Arabia. On the 10th, Lieutenant-General P. S. Gyani, of India, was appointed in General von Horn's stead.

U Thant's second report on UNYOM to the Security Council, on 30th October, was pessimistic, and he said that as Saudi Arabia would not provide any more funds, the Mission would have to terminate on 4th November. He confirmed that no progress had been made towards implementing the Disengagement Agreement, that aid was still being given to the Royalists, and that there was no evidence of the withdrawal of UAR troops from the country. He went on to say that he was dissatisfied with the UNYOM mandate, which, being limited to observation only, was too restricted to enable it to take on a constructive role. He thought there might be some scope for UN civilian representation in the Yemen, for which the cost could be met from the UN emergency fund. However, the next day the Saudi Arabian Government changed its mind and agreed to pay a share of the cost of UNYOM for another two months. The United States had exerted pressure on Saudi Arabia to bring about a change of mind by giving warning that it would be difficult for the US to give air cover over Saudi Arabian frontiers should the UAR attack.

In November the character of UNYOM changed, when on the 4th, U Thant appointed Signor Pier Spinelli, Director of the UN European Office at Geneva, to be head of the Mission and his special representative for the Yemen. Spinelli's task was to encourage discussion with a view to implementing the Disengagement Agreement. He arrived at Sana on the 8th, and later visited both Saudi Arabia and the UAR. A further report by U Thant on 2nd January (1964) stated that as both the UAR and Saudi Arabia had agreed to continue financing UNYOM, it would continue in existence for another two months. It had accomplished nothing, and the combatants resented its presence unless it could be turned to individual advantage. To be fair, it was far too small to carry out even an observation role properly, there being a total of only 25 Observers with the Mission instead of the 200 originally anticipated. On the 21st, U Thant at a press conference claimed that fighting in the Yemen had practically stopped and the 'portents of the future were brighter than a few weeks ago', but the ensuing two-monthly reports made depressing reading. UNYOM struggled desperately to gain new leases of life, until it was finally terminated on 4th September 1964.

It was stated that the total expenses of the Mission for the time it had been in existence amounted to about $2 million, of which the UAR and Saudi Arabia had each contributed about $800,000. It had been impracticable from the outset, seeking to implement long-distance good intentions that had little chance of success because of the hostility and mutual suspicion of the contending factions. UNYOM achieved nothing, but detracted much from UN peace-keeping prestige. It had not had the slightest effect on stopping the war.

CHAPTER SIX

Early Stalemate

MAIN EVENTS

1963	
April 13th	New Republican Constitution announced.
April	Royalist and Saudi Arabian leaders confer.
June	As-Sallal's foreign tour.
June 12th	Plot against as-Sallal discovered.
22nd	British military party strays into the Yemen.
July 8th	First report of UAR using poison gas bombs.
August	Unofficial meeting between Royalists and Republicans.
August 12th	Abdul Rahman Baidani speaks out against as-Sallal in Aden.
September 17th	Abdul Rahman Baidani arrested in Cairo.
September	UAR offensive in the Jauf.
September	Extensions to the Rahaba airfield completed by Soviet personnel.
November	As-Sallal to Egypt for medical treatment.
November–December	UAR offensive in the Jauf.
December	UAR Commander-in-Chief wounded and replaced.

The Republicans were anxious to establish their regime on a sound basis, and on 13th April at a gathering in Sana of delegations from most parts of the country, as-Sallal announced a new interim constitution which was to replace the provisional one of the previous October. As-Sallal was acknowledged Head of State and Commander-in-Chief of the Yemeni armed forces, and a re-shuffle of personalities in the Cabinet was planned. The supreme body to decide political, economic, social and administrative policies was to be the Presedential Council, under as-Sallal's chairmanship, while an Executive Council, led by

Abdul Latif Dhaifallah, was set up to implement them. It was grandly announced at the same time that there was to be a parliament of some twenty-five sheikhs to represent the major tribes and tribal federations, and although a few came forward for this purpose, the project never amounted to much. Neither did the compulsory conscription that was decreed, since the casual method of compulsorily enrolling men into the Yemeni army as they were needed went on as before.

In June, as-Sallal went off on a foreign tour that included Arab capitals and some Iron Curtain countries, to try and ensure that aid given to the Yemen came to him directly. In this he was unsuccessful. Nasser insisted that all such material assistance be sent to the UAR for re-distribution, which meant in practice that the bulk was kept back by Egypt for its own use. Only a small proportion got through to the Yemenis, and this amount was regulated according to how the Yemenis responded to current Egyptian wishes. UAR displeasure meant a curtailment of foreign supplies intended for the Yemeni Government.

While as-Sallal was away Hassan al-Amri acted as Head of State. On 12th June, while as-Sallal was still absent from the Yemen, it was announced by the Republican Government that a plot against the regime had been discovered, and that several people had been arrested. On his return, as-Sallal announced that he would let the country's religious leaders decide the punishment of the plotters, and on 11th July nine were sentenced to death and twelve others to imprisonment. In its customarily violent way the Yemen was showing that as-Sallal and his colleagues were not popular with everyone. There was an assassination attempt on him in August, and rumours of several others, as well as evidence of attempts from time to time on the lives of certain members of the Republican Government. It also became known that in September 1962 a group of senior officers in the Yemeni army had petitioned Nasser to remove as-Sallal from his position as Head of State. As a deterrent, public executions remained a feature of the Yemeni scene, especially in Sana. On 28th May, for example, three former Imamic officials including the former chief executioner had been shot before a crowd of citizens in the large square[1] in the

[1] Newly named Liberation Square.

Capital, and another two men suffered the same fate on 10th June. International dismay at this prompted later executions to be carried out within prison walls, but this conversely gave rise to suspicions that the Government was killing many of its enemies in secret.

The UAR Expeditionary Force remained at about 28,000 strong, but was re-organized for an occupational role in which its main responsibility was to hold the key cities and towns and to keep the communications between them open for the Republican Government. Large numbers of armoured fighting vehicles and guns were shipped to the Yemen from Egypt and were very much in evidence. The UAR troops directed fire into the countryside at the least excuse, to deter hostile tribesmen from attacking and to impress those who were uncommitted. The number of aircraft allocated to the Yemen was also increased, and daily bombing sorties into the Royalist-held mountains became the order of the day, while vicious air strikes were continually embarked upon to cow unruly tribal warriors.

Now that the Ramadan Offensive had pushed the encroaching tribesmen back a little way into the mountains, fighter and light strike aircraft were again operating from the Rahaba airfield, just north of Sana, as well as from the dozen or so others. Heavier bombers remained based on airfields in Egypt, and had to make the lengthy trip over the Red Sea for each sortie into the Yemen, until, in September, the extensions to the Rahaba airfield were completed by Soviet personnel[1] and bombers were able to operate from it. This was a big advantage to the UAR Expeditionary Force, since it gave it a much quicker reaction time to hit heavily at any hostile movement.

The Ramadan Offensive had certainly rocked the Royalists and brought home to them the fact that traditional tribal warfare could not defeat, or even stand up to, the modern arms and equipment of the UAR Expeditionary Force. Its leaders had to pause and think out a new strategic policy. Saudi Arabia, concerned at the UAR military successes, called in April a conference lasting several days, held in Saudi Arabia, to hammer out future Royalist policy and strategy. The Royalist representatives were Prince Mohammed Hussein, Prince Abdul-

[1] It was estimated that at least five hundred Soviet personnel had been working on the Rahaba airfield for several months.

lah Hussein and Ahmed al-Sayaghi, who met Prince Faisal, Saudi Arabian cabinet ministers and senior army officers.

It was decided that Saudi Arabian aid to the Imam would be increased[1] to enable him to bribe the Zeidi tribes into supporting him and to form a Royalist army. Now that the former supply route through Beihan was blocked by UAR soldiers, arms, ammunition and military material would be sent on camels by devious routes, through the mountains and at night to avoid detection by UAR aircraft. Saudi Arabian military experts advised that a conventional army should be formed and trained to assault fortified positions, and that, in particular, the Imam should strengthen his forces in the north-west. The suggestion that there should be a Royalist air force with mercenary pilots was firmly vetoed by Prince Faisal who did not want his country to become openly involved in the Yemen war, particularly since such an air force would have had to operate from Saudi Arabian territory and would have invited UAR reprisals.

Immediately after the Saudi Arabian conference, the Royalist commanders met under the Imam's chairmanship to discuss the strategy to be adopted. Basically, they had to decide whether to resort to guerrilla warfare or whether to form, arm and train an army able to undertake conventional operations. The outcome was a vague compromise between the two courses which was detrimental to both. They had already captured a few UAR tanks, armoured cars, guns and radios, and the prospect of possessing modern armaments and equipment obviously fascinated the Royalist commanders, who urged Saudi Arabia to send quantities of supplies, together with instructors. But Prince Faisal was cautious, and the arms he sent the Royalists consisted mostly of rifles, grenades and explosives, although he did send a few field guns as well.

The Royalists boasted, rather imaginatively, that they had three major Fronts, encircling Sana from the west, north and east, each with about 2,000 fighting men and able to call upon another 100,000 armed warriors when necessary. Although elementary and disjointed, their military organization was in fact beginning to take shape. Prince Mohammed Hussein re-

[1] It was estimated that up until March 1963, the Imam had received about $15 million of aid from Saudi Arabia.

mained in charge of the rear bases near Najran, and concentrated upon recruiting, arming and training volunteers, while the Imam remained at his headquarters near Jebel Qara, and dealt with political matters rather than strictly military affairs.

Prince Hassan, established in Wadi Amlah to the east of Sada with a small group of supporters grandly known as the 1st Army, was the nominal commander of the eastern part of the country, that is, east of the road from Sana to Sada. His control was nominal partly because of poor radio communication and partly because of the independent character of his two subordinate commanders. These were Prince Abdullah Hassan, who had moved his headquarters near to Sinwan so as to be able to close in on Sana and deal with targets to the north of the capital, and whose followers were known as the 2nd Army, and Prince Abdullah Hussein, with the 3rd Army, who had moved northwards from the area of the Sana-Marib Corridor into the Jauf, and eventually established his headquarters a few miles to the east of Harf.

To the west of the Sana-Sada road, with the 4th army in the mountains to the west of Harf, the overall field commander was Prince Mohammed Ismail. His subordinate commanders were Prince Abdul Rahman, with the 5th Army, near Sudah, and Ahmed al-Sayaghi, with the 6th Army, in the region of Hajja. These six armies were in fact merely groups of armed tribesmen, who came or went much as they pleased, and probably only amounted to two or three hundred at a time. They were little more than large bodyguards for the commanders and had no military shape at all. When an ambush or raid was mounted, the Royalist commanders had to persuade armed tribesmen in their regions to provide the manpower, and the quality and quantity of Royalist activity depended greatly upon the persuasiveness of the commanders and the whims of the local tribes.

The Royalist forces in one sense surrounded Sana on three sides, as they were in the mountains to the west, north and east of the capital, but as the UAR troops held the centres of communication, had control of the air, and possessed a much wider range of armaments, the poorly-armed and equipped Royalists were at a considerable material and tactical disadvantage. Despite loud boasts, individual Royalist commanders were privately determined to ensure their own security, build up their following and increase their stocks of arms and ammunition, and so for most of the time they remained inactive. Communiqués used to be issued from Royalist sources, claiming advances and the capture of villages, territory, arms and prisoners during the course of the months, but when closely examined they were always found to be empty and false. Despite a grandiose announcement by the Imam on 28th May that the Royalists everywhere were taking the offensive again, as a measure of confidence was regained after the Ramadan Offensive, hardly any planned hostile activity was carried out by the Royalists during the summer or autumn.

In fact, in many places a sort of impasse set in, inconvenient to both sides, with the UAR troops capable of intercepting Royalist supplies, and the Royalists able to interrupt those of the Republican garrisons, many of which were isolated in the mountains. Secret, unofficial arrangements began cautiously to be made by some Egyptian and Royalist commanders on a 'live-and-let-live' basis, so that neither would be completely deprived of essential food supplies. For example, Prince Abdullah Hussein made contact with the Egyptian commanders at Hazm and Lebena in the Jauf, and made a private truce so that supplies could get through to both of them. He also made a secret agreement with the Egyptian commander at Marib on similar lines, so that the Royalist supply route through Beihan would remain open. In return, the Royalists secretly agreed to refrain from attacking UAR supply columns in the Sana-Marib Corridor. By mutual consent the Royalist camel trains made their way silently past UAR-held garrisons by night, avoiding detection by UAR troops and aircraft alike.

In the west of the country there was a long lull in engagements between the Royalists and the UAR-held garrisons, and it was rumoured that each was exchanging secret safe-conduct guarantees and that many of the local war communiqués issued by both sides fabricated minor actions to allay suspicion. The one activity that did continue with unabated ferocity was aerial bombing, but even this tended to lose something of its sting as populations evacuated villages that lay open and defenceless in valleys, and went to live in caves in the lower mountain sides.

At no stage did the Imam have the unswerving allegiance of

all the Zeidi mountain tribes, for reasons that have been mentioned, although when he was able to hand out gold and silver, some had begun leisurely to take the field on his behalf. The Ramadan Offensive set against the energy, example and ability of the Royalist commanders tended to unsettle them, since they wanted to be on the winning side and found the choice a difficult one. At first, small arms had been given out as bribes, but this practice had to be moderated because once a tribesman was given a rifle he regarded it as his own personal property and often promptly disappeared to sell both gun and ammunition in Saudi Arabia where there was a ready market for such commodities. He would then return and ask for another rifle, without having done anything to earn the one he had just sold. The Royalist commanders tried to persuade tribesmen to 'join' and stay with their own particular field army, and issued arms on that condition, but they did not have much success with this. They also tried to induce tribesmen to make their way to Prince Mohammed Hussein's training camps, but there was a great deal of suspicion to begin with about being sent so far from home. Besides this the sheikhs did not like to see their warriors leave the tribe, as this weakened its fighting ability.

Very few tribes were single-mindedly loyal to either the Imam or the Republican Government unless their position allowed them to be completely dominated by one or the other. Although one day a tribe might be reported loyal to the Imam —who then declared that his followers were 'in sight of Sana' or some other town—the next day it had been bought over by the Republicans. This accounted to some extent for the many confusing and conflicting reports which gave the impression that the fighting was raging to and fro in certain parts of the country, and that territory was being daily lost or won. It was also the reason why both sides frequently claimed to be in possession of the same piece of country at the same time. In general the countryside was passive, and the war was fought more with communiqués from GHQ's than with weapons. In the much-publicised Royalists' offensive of June hardly any fighting occurred at all.

Instigated by Nasser, as-Sallal played up the recurring friction along his border with the Federation of South Arabia, and in June he was provided with some excellent propaganda material of which he made good use. On the 22nd, a party of forty-four British Servicemen and women from GHQ Middle East Command (then at Aden) set off from Lahej on an adventure training exercise. Taking a wrong turning, they moved along a desert track that took them accidentally into the Yemen, where they were fired upon. A group of eighteen, including four women, escaped, but the remainder were pinned down by gunfire. Four were killed, two wounded, and they were forced to surrender. The other four women (there were eight) and the bodies of the dead were returned over the border to the British military authorities, and a British military doctor was allowed to visit the wounded Servicemen, who were also returned to British-protected territory. The remaining sixteen men were taken to Taiz as prisoners. After negotiations by the US chargé d'affaires they were released on 4th July in return for payment of about £7,500, it being alleged that three Yemenis were killed in the skirmish.

Uneasy relations persisted between Britain and the Yemeni Republican Government, because of British non-recognition and the fact that the Yemen claimed certain parts of the British-protected Federation of South Arabia. On 26th August, for instance, Hassan al-Amri, the Vice-President, protested against an alleged raid by the British on Harib. This was denied by the British Government who stated that Yemeni troops had been forced to evacuate a village in Beihan that they had occupied illegally. As part of the area adjacent to Harib Fort was disputed territory, it remained a source of trouble.

The spirit of the Disengagement Agreement began to wear very thin. Nasser alleged that Saudi Arabia was supplying arms to the Royalists in greater numbers than before (which was, of course, quite true) and threatened that UAR forces would stay on in the Yemen if this aid was not stopped. Radio Mecca stated on 6th June that UAR aircraft had bombed both Najran and Khamis Mushait (the latter town being the proposed site for British Bloodhound missiles) causing loss of life, and that two days later a UAR air raid on Qizan had killed thirty people and injured nineteen others. There was a strong foundation of fact in these reports, although the numbers of casualties were exaggerated. On the 17th, Saudi Arabia protested to the United Nations, saying that it might be provoked into grave counter-measures in self-defence. Further allegations were made, one of a UAR air raid on Abha, a small habitation about sixty miles north of the Yemeni border, in which a hospital had been hit, and another of an aerial attack on Najran. At a Saudi Arabian press conference it was said that the UAR had violated the Disengagement Agreement, both by bombing and by allowing its troops to fight the Yemeni tribes. The United States expressed concern to the UAR, but, having recognized the as-Sallal regime, stated that it was logical for UAR forces to fight tribesmen who continued to operate against the central government.

Nasser replied that by supplying the Royalists with the means to revolt, it was Saudi Arabia who had violated the Disengagement Agreement. He asked the UN to investigate, but UNYOM observers were unable to do so because the situation was such that neither side could, or would, guarantee their personal safety. In fact, it was most probable that the Royalists deliberately stirred up a certain amount of activity along the northern Yemeni border region to handicap UN observation, because at this stage, there was a considerable flow of Saudi Arabian military stores into the Yemen. The Disengagement Agreement was in any case a dead letter, if indeed it had ever been anything else.

The Republican leaders became concerned at the rising heat of the exchanges between Nasser and Prince Faisal. They did not want full-scale hostilities to break out again, and were content for the time being at least, with what the Ramadan Offensive had gained for them. Now they wanted to consolidate their position, taking the view that time was on their side in this respect and against the Imam. With this in mind, they put out feelers in July and August which resulted in a secret meeting at the Kirsh Customs Post, in Lahej, between a Republican delegation, led by Mohammed as-Zuberi who was dissatisfied by so much dependance upon the UAR, and a Royalist one led by Ahmed al-Sayaghi. Nothing came of this, but it paved the way for later similar meetings aimed at achieving a compromise solution between the two sides and without reference to the UAR or Saudi Arabia.

When he heard about this contact, Nasser was intensely displeased. He had not been consulted, and did not want to allow the Yemeni Government he was supporting (and was under the impression he was controlling) any freedom of negotiation, or indeed any freedom at all regarding external affairs. But despite his disapproval there were a few other secret contacts in the course of the year between Royalists and Republicans at various levels, and also between sheikhs with opposing loyalties. The United States, openly in favour of a broad-based Yemeni Government to include both Royalists and Republicans, encouraged these contacts.

These under-cover contacts revealed a trend that neither the UAR nor Saudi Arabia liked, and both deliberately slackened their support in case they should push the opposing Yemeni factions into each other's arms. In September, the Saudi Arabian Government insisted that its material aid to the Imam had ceased completely. This was not true, but for several weeks it markedly decreased in volume, enough certainly to alarm the Royalists and bring them to heel. On the other side of the fence, Nasser claimed he had withdrawn over 13,000 troops from the Yemen and was about to recall more. The actual figures of troop withdrawals might have been less than half that number, as the strength of the UAR Expeditionary Force declined to not less than 22,000 men, but the Republican Government was put firmly in its place. It was also reported in September that Field Marshal Amer, dubious about the wisdom of continuing to support the as-Sallal regime at such a huge cost, made secret contacts with the Royalists to see if they would take part in a coalition government. But the Royalists by this time had been frightened off by Saudi Arabian pressure.

Without fully realizing the depth of the implications, the Republican Government now found itself faced with rising Shafi discontent. The Shafeis had originally supported the as-Sallal regime, regarding it as a means of casting off traditional Zeidi domination. They had assumed that they would at the very least be equals in the new Republic, with equal representation, but they now began to realize that the as-Sallal Cabinet was composed mostly of Zeidis appointing Zeidi officials who were just as arrogant and domineering as in the past. The Shafeis were disturbed by the determination of the as-Sallal Government to placate the feared Zeidi mountain tribes and its attempt to coax them into the Republican fold. As-Sallal seemed to disregard the Shafeis and their interests, apparently considering them to be of little importance. In August, an underground Shafi organization was discovered working against as-Sallal and Zeidi oppression, and at almost the same time another subversive faction composed of both Shafeis and Zeidis was unearthed, which had the object of deposing as-Sallal.

Abdul Rahman Baidani, the one prominent Shafi leader, had been forced out of the Government by as-Sallal, but before that the two men had issued joint appeals to end sectarian hatred. Baidani constantly recommended that more Shafeis be included in the Government, but despite lipservice to equality and his Republican ideals, as-Sallal, a Zeidi himself, firmly believed that it was the lot of a Zeidi to rule and of a Shafi to be ruled. When the Shafi tribes in the south became restless, as-Sallal, on his foreign tour in June, had talks with Baidani in Cairo to seek his support. Baidani seems to have stuck to his guns and insisted on more Shafi representation in the Government and more Shafeis in the civil service, but this did not seem to be the attitude as-Sallal expected, or the answer he was seeking.

This unsatisfactory meeting with as-Sallal may have prompted Baidani into an extreme course of action. When he arrived in Aden on 12th August ostensibly to win support for the establishment of a development bank, he made political statements denouncing the as-Sallal Government, criticizing certain Zeidi leaders, and advocating the formation of an independent Shafi state in southern Yemen. As a reprisal, on the 29th the Presidential Council deprived Baidani of his Yemeni nationality, accusing him of being a foreign agent who sought to separate northern and southern Yemen. Persuaded to return to Cairo, Baidani on 17th September was detained, and although subsequently released he remained under house arrest. On 6th October, as-Sallal appointed Mohammed Othman and Abdul Rahman Iryani to be Vice-Presidents. Both were considered to by unsympathetic to Shafi aspirations for equality.

The inhabitants of Royalist-held territory, despite their military passivity, were having a very tough time of it. Reports brought out by journalists, visitors and refugees, began to indicate how the war was making its impact on them. Food was becoming scarce as cattle were killed in air raids or in retribution, and cultivation had been severely disrupted. UAR and Republican forces deliberately despoiled farms and arable land belonging to tribes suspected of being loyal to the Imam, and in some areas there was a water shortage where wells had become targets for UAR raiding aircraft.

Many people had been killed, although no one knew exactly how many. War orphans living as semi-starved beggars had already begun to appear. Air raids caused numerous casualties, and hundreds died for lack of medical attention since there were no hospitals at all in Royalist territory, and indeed no medical facilities at all except of the most primitive sort. For many months, the only hospital available to treat Royalist casualties was a small one at Najran, in Saudi Arabia, whose staff was augmented by a few foreign volunteer doctors and workers. But the difficulties of transportation through the almost roadless mountainous country were such that the badly wounded invariably died long before they reached Najran. The International Red Cross Society made an appeal to fifty nations for funds and medical facilities, but there was a poor response and it was not until towards the end of 1963 that a few mobile medical teams appeared, near the northern Yemen border. The first Red Cross field hospital to be established inside the Yemen in Royalist-held country was in November, at Uqd, a few miles due south of Najran.

Meanwhile, some other news had spread alarm in the Royalist camp. In July, the first report alleging that UAR aircraft were dropping poison gas bombs in northern Yemen was carried by a British newspaper.[1] The correspondent announced that he had seen the results in the Royalist village of Kawma, where seven people had died and twenty-five others had suffered from the effects. Photographs were produced, showing children with burns. The report was passed by the British Government to the United Nations and U Thant instructed General von Horn to investigate, but the General's Observers had no access into these parts of Royalist territory. The UAR flatly denied the allegation, and a UN spokesman said that Saudi Arabia had already made similar accusations, for which the UN had been unable to find any supporting evidence. The fact that the

[1] *Daily Telegraph* of 8th July 1963.

UAR was supposed to be dropping poison gas bombs had been kept quiet by both the Red Cross and the UN because of its grave political implications until the story was 'broken' by a British newspaper.

Fragments of the bombs dropped were brought to Britain to be examined, and on 8th September the War Office announced that it was considered most unlikely they had contained poison gas. The general evidence seemed to be that the bomb cases were made in the Soviet Union and the contents in Egypt. Also, a young Yemeni boy suffering from burns had been specially flown to a London hospital to be examined and treated, and it was stated that there was nothing to indicate the cause of his injuries. The allegations of poison gas were played down, and it was rumoured that some other sinister, possibly Western, source might be producing the controversial bombs.

It has been said that there was a general lull in the fighting between the Royalists and the Republicans, but this was occasionally broken, as when a UAR convoy was caught in an ambush mounted just south of Sada, and about one hundred Egyptians were killed and their bodies mutilated. At first any enemy killed was automatically mutilated in the traditional Yemeni fashion, but the Imam and his commanders put a stop to this practice, as much as they could, since it was not the best way of enlisting universal sympathy and understanding for their cause. It was said that the ambush was carried out on Prince Abdullah Hussein's orders when his private agreement with the Egyptian commander at Harf was treacherously broken by Egyptian soldiers. This may have been so, as the local 'live-and-let-live' pacts were only concluded as expedients, and both sides broke them whenever they felt it would be to their advantage.

In September, the Egyptians mounted a small offensive in the Jauf from their base at Lebena in Wadi Humaidat, where they had a fairly large garrison. Their object was to drive northwards and wipe out the Royalist training camps dotted along the northern Yemen border. Prince Mohammed Hussein, in charge of these camps, deployed some captured armoured fighting vehicles and some Saudi Arabian guns, mustered sufficient technicians to man them, and was able to put down a barrage on to the UAR force that made it halt and withdraw.

Some of the Prince's drivers and gunners were UAR prisoners who had been forced to fire on their own comrades.

The first European mercenaries hired to train Royalist volunteers did not arrive in Prince Mohammed Hussein's camps until November,[1] and neither Jordan nor Saudi Arabia would allow their military personnel with the Royalists to go into action with them. A number of Europeans, some of them characters in their own right, had begun to be attracted to the Royalist cause. One of these worthy of a mention was Bruce Conde[2] who became known to many Western visitors. Bruce Conde, an American, who had been a major in the US Army in World War II, went to the Middle East after the war and learnt to speak fluent Arabic. He visited the Yemen in 1953, and was allowed to stay and work for the Imam in a variety of jobs, including postal communications, stamp designing and archaeological tasks. He acted as a kind of PR man to the journalists who were invited to Imam Ahmed's solitary press conference in 1957, but although he had become a Moslem he was expelled from the Yemen two years later for an unstated reason. Conde then figured for some time as a stateless person, until he managed to obtain a British passport in Sharjah. After the *coup* in the Yemen, he appeared at the Royalist camp at Najran to offer his services, which were accepted. A sincere Yemenophile he pushed the Royalist cause as hard as he could, frequently briefing and accompanying Western visitors on their trips through Royalist territory. He was a romantic, and perhaps something of an eccentric, but he was extremely helpful.

The Nasser-Prince Faisal quarrel dragged on, and occasionally UAR air attacks were made on Saudi Arabian territory with bombs and rockets, but although there were some casualties little real damage was done. One such raid took place on villages near Najran on 4th September, and another on 21st November on a market place at Kuba, in both of which people were killed. When overwhelming evidence forced the UAR to admit these attacks, they blamed them on errors of navigation.

[1] According to Dana Adam Schmidt they were at first twelve in number—British, French and Belgian.

[2] According to David Holden, *Farewell to Arabia*, his full name, according to his own claim, was Bruce Alfonso de Bourbon Conde.

In the same month as this second attack, it was decided to mount an offensive against Prince Abdullah Hussein, who was beginning to harass some of the UAR garrisons in the Jauf. The offensive was commanded in person by Lieutenant-General Anwar al Qadi, the Commander-in-Chief of the UAR Expeditionary Force in the Yemen, but in December his column was badly ambushed in Wadi Ashia. The Commander-in-Chief was wounded by mortar fire and had to be evacuated to Egypt. He was replaced by Lieutenant-General Abdul Mohsin Kamal Murtaji, but the UAR offensive fizzled out, leaving Prince Mohammed Hussein in a stronger position than ever in the Jauf.

Also in November, as-Sallal went to Egypt for medical treatment after an alleged heart attack, although there were strong rumours that he had been wounded in an assassination attempt. He stayed in Egypt for two months, and again Hassan al-Amri acted in his stead. This meant that the year ended for the Yemeni Republic with an absentee Head of State, and the knowledge that the UAR Commander-in-Chief had been wounded in battle. It had been a year in which little drastic had occurred besides the Ramadan Offensive, after which, with minor exceptions, a passive stalemate set in—but it was the year when the effect of the war first bit deeply into the country.

CHAPTER SEVEN

Continued Stalemate

MAIN EVENTS

1964	
January	As-Sallal returns from Cairo.
January and February	Minor Royalist offensive.
April 23rd–29th	Nasser visits the Yemen.
May	Brief successful UAR punitive campaign.
May	Radfan Rebellion, in Federation of South Arabia.
June–July–August	Successful UAR offensive. Imam forced to move his HQ.
August 25th	Shafi incident at Taiz.
November 1st–3rd	Erkwit Conference, in Sudan.
November 8th	Cease-fire comes into effect.
November	King Saud deposed and Prince Faisal declared King of Saudi Arabia.
December	Royalists break the cease-fire agreement.
December	Shafi incidents at Hodeida.
	Formation of Yemeni Youth Organization of Shafeis, and its visits to Saudi Arabia and Syria.
December 13th	National Congress postponed indefinitely.
11th	Ahmed Numan resigns as President of the Consultative Council.
December 26th/27th	As-Sallal's ministers resign.
27th	As-Sallal flies to Cairo.

In the first week of January 1964, as-Sallal hurriedly returned to the Yemen from his health cure in Cairo to take control of his rudderless ship before it crashed on the rocks. He immediately reorganized the political structure by establishing a

Political Bureau as the supreme authority for political and legislative matters, under himself as President. He also made himself President of a new National Security Council, to deal with the conduct of the war, which had a number of UAR officers as members, including General Murtaji, the Commander-in-Chief of the UAR Expeditionary Force.

This done, as-Sallal rushed back to Cairo to attend an Arab Summit meeting, which was attended not only by Nasser and King Hussein of Jordan, but also by King Saud of Saudi Arabia. At this conference, Nasser was able to detach King Hussein from the Saudi Arabian side, although it was not until July that Jordan formally recognized the Yemeni Republican regime. Jordanian aid to the Royalists, which had dwindled to very little, now ceased completely. King Saud did not emerge very advantageously from this meeting, and there were signs that Saudi Arabia was in danger of losing its monopolist control over the Royalists. However, the meeting led to much improved relations between the UAR and Saudi Arabia, and early in March a UAR delegation led by Field Marshal Amer visited Riyadh to talk with Prince Faisal, the Saudi Arabian Premier, and other Saudi Arabian leaders. At the end of these discussions, it was announced that the two countries would resume diplomatic relations without delay. Both declared that they had no aims in the Yemen and were in favour of its complete independence, adding cautiously that they were both equally ready to oppose any imperialist attempt to restrict the freedom of the Yemeni people. In April, Prince Faisal visited Cairo for talks on how to end the Yemeni war.

In the field, meanwhile, the Royalists took the offensive in a minor way in several places during January and February. They successfully closed the Sana-Hodeida road for about a month, and also managed partially to block the Sana-Taiz road, too. Elsewhere, attacks were made on the small town of Jihanah, south-east of Sana, on Republican camps near Harib, and on UAR-held positions near Lebena in the Jauf. An unsuccessful attempt was also made to seize Hajja. All these activities prompted sharp UAR aerial reprisals, and gradually the force of the Royalist offensive died down as tribesmen faded away to their homes, tired of the fighting. Little had been accomplished. During February Algeria and Iraq took part in further mediation attempts, both secret and open, to try and bring about a cease-fire.

The attitude of many of the tribes remained uncertain, and in January (1964) a British observer[1] who had made several visits to Royalist territory, said he thought that the Bakil, whom he regarded as the largest Zeidi tribal federation, supported the Imam, together with a large part of the Hashid federation; although he admitted that a proportion of the latter openly supported the Republicans. He claimed that a number of Shafei tribes had promised the Imam their support, while pointing out at the same time that many of them were strongly committed to the Republican cause. This suggested that there were many tribes who supported neither camp, despite threats and blandishments. Some were waverers, and some simply wanted to be left alone and have nothing to do with either side.

In the spring, Sheikh Ali al-Gadr was elected Paramount Chief of the Bakil tribal federation. Republicans hoped he would influence a large sector of the Khawlan region to opt for them, as they had some dealings with him, but the new leader was as wily and shifting as any of his fellow sheikhs, and had been elected to this high position mainly because he had subverted two large tribes from the Hashid tribal federation and brought them into the Bakil one. The Sheikh had acted as an unofficial link between the Royalists and the Republicans, and was allowed free passage from Sana to Qara. There had always been intense rivalry between the two major tribal federations, and Sheikh Abdullah al-Ahmer, the paramount chief of the Hashid tribal federation who had been appointed Governor of Hajja and was at this stage a declared Republican, was losing some of his influence. In true Yemeni tradition he had taken hostages from the tribes in his federation as a bond for their good behaviour, but these through bribery and trickery had been released, which left him in a weak position, unable to exact retribution on any defectors.

Suspecting that Nasser might want to disentangle himself from the Yemen and reduce his support, and that any friendship between the UAR and Saudi Arabia might be to the detriment of his Government, as-Sallal in March visited the

[1] Lieut.-Colonel McLean, writing in *The Times*, 4th January 1964.

Soviet Union to ask for direct assistance. In April, a meeting of Zeidi Ulema was held in the Jauf region under the chairmanship of Prince Mohammed Hussein, ostensibly to draft a Royalist constitution which would cater for an elected Imam and Cabinet Government, and an independent judiciary. These two occurrences prompted Nasser to make a surprise visit to the Yemen, his first, on 23rd April. He was worried about the spirit of independence shown by as-Sallal in visiting Moscow and attempting to obtain direct material aid, and at the same time he wished to reconcile the opposing factions within the Republican Government. The Imam's attempt to gain the full support of the Zeidi Ulema and the talk of a Royalist constitution were also disturbing factors which had to be countered, and so Nasser determined to appraise the situation at first hand.

On the 27th, while Nasser stood by, as-Sallal was forced to proclaim yet another new constitution which provided for a Cabinet, under a Premier, and a Consultative Assembly with legislative powers. The new Premier was Hamoud al-Jaifi, who had been the Defence Minister in the first Republican Government, and then Ambassador to the UAR. Both Abdul Rahman Iryani and Mohammed as-Zubeiri, who exercised great influence over sections of the population, were brought back into the Government as Deputy Premiers, although each was an advocate for ending all foreign aid to either side and for the negotiation of a settlement by the Yemenis themselves. Ahmed Numan, the most prominent and widely-respected Shafi Republican, was appointed President of the Consultative Council. It seemed that a serious effort was being made by as-Sallal, perhaps under Nasser's direct pressure, to try and bring all factions together and heal the breaches threatening Republican security.

On 29th April, the day he left the Yemen, Nasser stated that a council would be established to co-ordinate the policies of the UAR and the Yemen, and this was complemented on 13th July by an agreement signed in Cairo by Nasser and as-Sallal to co-ordinate their political, military, economic and social policies as a step towards complete unity. An attack on one country would be regarded as an attack on both. The UAR would contribute 90 per cent of the budget of this council, and the Yemen the remaining 10 per cent. It was to have two Presidents—Nasser and as-Sallal.

Like as-Sallal, Imam Mohammed al-Badr was also very suspicious of the sudden friendship between the UAR and Saudi Arabia. He suspected he might be left out in the cold, so in May another Royalist conference was held under Prince Abdullah Hussein. It was attended by many sheikhs and the future policy of the Royalist Government was discussed, but it did not produce anything of any value. The one big weakness in the Royalist cause was the total lack of anything even vaguely resembling a constitution which would bind the Royalists together and give them some form of unity and centralized administration. Despite the promises given Nasser by King Saud and Prince Faisal, Saudi Arabian money, arms and supplies continued to reach the Royalists in quantity, and thus enabled the Imam and his commanders to prepare for an offensive which would aim to gain as much territory as possible, so that should a cease-fire suddenly become effective, they would be placed in a strong bargaining position.

Meanwhile, as-Sallal went off on his tour of the Communist capitals, and it was reported that the Comcon Bank would grant the Yemen an interim credit of $7 million, that Czechoslovakia would provide clothes, shoes, medicines and tractors, and help to train the Yemeni army and air pilots, and that Czech arms would be delivered not through Egypt but directly to the Republicans. East Germany was to supply agricultural machinery, a textile factory and two hospitals with experts in tropical diseases. In the first fortnight in June, as-Sallal visited China, where on the 9th he signed a Ten-Year Friendship Treaty, replacing the former one signed by the Imam, which made agreements on technical and cultural co-operation. All this sounded very grand, but it did not mean a great deal in practice. Goods went first to Egypt, and only a small proportion was allowed to trickle through into the Yemen. As-Sallal was regarded by all his hosts as Nasser's puppet, and his attempt to prove he was an independent national leader was not successful.

However, Nasser also was of the opinion that the more territory the Republicans held at the time of any cease-fire the better, and he was quicker than the Imam in launching an offensive in the field. Although the Republican forces were firmly in position in the cities and towns, Royalist guerrillas were frequently able to mine the roads between them, and many of the garrisons, both for convenience and safety, were supplied by helicopter. Such convoys as moved along the roads had to be heavily escorted by armour and guns, with overhead aircraft cover, especially convoys to Hajja and Sada. The UAR Expeditionary Force had been increased to at least 36,000 men, with a large complement of tanks and guns, and two strong armoured, mobile columns were formed for the purpose of pacifying these two troublesome areas.

Early in June, one column began to make for Hajja, and soon became involved in a battle around Beit Adaqah, about ten miles south of Hajja, now the HQ of Prince Abdullah Hussein. Aircraft showered rockets, bombs and napalm on the tribesmen, and shells were poured into their positions, causing them to break and escape deep into the shelter of the mountains. The Royalists admitted losing over 250 dead in this battle, in which Prince Ali Hassan, one of the fighting princes, was killed. The UAR armoured column then pushed northwards towards Sudah (about twenty miles from Hajja) which fell by a combination of trickery and bribery. In the Sada area, Royalist tribesmen were pushed backwards by similar methods. The UAR Expeditionary Force was able to call upon YAK 11's, MiG 16's, MiG 17's and Ilyushin 28's which were stationed at airfields within the Yemen, as well as Tuplov bombers, which had to come from Egypt to carry out their missions, with suspected Soviet-UAR crews on board. A number of Mi 4 helicopters were in use. The UAR aircraft also took to dropping small objects, booby traps which exploded when picked up and caused many casualties and much apprehension. The Royalists poured machine gun and rifle fire at aircraft whenever they came close enough and brought about a dozen down by this method, although they claimed to have accounted for many times that number.

The Royalist tribesmen rushed into the shelter of the mountains expecting that as was customary by now the Republicans would let them go and retire to their cities and camps again. But this time it was rather different. The UAR troops stayed right on the heels of the fleeing Royalists, methodically picketing the heights and mountain ridges as they moved forward, systematically clearing the valleys and razing villages with shell fire. The tribesmen were ruthlessly hunted down in these two minor operations which penetrated well into mountain areas where the Egyptians had not set foot before. Many thousands must have been killed before the UAR commanders called a halt and withdrew, and it was many weeks before tribesmen could be roused into action once more in the Royalist cause. Egyptian air activity increased in certain areas, and bombs were scattered on civilian, as well as military, targets.

Nasser also worked to stir up trouble in the British-protected Federation of South Arabia, and since December 1963 had given aid to dissidents which enabled them to instigate the Radfan Rebellion of May 1964. Throughout the spring and summer, supplies from Saudi Arabia continued to reach the Royalists by several routes, and because one of these was through Beihan State, there were allegations that this was happening with the knowledge and consent, and even active assistance, of Britain. It was additionally frequently alleged that there were British military advisers and mercenaries with the Imam's forces, which was, of course, quite true, although they acted as individuals and had no official recognition or support from the British Government.

Some substance was given to these accusations on 1st May, when the Cairo newspaper, *Al Ahram*, published letters said to have been intercepted near the Yemeni frontier with Beihan State, which dealt with the activities of an organization existing to provide personnel and supplies for the Royalists. A former British officer was named, and there were references to sabotage operations and dropping arms to Royalists by parachute. The letters were addressed to a 'Major Cooper'. They were written in English, and some of them were signed by 'Tony', who was later identified as Flight-Lieutenant Anthony Boyle, ADC to Sir Charles Johnston until June 1963, and then to his successor, Sir Kennedy Trevaskis. The letters, all dated after he had relinquished his post, were later admitted to be genuine by a British Government spokesman. On 21st July, the British Prime Minister, Sir Alec Douglas-Home, said in the House of Commons that no one had authorized Boyle's activities and that the two High Commissioners he had served knew nothing of them. The British denial was widely disbelieved, especially as Boyle later appeared in the Imam's camp as a military adviser, and UAR and Yemeni Republican propaganda made much of these letters.

The brief, punitive campaign of May had shown what could be done against disorganized mountain tribesmen, and it was decided to mount a large summer offensive designed to clear a wide section of mountainous country dominated by Royalists which was adjacent to the Yemeni frontiers in the north-west and north. It was to be a two-prong thrust with the object of closing on and capturing the Imam at his HQ near Jebel Qara. The Egyptian Expeditionary force was further reinforced until it was over 50,000 strong, more armoured vehicles and guns were shipped to the Yemen, and more aircraft allocated to its support. One large armoured column with heavy fire support pushed northwards from Hajja in late June, and another moved south-westwards from Sada, slowly and systematically clearing the valleys as they progressed.

For nearly ten weeks this pressure was maintained, and the two prongs closed in on Jebel Qara. There was resistance, but on 26th August the Republicans claimed to have occupied the Royalist HQ and driven the Imam out. Towards the end of this offensive, co-ordination became ragged, and the trap was not closed in time. Imam Mohammed al-Badr escaped to Jebel Sheda, close to Nadir, not far from the point on the Saudi Arabian frontier where he had formerly held his dramatic press conference after the *coup*. Despite a certain amount of confusion and disloyalty among the tribes supporting the offensive, it was successful from the Republican point of view, because it had demonstrated their superiority over the Royalists in the mountains. Although they had not captured the Imam, it had been a very close thing, and the Royalists in the north-west were rocked back on their heels and demoralized. It was claimed that many casualties had been inflicted, and it was undoubtedly true that many thousands had been killed and wounded, especially by aerial action. A large quantity of military equipment had been seized, which was later displayed in Sana and other cities to foreign journalists. The Royalists established their POW camp near Washa, close to Qara, when the UAR troops withdrew from that region in September after chasing the Imam out. Later five such camps for prisoners and political detainees were set up, and Red Cross representatives were eventually allowed to visit them. Also, in the same area, a small British hospital unit was set up, to which wounded were brought by night.

Despite this severe military setback the Royalists were by no means beaten, and they made plans for hitting back. The training camps which had formerly been scattered along the Saudi Arabian border, had now concentrated and moved into the Yemen. One group was located near Amara, about thirty miles south-east of Najran, and the other around Hanjar, a further forty miles south-east where the desert terrain meets the foothills of the Jauf. At these camps some elementary training was given with what weapons there were to hand, and then the volunteers were sent to one of the field commands. Many of these semi-trained men simply returned home with their new weapons, the reason perhaps being, in the early part of the war, that the terms of service were too vague, and the Royalist commanders too exacting and despotic. Later, these men were encouraged to serve in the field for a year, or at least a season, and then to be available when called upon for some particular action. But throughout the war the Royalist commanders had difficulty in mustering sufficient men for a particular operation at the right time, in the right numbers, and in the right place.

Each of the Royalist commanders succeeded in maintaining a small group of volunteers, still little more than a large body-guard, to which were added a shifting body of recruits. The first motivation was to fight the Egyptians, who were regarded as invaders, and the second was the age-old lust for loot. The training given at the camps did not seem to make a very deep impression on the men who received it, because they invariably reverted to primitive tribal methods of fighting which were costly in military terms and less effective against modern fire power and tactics.

A handful of foreign mercenaries were helping to teach the Royalists fighting methods, and were advising the Royalist commanders on strategy and tactics, but the task was proving difficult. The Yemenis were on the whole unreceptive to modern military ideas, and often unable to comprehend the need for them. About half the mercenaries were French and Belgian, who were mostly weapons instructors, and the other half chiefly British, working on communications and as medical assistants. There were seldom more than fifty mercenaries with the Royalists at any one time, but a small permanent cadre did enable the Imam to keep up a semblance of a military command

and a communication network of sorts between his various commanders. Material aid came, of course, consistently from Saudi Arabia, but there were other donors, practically all of whom were Nasser's enemies. At first there had been Jordan and Pakistan, but they had soon dropped out, to be replaced by Iran whose Shah was a long-time opponent of Nasser. Valuable aid was also given by several of the British-protected states of the Federation of South Arabia, especially by the Ruler of Beihan. By mid-1964, the Royalists had received quantities of small arms, mainly Soviet and Chinese, 81-mm. mortars and a few 75-mm. recoilless guns. Later they were to get some 105-mm. and 155-mm. howitzers.

There was one brief break in Saudi Arabian support for the Royalists. During the summer its financial contributions to the Imam had begun to dwindle and the Royalists began to look elsewhere for assistance. Without consulting the Saudi Arabian Government, Prince Mohammed Hussein went to Jordan and Iran to see if he could get help from them, and also visited London, Rome, Bonn and Paris. The Saudi Arabians did not like the Royalists to take any independent action without their permission, and Prince Faisal stopped sending money to the Imam. In protest, Prince Mohammed Hussein refused to return to the Yemen until Saudi Arabian financial support was restored. Mohammed al-Shami, the Royalist Foreign Minister, acted as peace-maker, and eventually Prince Faisal relented, while insisting that the Royalists should co-operate with dissident Republicans, and tribesmen who were anti-UAR rather than pro-Royalist. Although they disliked the conditions imposed, financial considerations forced the Royalists to comply with them. Their feeble attempt to assert independence from Saudi Arabia had been a failure from the start.

During the summer the Shafeis became restive and more openly discontented with the way they thought the Zeidi-dominated Government was discriminating against them. A major incident occurred on 25th August at Taiz, the main Shafi centre, when a group of Zeidi soldiers surrounded the house of the Governor, a Shafei, in an attempt to depose him and put a Zeidi in his place. Instead of meekly acquiescing to such an outrageous demand, as the Shafeis had been accustomed to doing for over a thousand years, the Governor sat tight and sent out a rallying call for all Shafeis to come to his assistance. Within a couple of days some 30,000 Shafi tribesmen, about one-third of them armed, flooded into Taiz. It was probably the biggest gathering of Shafeis for hundreds of years, and this sudden and unexpected display of their strength brought as-Sallal and Hamoud al-Jaifi, the Premier, hurrying down to Taiz to sort the matter out. A compromise followed. The Governor stayed in office, but the Zeidi soldiers were not punished.

The Shafeis had several times put forward demands for equal representation in the Government. As there were as many Shafeis in the Yemen as Zeidis, this seemed fair and logical, but neither as-Sallal nor Hamoud al-Jaifi would listen. In Sana, Hassan al-Amri, a Vice-President, was also firmly against equal Shafi representation, and threatened to arrest anyone who dared to suggest this openly or to protest. In September Ahmed Numan, the only prominent Shafi in the Government, attended an Arab summit meeting in Cairo in his capacity as President of the Consultative Council, and in protest against as-Sallal's decisions refused to return to the Yemen. This open breach between the two religious sects in the Yemen embarrassed the Egyptians, who, like the Shafeis, were Sunnis, but at the same time they realized that the Zeidis still dominated the country and so reluctantly had to endorse as-Sallal's policy in this respect.

Deadlock in the war continued, and the thoughts of Arab statesmen turned to projects for peace in the Yemen. President Ben Bella of Algeria and President Arif of Iraq, acting as intermediaries between Nasser and Prince Faisal, were largely responsible for the holding of peace talks at Erkwit, in the Sudan, from 1st to 3rd November. This conference was a secret one, with Mohammed as-Zubeiri leading the Republican delegation, and Mohammed al Shami the Royalist one. UAR and Saudi Arabian observers were present. An agreement was soon reached, and it was announced that a cease-fire would become effective on 8th November. It was also arranged that a National Congress, consisting of 63 Ulema, 63 tribal leaders and an 18-member preparatory committee, was to meet in some Yemeni town on the 23rd to compose terms for settling existing differences. The UAR and Saudi Arabia were to be asked either jointly or separately to implement the National Congress' decisions.

The cease-fire came into effect on 8th November as arranged, but both sides remained watchful and suspicious of each other, and as there was no clear victor or vanquished, each felt that it should be able to dictate peace terms. Despite the devastated state of the country, especially in the Royalist sector, there was no cowed loser anxious to seek peace for the practical reason of continued survival. At a press conference on the 7th, Mohammed al-Shami, the Royalist Foreign Minister, estimated that so far during the war some 25,000 Egyptians had been killed, of whom about 3,000 were officers, and about 220,000 Yemenis. These figures were exaggerated, but no one seemed to be able to prove or disprove them with solid facts. Certainly, a great many had died.

The proposed National Congress was never held. It was postponed first for one week, and then, on 13th December, indefinitely. The reason given was that there were disagreements as to where it should take place. The Republicans favoured Harad, and insisted that three-fifths of the delegates should be Republicans, and the Royalists insisted that the Congress should be held at Sada, the centre of traditional Zeidi support, and that there should be equal Royalist and Republican representation as agreed at the Erkwit talks. There were other differences too, and successive announcements by both sides only made the situation worse. On 10th November, Hamoud al-Jaifi, the Premier, said that his Government would be prepared to discuss the return of Royalists and certain compensations for them, but would not countenance any modification of the Republican regime, the return of the Imam or the withdrawal of the UAR Expeditionary Force.

In reply, on the 11th, Mohammed al-Shami said that it was out of the question for the Imamate to disappear, and demanded guarantees that the Egyptian troops should leave the country. He also insisted that it would be up to the National Congress to discuss whether the Yemen should be a Republic or a constitutional monarchy. Mohammed al-Shami said that if no agreement was reached quickly, the Royalists would take the field again. Even though many tribesmen had left Royalist areas to return to homes in Republican-held territory, in anticipation of the cease-fire becoming an armistice, Royalist leaders were soon making fiery speeches and threats. The Imam declared that the withdrawal of Egyptian troops was an essential prerequisite to any peace move and must be guaranteed before the National Congress could meet. These bellicose utterances were made despite the very weak political and military position of the Royalists. Nevertheless, in November there was a secret meeting in Paris between Prince Mohammed Hussein and Field Marshal Amer, to sound out the possibilities of Nasser making peace directly with the Royalists without involving Saudi Arabia, and it is thought that Prince Mohammed Hussein agreed at this meeting to allow the UAR forces to withdraw unmolested from the Jauf and the north.

Also in November, there was a crisis in Saudi Arabia. King Saud was deposed by the ruling family, and his brother, Prince Faisal, was appointed King in his stead.[1] King Saud, who was reported to have spent £2 million to finance an assassination attempt on Nasser in 1958, was a deadly enemy of the President of the UAR, and as such had been in favour of unstinted aid to Imam Mohammed al-Badr. The shrewd and cautious King Faisal clamped down on princely extravagances and government waste. He continued financial aid to the Imam, but at a lesser volume, as he was not very impressed by him. The King never spoke of helping to put the Imam back on his throne in Sana.

The cease-fire was broken by the Royalists during the first days of December, as they flooded back into sectors of territory that had been taken from them by UAR troops in August but since vacated, and this movement, with some attendant skirmishing, continued throughout December and January (1965). Nasser did not at all mind the Royalists breaking the cease-fire agreement, as it showed them up in a bad political light. He had been sorely tempted to launch an offensive himself, at this time when so many tribesmen had gone to their homes for the winter and would be reluctant to turn out to fight again until the spring. He had thought that a swift assault on the remaining Royalist positions would lead to the killing or capture of the Imam. This might have been possible, but somehow his projected offensive never really got under way. Egyptian soldiers did not like fighting in the Yemen in winter any more than the

[1] Faisal was proclaimed King of Saudi Arabia and Omam, and recognized as the religious head of the nation.

Yemenis did, and their officers found many excuses to postpone an offensive. As a result, the Royalists were allowed, almost unhindered, to return to areas from which they had so recently been driven. The military position crystallized into what it had been before August, and the stalemate hardened once more.

All was not well in the Republican camp. Early in December, sixty dissident Republicans, including eight senior army officers and officials, all Shafeis, fled to Aden after staging a protest at Hodeida, a Shafi stronghold. Hundreds of arrests were made in Taiz and Hodeida, and there was a general exodus of Shafeis from Sana to the southern part of the country. These Shafi dissidents formed themselves into what became known as the Yemeni Youth Organization, and a deputation went to Saudi Arabia to be received by King Faisal and to ask the UAR Ambassador in Saudia Arabia to obtain permission for it to visit Nasser, so that it could lay its case before him. The deputation then moved on to Beirut, where on 30th December it held a press conference at which it condemned the as-Sallal regime but declared its opposition to the return of the monarchy. It demanded the establishment of a provisional government and the election of a constituent assembly to decide the country's future form of government. The Yemeni Youth Organization also wanted to end all foreign aid to either side in the Yemen war, and called for the withdrawal of UAR troops.

The Republican Shafi-Zeidi split had severe repercussions in the Government. On 11th December, Ahmed Numan resigned as President of the Consultative Council (having decided to return from Cairo). Then Mohammed as-Zubeiri and Abdul Rahman Iryani resigned from the Cabinet, accusing as-Sallal of alienating popular support through corruption and in competence, and proposing that his powers should be transferred to a five-man Council of Sovereignty for an interim two-year period. On the 26th, six other ministers resigned, and on the following day all except one of those remaining in office resigned too. As-Sallal immediately flew to Cairo, to avoid being pressured into resignation by this powerful group of politicians and to seek Nasser's moral and physical support. The year of 1964 drew to a close with an absentee President, a Republic without a Government, and a Royalist offensive in full swing.

CHAPTER EIGHT

Republican Differences

MAIN EVENTS

1965	
January 5th	As-Sallal returns to the Yemen from UAR.
14th	The Imam forms a Council of Representatives.
25th	As-Sallal forms the Yemeni Arab Union.
—	Royalist successes at Jebel Razeh and Beit Maaran.
March 10th	Harib falls to the Royalists.
April 1st	Mohammed as-Zubeiri assassinated.
15th	Ahmed Numan forms a Government.
May 2nd/5th	The Khamir Conference.
12th	Ahmed Numan dissolves the Presidential Council.
24th	Royalists take Sirwah.
June 14th	Royalists take Qaflah, seat of the Hashid Federation.
28th	The Numan Government falls.
July 18th	Hassan al-Amri forms a Government.
20th	Khamir sheikhs go to Saudi Arabia.
23rd	Taif Talks between dissident Republican sheikhs and Royalists.
24th	Royalists seize Jihanah.
25th	Royalists seize Marib.
August 18th	Nasser holds a meeting of Republican leaders in UAR.
22nd–24th	Jedda Meeting between Nasser and King Faisal.
25th	Cease-fire becomes effective.
September	Reduction of UAR forces in the Yemen.
September	As-Sallal flies to Cairo for medical treatment.

On 3rd January 1965 the ministers who had resigned sent a message to Nasser asking him to remove as-Sallal and Vice-

President Hassan al-Amri. On the 5th as-Sallal returned to the Yemen, and immediately announced that a state of emergency was in force in Sana and that a tribunal would be set up to try several former ministers and other dissident Republicans. He 'accepted' the resignation of the former Premier, Hamoud al-Jaifi, and asked Hassan al-Amri to form a government. Hassan al-Amri did so, and thoughtfully included Hamoud al-Jaifi and several other ministers who had so recently and dramatically resigned. Wholesale dismissals and arrests followed as as-Sallal sought to re-establish his authority, and within days five members of the old al-Jaifi Government had been placed in detention. There were refusals to take office that included four men nominated for the new al-Amri government. Mohammed Othman refused to accept the post of Chairman of the Consultative Council, and Abdul Ghani Motahar would not take the Governorship of Taiz. Ahmed Numan was dismissed as Permanent Representative to the Arab League, and Ismail al Gurafi was appointed in his place. On the 25th, as-Sallal announced that there was to be a single political party, which would be called the Yemeni Arab Union.

It was an uneasy President who had to turn and face the Royalist offensive as it mounted in intensity. The UAR forces amounted to over 48,000 men, and new Soviet armoured vehicles, guns and aircraft had been shipped over from Egypt. But the Yemeni Army itself was still a poor and weak organization, ill-trained, ill-armed, and less than 6,000 strong.[1] Many decrees had been issued about the Yemeni Defence Forces, but Egyptian disapproval and deliberate hindrance had seen to it that little had been done. For example, in October 1964, some 200 sheikhs of tribes alleged loyal to the Republican cause had met at Sana and been talked by as-Sallal into agreeing to raise a total of 20,000 armed tribesmen to help fight the Royalists. Nothing had been done to implement this decision because of Egyptian obstruction, but at the time it had made good propaganda and dismayed the Royalists. On 9th January in an effort to put defence and internal security on a sounder footing, as-

[1] The number quoted is that estimated actually to have been serving in the Yemeni Army. Additionally, there were probably between 6,000 and 8,000 Yemeni auxiliaries serving with the UAR, including a horde of labourers, servants and camp followers.

Sallal re-established the National Defence Council which consisted of the Premier, the Ministers of Defence, the Interior and Tribal Affairs, the Chief of Staff and other army officers and sheikhs, with himself as Chairman. It was given authority to develop and improve the Yemeni Army and to raise such other forces as were necessary for the defence of the country.

In the mountains, Imam Mohammed al-Badr and his Premier, Prince Hassan, were preparing a political front for world consumption, and on 14th January it was announced that the Imam had formed an Interim Council of Representatives under Ali Abdul Karim al Fadheel, which was to be divided into separate committees responsible for administration, defence, political affairs and legal matters. The Royalists had never had an effective government and so had been unable properly to administer and control any territory they occupied or had paramount influence in, and accordingly there had never been any serious threat of a strong rival government to the Republican regime.

By this time most of the dwellings were deserted because of UAR aerial activity, and the Imam and his followers, including the Premier and the Royalist field commanders, all lived in mountain caves which, being widely scattered, brought serious communication problems. There had never been a convincing command structure, and there was neither a general staff to formulate plans and systematically prosecute the war, nor a good organization for supply for the Royalists. The Zeidi tribes very much cherished their individual independence, resenting and resisting the imposition of any authority, and to retain their vital support the Imam had to tread very cautiously. The Royalist prosecution of the war was by force of circumstances a spasmodic, casual, hit-or-miss affair. Mohammed al-Badr now felt that the moment had come to put together a framework of government structure.

In an attempt to rally dissident Republicans and waverers to his banner the Imam now announced a National Charter which promised them an amnesty. To attract the Shafeis, he promised them equality, and freedom of speech and publication within the Islamic law. Demanding the withdrawal of UAR forces, he called for self-determination for the people of the Yemen, saying that he would establish a constitutional monarchy and give the power to a Council of Ministers and a Consultative Assembly. He also declared that future Imams would be elected by the people. In actual fact, very little changed. The Imam retained absolute power, although as he was at this stage a sick and tired man, this was wielded by Prince Hassan, the Premier, assisted by Prince Mohammed Hussein.

The Royalist offensive that had begun in December 1964, continued sporadically on most fronts until July, and enabled the Royalists to occupy large areas formerly held or influenced by the Republicans. These Royalist successes were due not only to the energy of individual Royalist commanders in the field, but also to increased financial and military aid both from Saudi Arabia and from Iran, which granted large credits enabling supplies to be purchased and delivered. The Iranians, Shiite Moslems, were of the same religious persuasion as the Zeidis, and the Shah considered Nasser's ambitions to be a danger to himself and his country. Support for the Royalists continued to be given by some states of the Federation of South Arabia also. The Republican Government protested to the UN and the Arab League about King Faisal's aid to the Imam, declaring that without it the Royalists would have been defeated, which was most probably true. Later (in June) King Faisal confirmed he was actively assisting the Royalists, maintaining that since Egypt had not kept the agreement for the cease-fire, he was not bound by it either.

During January the Royalists had two major successes in the northern part of the Yemen, when they captured a massif, known as Jebel Razeh, in the north-west, close to the Saudi Arabian border, and then another called Beit Maaran, which was about twenty miles north-east of Sana. In an attempt at brinkmanship, a large Republican force of about 7,000 UAR troops with 3,000 Yemeni auxiliaries had assembled near Maidi on the coast, with the object of making threatening moves against Qizan. It was immediately turned against the Royalist thrusts, but all its attempts to penetrate the mountains were repulsed.

On the 10th, the Royalists stated that 500 UAR troops had been killed when the Republicans launched a punitive campaign against the Harith tribe, near Sada, and the Naham tribe at Beit Maaran, after they had both changed sides and joined the Royalists. On the 13th, visiting Aden, Hashem bin Hashem, the Royalist Information Minister, gave details of the battles for Jebel Rezeh, which was adjacent to the Imam's new headquarters. He claimed that over 6,000 UAR and Yemeni soldiers had been engaged, that over 1,000 UAR personnel had been killed, and that 335 (including 17 UAR officers and 25 Yemeni officers) had been taken prisoner. He would only admit to about 100 Royalist casualties. These figures were denied by the Republicans, but they stung Field Marshal Amer into announcing that the total number of UAR personnel killed in the Yemen since 1962 was 105 officers and 1,502 soldiers.

While in Aden, Hashem bin Hashem took the opportunity of launching an appeal to international organizations to help the 'hundreds of thousands of Yemenis homeless, hungry and destitute as the result of Egyptian intervention'. He said the Imam was inviting Moslem delegates from all over the world to attend an 'Islamic conference' at his new headquarter caves near Jebel Nadir. The Royalist Information Minister also alleged that on 23rd January, UAR aircraft had dropped gas bombs in the Beit Maaran area, killing some 200 people. This charge that the UAR was using gas bombs again was repeated by some Republican dissidents who reached Aden early in February, but on the 13th of that month it was reported that the International Red Cross had refused a Royalist request to look into this matter. Obscure political pressures seemed bent on befogging this issue.

After a pause, fighting broke out again in south-east Yemen, and Royalist pressure grew in intensity until the successful capture of the fort and town of Harib, near the Beihan State border, on 10th March. A force of irregulars had crossed over from Beihan, taken the Republican garrison in the fort by surprise, and then in conjunction with Royalist forces from the north, had driven the defenders out westwards where they retreated to Haqla, a mountain pass area. In Republican hands since March 1963, Harib was the first town the Royalists had taken by force, and it considerably boosted their morale. In mid-April, a mixed UAR and Yemeni force striking from Haqla mounted a counter-offensive to re-take Harib, but this failed, and the town and the fort remained in Royalist hands.

Spasmodic fighting continued throughout the spring in the northern parts of the Yemen, with the Royalists pressing forward whenever and wherever they could. In the north-east, Prince

Mohammed Hussein now had a fairly large group of trained volunteers, and a handful of field, anti-aircraft and anti-tank guns. He was able to defeat a UAR attempt to sever the supply routes from Saudi Arabia in the region of the Humaidat Valley, but this offensive failed largely because the Egyptians tended to remain inside their armoured vehicles as much as they could, and the mountainous terrain was unsuitable for tracks or wheels. Another similar UAR offensive in the same region was launched in May, but this also was repulsed by Prince Hussein.

But the Royalists did not have it all their own way. They suffered heavy casualties in the attacks and raids they made, because of superior UAR fire power and close air support. The co-ordination and movement of the Royalist volunteers on the battlefield left much to be desired, and contributed to their casualty rate and their occasional defeats. On 7th June, UAR forces halted and broke up a Royalist attack in the north-west near the Saudi Arabian frontier, in the Harad region, and on the 14th, in a similar action, it was claimed that forty-nine of the Imam's soldiers had been killed, and quantities of arms seized, in an unsuccessful attempt to filter in, near Barat, men and supplies from the north and east.

Another group of Royalists, under Prince Abdullah Hussein, concentrated upon pressing closer to Sana. They swarmed in from the eastern mountains, and succeeded in cutting the road from Sana to Hazm, where there was one of the strongest UAR garrisons in the Jauf. A heavy UAR counter-attack re-opened the road temporarily, and drove back the tribesmen with heavy loss, but Prince Abdullah Hussein managed to block the road again a fortnight later.

To the north-west of Sana, the Royalists under Prince Abdul Rahman temporarily blocked the road northwards to Sada, about fifteen miles from the capital, while to the south-east Prince Abdullah Hassan marched against Jihanah, which fell to him after weeks of fighting, on 24th July. Meanwhile, Royalist troops had swarmed into the Sana-Marib Corridor, and on 24th May had seized the Republican positions at Sirwah. Next, they concentrated upon the city of Marib, which fell to Prince Abdullah Hassan on 25th July, after being held by the Republicans since February 1963. Although it was empty, such inhabitants as remained living in caves in the surrounding mountains, it was a prestigious gain for the Royalists. On 14th June, they had occupied another valuable town in the north-west, that of Qaflah, the traditional seat of the Hashid federation.

This six-month Royalist offensive had been a huge success, and it was claimed that by August 1965 the Royalists had retaken over half the total area once held by the Republicans. While this may not have been completely accurate, it is probable that by this stage approximately half the country was in their hands. They had taken a few key objectives, Harib, Marib, Sirwah and Qaflah, had seized large quantities of arms, vehicles and equipment, and had captured several hundred UAR prisoners. With only a few exceptions, UAR offensives and counter-attacks had been failures, or limited successes at best.

Earlier in the year, Prince Mohammed Hussein had assumed command of the whole of the eastern sector of the Yemen, taking over from Prince Hassan, the Premier, who now devoted himself mainly to political matters since the Imam, despite the success of the Royalist offensive, was a sick and disillusioned man. Most of the credit for victories, at least in the eastern part of the country, was due to Prince Mohammed Hussein, who was the key personality in training, organizing and equipping volunteers, and instrumental in persuading so many to agree to serve for a year in the field. At last some semblance of military organization was beginning to show through. There still remained six major 'armies' in service, or now perhaps seven if Prince Mohammed Hussein's own group could be counted, although it was never, as far as I can discover, given a formal number. Each of the field armies now had anything up to 2,000 armed and semi-trained soldiers, and for the first time the commanders had something with which to hit back at the Republican forces, when and where they wanted it. The Yemeni Royalist soldiers were fed and paid a small sum of money for their services, which gave them some material motivation, although some of the commanders could still inflict barbaric punishments at times.

The UAR Expeditionary Force was in bad shape. It had suffered heavy losses in arms, vehicles and men, and was certainly in no position to retake any of the territory so recently lost, or to mount anything of an offensive. Nasser badly wanted a breathing space and was seriously considering withdrawing his outlying forces and concentrating them all in the coastal region of the Taiz-Sana-Hodeida triangle. He was saved from that indignity by being able cunningly to engineer a cease-fire, in the nick of time, which gave him the respite he needed to re-group, re-equip and reinforce his badly-battered forces.

The people of the Yemen were disillusioned with the leadership and dominance of Nasser, and after a meeting of the senior sheikhs in March, both the Hashid and Bakil federations, in a rare moment of accord, issued a joint ultimatum,[1] demanding that the Egyptian troops be withdrawn, and promising that no action would be taken against them if this happened. Although some elements of the two federations were pro-Republican, the majority had fought with the Royalists in the Imam's recent offensive. Those Republicans who strongly supported Nasser and his line were of little use to him at the moment because of the major schism within their ranks. A few, like the faithful as-Sallal, accepted UAR policy, but there were many others who advocated an end to all foreign aid to either side and were in favour of the Yemenis negotiating their own peace settlement amongst themselves. A Third Force was definitely emerging, and seemed to gather support not only from the intellectuals of the revolution but now from among the tribes as well.

Early in 1965, Mohammed as-Zubeiri, who came to symbolize the Third Force, had left Sana and taken to the mountains in the north in the region of Barat, where he formed a political organization known as 'Allah's Party'. This had the objective of working for a peaceful settlement of the war, and attracted many dissident Republicans who had become disenchanted with as-Sallal. As-Zubeiri, who had been a minister in the al-Jaifi Government until he resigned in December 1964, was appalled at the continuing corruption and the general lack of security under as-Sallal's regime, and considered the government to be much too subservient to the UAR. He was dismayed that the reforms promised so often were never put into effect, and he was not impressed by the fumbling efforts of the al-Amri Government. As-Zubeiri's main aim was to form and keep in existence a 'middle' party, and he tried to project this idea to the sheikhs,

[1] At this meeting it was claimed that the Hashid could put 30,000 armed warriors into the field and the Bakil about 80,000, which went to show how these two federations fluctuated in strength, through tribal intrigues and changes of loyalty.

with some success. For example he issued crude cartoons depicting the Yemeni people as a dove attacked by two serpents, one representing Egypt and the other the as-Sallal clique.

On 1st April Mohammed as-Zubeiri was assassinated in north-east Yemen, in obscure circumstances, while on his way to a meeting with King Faisal at Mecca. The Republicans vaguely blamed the Royalists, but evidence did not support this charge. The assassination embarrassed both the UAR and the Sana Republican regime, although both would have liked as-Zubeiri out of the way. The assassination sparked off a huge wave of resentment against both Nasser and as-Sallal. The Hashid and Bakil federations, and some other tribes, threatened to march on Sana at once if Ahmed Nuhman, a friend of Mohammed as-Zubeiri and himself a Shafi with similar Third Force views, were not at once made Premier. After hesitating briefly Nasser and as-Sallal gave way before this threat. They had little choice if they wanted to save the Republic. On 15th April, the al-Amri Government resigned, and Ahmed Numan became the Premier. His conditions were freedom of action, the choice of his own ministers, the abolition of the Presidential Council and the holding of a peace conference. All this meant that as-Sallal would be shorn of most of his power, but the seriousness of the situation was such that, for the moment at least, the Premier's demands were conceded.

Ahmed Numan's Government consisted of nine Zeidis and nine Shafeis, with Mohsin al-Aini as Foreign Minister and Colonel Mohammed al-Riani as Defence Minister. Two, Ahmed al Marwari, Minister of Information, and Hussein al Maqdami, Minister of Health, were regarded sympathetically by the Baathist Party of Syria, and each had a considerable following amongst the younger officers and intellectuals. Numan's Government did not include Hassan al-Amri nor a Minister for 'South Yemen' as had previous ones, which may have indicated a desire for better relations with Britain over the Federation of South Arabia. Sheikh Abdullah al-Ahmer, paramount chief of the Hashid federation, became the Minister of the Interior. The Sheikh held Mohammed as-Zubeiri's assassins in one of his own prisons and this was used as a lever by Ahmed Numan to obtain more freedom from Egyptian control, since the prisoners had incriminated the UAR.

The reformation of the Presidential Council on 20th April stripped as-Sallal of most of his powers, although he was allowed to retain the face-saving title of President and Hassan al-Amri that of Vice-President. New members of the Council, whose tasks were defined as being to plan, direct and supervise the execution of state policy, included Abdul Rahman Iryani, Mohammed Othman, and two Shafeis, Mohammed Numan (son of the Premier) and Sheikh Numan Ben Qaid Rajeh. Ahmed Numan declared he would work for the consolidation of the Republican political system and prepare for elections to be held within two years. He also said that a Yemeni national army would be formed with assistance from Arab countries, and made other statements, to do with non-alignment in international affairs, implementation of agreements with the UAR and economic development, that were little different from those issued by his predecessors. The appointment of Ahmed Numan as Premier was a setback to Imam Mohammed al-Badr's newly-declared policy of freedom from Egyptian domination. The Royalist political platform had now been stolen from him.

The policies of Ahmed Numan attracted the allegiance or interest of several uncommitted tribes. It was reported, for example, that he had a secret meeting with Sheikh Naji bin al Khadir, the paramount chief in the Khawlan region, who was nominally pro-Royalist. This and many similar contacts enabled him to call a conference, at Khamir, in Hashid territory about twenty miles north of Sana, which was attended by some 5,000 sheikhs and lasted from 2nd to the 5th May. Many pro-Royalist tribes refused the invitation, largely because the meeting, which became known as the Khamir Conference, was held in Republican territory. The gathering together of such a large number of tribal representatives seemed to indicate that the Imam could only count on the undivided and unswerving loyalty of a very small minority, mainly those in the mountainous north-west, and that the majority wanted nothing to do with either the Imam or as-Sallal.

Abdul Rahman Iryani was the chairman of the Khamir Conference, which was addressed by Ahmed Numan, who said he was prepared to extend the hand of friendship to King Faisal of Saudi Arabia. The Conference approved several resolutions, including one to send delegations to Arab countries to seek co-operation in ending the war, and another to appoint a committee to make contact with the Royalists. It was also decided that a Yemeni Peoples' Army, about 11,000 strong, should be formed, which would gradually take over internal security duties from UAR soldiers. The Yemeni army was still less than 6,000 men in strength, and was made up of a jumble of small infantry units scattered about the country, some of which were either incorporated in the UAR formations or in some other way under UAR command. Steps taken to try and implement conscription had been frustrated by the Egyptians, and the Revolutionary National Guard which had been formed immediately after the revolution had early on fallen apart for a similar reason. There were very few effective Yemeni fighting units, perhaps for a very good reason from Nasser and as-Sallal's point of view since they might have presented a serious danger to stability. As-Sallal retained his UAR bodyguard.

On 8th May yet another Interim Constitution was announced, which further decreased as-Sallal's powers. It provided for a Consultative Assembly of ninety-nine members to act as the legislative body, paving the way for a permanent constitution which, when evolved after a two-year transitional period, was to be the subject of a national referendum. It was also announced that there was to be a single political party, to be known as the National Congress and modelled on the permitted political parties of the UAR and Iraq, which was to supersede as-Sallal's briefly-initiated Yemeni Arab Union. Ahmed Numan's independent line for making peace with the Royalists brought him into sharp conflict with the as-Sallal faction. Hassan al-Amri resigned as Vice-President[1] of the Presidential Council, nominally for health reasons, and on 12th May, Numan replied by dissolving the Council, and forming in its place the Republican Council, which consisted only of as-Sallal, Abdul Rahman Iryani and Sheikh Numan Rajeh.

On 17th May, Abdul Kawi Hamim[2] and Kassem Ghaleb, both former ministers in the al-Amri Government, arrived in Aden and asked for political asylum. They claimed that the Numan Government had tried to arrest and murder them, and

[1] At the same time he was granted the rank of lieutenant-general.

[2] Hamim, who later returned to the Yemen after the Numan Government fell, was reported killed in a gun battle in south Yemen on 23rd August.

when this had failed, had sent troops to destroy their home town of Rahida near the border of the Federation of South Arabia. They alleged that Ahmed Numan wanted to establish a tribal system of government, while they wanted a national, democratic and progressive one.

In accordance with the Khamir Conference proposals, Ahmed Numan and Mohsin al-Aini began talks with the UAR Commander-in-Chief and the UAR Ambassador, at Sana, and on 15th May a Republican delegation led by Abdul Rahman Iryani, which included Mohsin al-Aini, left to tour Arab countries to explain the resolutions of the Conference. On 6th June, a Jordanian spokesman said that King Hussein was working to obtain a settlement of the Yemeni problem and that his initiative had led to a preliminary agreement on basic principles. A letter from King Hussein to both Nasser and King Faisal, dated the 14th, contained proposals to establish a joint Republican and Royalist administration under a neutral leader to govern the country until the people's wishes could be determined by a national referendum, the replacement of the UAR Expeditionary Force by an inter-Arab peace force, and the establishment of an inter-Arab fund to finance the reconstruction of the Yemeni economy.

Other Arab statesmen rushed forward to act as peace-makers. President Ben Bella of Algeria had a peace plan ready, and sent an envoy to have talks with Ahmed Numan, Nasser and President Aref of Iraq. A Kuwaiti delegation, headed by the Crown Prince, also tried to mediate in the Yemeni dispute and at Ahmed Numan's request visited King Faisal. On 17th June, Numan was able to announce that the Saudi Arabian ruler had agreed to accept Yemeni Republican representatives to discuss matters. It was also expected that the Yemen would be prominently placed on the agenda for discussion at the Afro-Asian Conference due to be held at Algiers on the 28th, but this did not take place. These and other well-meaning peace negotiations were suddenly dropped for another reason—the ousting of Ahmed Numan by as-Sallal.

Since Ahmed Numan had become Premier, relations between him and as-Sallal had been extremely strained, and Numan had also deeply offended the UAR by his support for the withdrawal of Egyptian soldiers from the Yemen, by establishing relations with Syria over Nasser's head, by including suspected Baathists in his Government, and by forming a political party not under Egyptian auspices. The UAR consistently backed as-Sallal against Ahmed Numan on all military issues and was in a strong position to nullify many of Numan's proposals. For example, Nasser refused to allow money to be used to set up the Yemeni Peoples' Army, as proposed by the Khamir Conference resolution. Perhaps the most important difference of all was between Numan's policy of conciliation towards the tribes and the Royalists, and Nasser's implacable belief in the use of force against them as the only means of total victory.

On 27th June, without consulting the Numan Government, as-Sallal appointed a Supreme Council of the Armed Forces, and sent soldiers to force Radio Sana to broadcast his order. Ahmed Numan protested, and the next day when his protests were ignored by as-Sallal he resigned as Premier, because of 'acts and resolutions in total contradiction to the letter and the spirit of the Constitution'. As-Sallal at once sent troops of his UAR bodyguard to arrest Numan, but was persuaded by the UAR Ambassador to allow him instead to leave the Yemen. Ahmed Numan went off to Cairo.

Numan's resignation caused a big upheaval in Yemeni Republican circles as he had a large personal following, and on 1st July the committee set up to implement the resolutions of the Khamir Conference asked him to continue in office. He would not agree. On the 4th, a delegation headed by Mohsin al-Aini flew from the Yemen to Cairo to try and persuade Numan to return as Premier, but it was unsuccessful.

On 6th July, as-Sallal formed his own Government with himself as Premier and Hassan al-Amri and Hamoud al-Jaifi as Deputy Premiers. He immediately arrested over forty Numan supporters believed to have Baathist sympathies. Nasser was at the height of one of his anti-Baathist campaigns. However, this Government was short-lived. On the 9th, as-Sallal withdrew his order forming it, and hurriedly flew off to Cairo to consult Nasser. It is most probable that he was urgently sent for, as Nasser felt that such an as-Sallal Government would not have enough support to function, and would merely widen the Republican split.

On the 18th, as-Sallal returned to announce that a compromise had been found, and he publically re-affirmed the Khamir Conference resolutions. Hassan al-Amri formed a Government which consisted of thirteen civilians and six army officers, but several nominees refused to serve in it. Official appointments were refused by other Numan supporters, including Mohammed Said al-Attar, who turned down as-Sallal's invitation to become President of the Yemeni Reconstruction and Development Bank, as a protest against the 'arrests and other measures taken against my colleagues and intellectuals'.[1]

The Numan resignation had a deep affect on the Third Force Republicans, who were of the opinion that UAR forces should be withdrawn and that the Yemenis should make peace amongst themselves. On 20th July, a delegation, led by Sheikh Abdullah al-Ahmer and Sheikh Numan Rajeh, of nearly 250 people, all of whom had taken part in the Khamir Conference, arrived in the Federation of South Arabia. They had been allowed to travel through Royalist-held territory, because the Imam regarded them as 'brothers fleeing from the Egyptian invasion'. Sheikh Abdullah al-Ahmer sent messages to the UN and the Arab League asking them to ensure the withdrawal of the UAR forces from the Yemen, to reinstate the Numan Government, and to urge the Yemeni regime to fulfil the Khamir Conference resolutions.

Hussein Maqdami, another of Numan's former ministers, and Mohammed al-Fuseil who had been the secretary at the Khamir Conference, made their way to Beirut, where on the 26th, Maqdami announced that the Yemeni people could no longer tell the difference between the present Republican regime and the old reactionary one of the Imam. He called for the ending of aid to the Royalists from Saudi Arabia, and for a conference of Republicans and Royalists to end the war. Mohammed al-Fuseil claimed that, so far, between 80,000 and 100,000 Yemenis had been killed in the war, as well as between 5,000 and 8,000 Egyptians. These figures seemed to be more credible than any previous ones issued.

On 23rd July, the delegation of Republican sheikhs moved on to Saudi Arabia, where it was received at Riyadh by King Faisal. It also met the Federation of Popular Forces, a group

[1] He later accepted this post.

headed by Ibrahim al-Wazir, a prominent member of the Wazir family which was opposed to the Imam. This political faction was encouraged by King Faisal, as he hoped it would attract other dissidents, both Republican and Royalist, and so develop into a real Third Force which would eclipse other contenders. Under Saudi Arabian auspices, the Khamir sheikhs went to Taiz to meet Royalist representatives led by Prince Abdul Rahman, and on 13th August, it was stated that an agreement had been reached between them. The Yemen would be known as a Moslem State, thus avoiding the use of either the words Republic or Monarchy, a Presidential Council assisted by a Council of Ministers would act as Head of State, and there would be an Advisory Council to consist of representatives of all tribes and leading personalities. The people of the Yemen would be called upon to choose between an Imamate, a constitutional monarchy and a republic. As-Sallal immediately denounced the Republican sheikhs as traitors, and Mohsin al-Aini, who had remained at Sana, insisted that any settlement must be based on the maintenance of the Republic and the permanent removal of the Imam and his family. This was well received by both Nasser and as-Sallal, and did something to prevent the Republican breach from widening.

Meanwhile, Nasser had not overlooked the fact that his battered UAR Expeditionary Force must have a respite, and as a prelude to angling for a cease-fire, he made loud threats in the direction of Saudi Arabia. On 22nd July he said that UAR troops could not indefinitely tolerate attacks by British and Saudi Arabian mercenaries, and that if the negotiations he had just started with Saudi Arabia failed, the UAR would have to liquidate the centres of aggression. On the 29th, Nasser's representative visited Riyadh, and King Faisal declared that he would not negotiate under threats. The Yemeni Republican Government also came into the act, when Hassan al-Amri, the Premier, blustered that all Yemeni Republicans were prepared to wage war against Saudi Arabia, the Yemeni peoples' 'only enemy'. On 4th August it was reported that over 10,000 Saudi Arabian troops were massing near the Yemeni border in anticipation of a UAR invasion.

Having put down a smoke screen, Nasser worked for a quick cease-fire in the Yemen on his own terms to enable his troops to recover and make ready to regain lost ground. Messengers and envoys flitted to and fro. On 16th August it was announced that Nasser and King Faisal would meet at Jedda to talk about the Yemen. Nasser had apparently offered to meet King Faisal either in the UAR or in Saudi Arabia, but had rejected King Faisal's suggestion that they meet at sea, as Nasser said he did 'not wish to deal with King Faisal as an enemy and stranger'. On the 18th, at Alexandria, Nasser held a meeting of prominent Republican Yemenis, who included as-Sallal, Hassan al-Amri, Mohsin al-Aini, Abdul Rahman Iryani and Ahmed Numan. The talks were reported to be very heated, and Nasser accused Ahmed Numan of having formed a Government composed of anti-Egyptian elements. However, after this conference, Ahmed Numan said he was convinced that Nasser was determined to bring the war in the Yemen to a close, and spoke well of his intentions. Ahmed Numan did not yet know his Nasser.

Nasser and King Faisal met at Jedda from 22nd to the 24th August. The meeting was described by journalists as brotherly, and they signed an agreement providing for an immediate cease-fire in the Yemen. Other points of the Jedda Agreement, as it became known, established the withdrawal of the UAR forces from the Yemen by September 1966, the ending of Saudi Arabian military aid to the Royalists, the setting up of a provisional Yemeni Government, the holding of a plebiscite in November 1966, and the formation of a joint UAR-Saudi Arabian force to prevent any violation of the cease-fire. King Faisal said he would deny the use of his territory to the Royalists for any warlike operations in the Yemen, and would only allow food to pass to them. A conference of fifty representatives from all Yemeni national persuasions including major tribes and leading political personalities, was to meet at Harad on 23rd November to form a provisional government, make arrangements for the transitional period and organize the plebiscite. Both Nasser and King Faisal undertook to respect the decisions of the Harad Conference, and help implement them. One major factor that later had repercussions was that neither Republicans nor Royalists were present at the Jedda talks, or were consulted about the decisions reached by Nasser and King Faisal.

The UN and most countries welcomed the outcome of the Jedda meeting, especially America, the Soviet Union, Jordan, Iraq and the other Arab and Moslem countries. The exception was Syria (then in the throes of a 'hate Nasser' campaign) who accused Nasser of 'foully murdering the Yemeni revolution'. The Syrian Baathists at this stage were Nasser's most virulent opponents.

It was announced from the Royalist headquarters, now back in the original caves near Jebel Qara, that Imam Mohammed al-Badr had ordered his followers to cease fire on 25th August, but to maintain their present positions and not cede an inch of territory until the outcome of the proposed Harad Conference was known. The next day, UAR troops began to withdraw from the Saudi Arabian frontier areas. On 5th September, it was stated in Cairo that the joint UAR-Saudi Arabian force manning the border observation posts to supervise the cease-fire, would consist of an infantry brigade and two squadrons of aircraft from each country, to be commanded by an Egyptian and a Saudi Arabian officer on alternate months. This force was to be in position by 25th September. During September there were some UAR troop withdrawals from the Yemen, and although they were relatively small in size, each was accompanied by much publicity.

In late August, no doubt under strong UAR pressure, as-Sallal made a declaration of friendship towards the group of dissident Republican sheikhs of Taif fame, and also to some others who had differed with him politically, and invited them to return to the Yemen. He said he would release any Republican political prisoners, and a few lesser fry were indeed freed from detention. On 4th September it was announced that as-Sallal would lead the Yemeni delegation, planned to include his former enemy, Ahmed Numan, to the forthcoming Arab summit conference to be held at Casablanca. However, as-Sallal, allegedly for health reasons, parted company with it at Cairo, where he remained.

The picture in the Yemen was brighter than it had ever been before. It seemed as if the fratricidal war was about to end, that a solution was about to be found and forced through by the UAR and Saudi Arabia, and that all Republican differences were to be healed. Moreover, it seemed that Nasser and King

Faisal were fast becoming friends. On 10th August, King Faisal visited Cairo and was fêted, and a few days later Nasser withdrew the sequestration order on Saudi Arabian property in Egypt, which mainly affected the Saudi Royal Family and had been imposed in 1962 when the Yemeni war had erupted. Both leaders made statements about their firm intentions to develop cultural and economic co-operation between their respective countries. It seemed far too good to be true—and it was.

CHAPTER NINE

The Harad Conference

MAIN EVENTS

1965	
November 24th	Harad Conference.
December 24th	Harad Conference recessed.
December	UAR Expeditionary Force withdrawals begin.
1966	
February	British White Paper on Defence—to leave Aden by 1968.
February	Strategy of the Long Breath begun.
April	Imam Mohammed al-Badr moves to Taif, in Saudi Arabia, for medical treatment.
April	UAR announces whole of north and north-east of Yemen evacuated by UAR forces.
April 13th	Assassination of Abdullah Iryani.
May	UAR Expeditionary Force down to about 20,000 men.
August	Royalist Council of War at Taif, in Saudi Arabia.
August 12th	As-Sallal returns to the Yemen after a year's absence.
17th	The Kuwait Meeting.
September 16th	Hassan al-Amri and supporters arrested in Cairo.
18th	As-Sallal forms a Government.
September	End of Long Breath strategy.
October 14th	UAR bombs Najran and Qizan.
19th	State Security Courts set up.
November	UAR Expeditionary Force strength rises to about 60,000.
December 5th	Imam Mohammed al-Badr hands over powers to Imamic Council.
December	Abdul Rahman Baidani appointed Yemeni Ambassador to the Lebanon.

On 24th November 1965, in accordance with the Jedda Agreement, twenty-five Yemeni Republicans and twenty-five Royalists met at Harad, only a few miles from the Saudi Arabian border, to discuss the formation of a provisional government and the proposed plebiscite. The UAR and Saudi Arabia were each represented by two observers, while a liaison committee of two Republicans and two Royalists acted as a link with the joint UAR-Saudi Arabian peace commission. This was headed by Prince Abdullah Sudari, of Saudi Arabia, who commanded such of the joint force as had been assembled.

The Republican delegation, led by Abdul Rahman Iryani, only included three members who could be regarded as being of the as-Sallal clique, one of them the Deputy Premier, Abdullah Jizailan. Besides Iryani himself there were at least three others with marked moderate Republican views, Ahmed Numan the former Premier, Mohammed Othman, and Sheikh Abdullah al-Ahmer of the Hashid federation. The Royalist delegation, led by Mohammed al-Shami the Foreign Minister, was composed mainly of leaders of Zeidi tribes traditionally loyal to the Imam. In view of strong Republican objections, and under Saudi Arabian pressure, the Royalists had agreed to exclude any member of the Imam's family. Included in the Royalist delegation were three prominent dissident Republicans, one of whom, claiming to represent a 'third force' in the Yemen, was Sheikh Numan Rajeh.

From the very first day the Harad Conference found itself at a complete deadlock. Neither side was able even to agree to the agenda. The Republicans demanded that any provisional government must operate within a republican framework and on republican principles, and that members of the Royal Family be excluded. The Royalists would not accept this, insisting that the Jedda Agreement implied that the provisional government should be neither Republican nor monarchist. Royalists demanded the immediate withdrawal of all UAR forces and the holding of a plebiscite as soon as possible, and while the Republicans had no objection to a plebiscite, they insisted that time was necessary to arrange the UAR military withdrawal.

The delegates never got past these main points of difference, and the Harad Conference recessed on 24th December, the beginning of Ramadan. Both sides agreed to meet again on

20th February (1966), and in the interim period to continue the existing armistice in the present military positions. Each also agreed to refrain from propaganda against the other.

Subsequent consultations took place between the UAR, Saudi Arabian and Yemeni leaders on the interpretation of the Jedda Agreement, but these did not yield any fruitful result. On 19th February, Abdul Rahman Iryani stated that no interpretation on agreement was required, and that the Republicans were ready to resume the Harad Conference on the date suggested. But the points in dispute were so obtrusive that the delegates could not be assembled again. In mid-March, King Faisal rejected a UAR proposal for resumption since certain leading Republicans, on a visit to Cairo, had re-affirmed views they had expressed during the Harad Conference. In fact, the Harad Conference never was resumed. The only development had been an exchange of prisoners between the two sides. While all this futile argument had been going on as-Sallal had remained in Cairo, saying nothing.

Meanwhile, there had been a considerable reduction in the size of the UAR Expeditionary Force, and a resultant regrouping at the main centres of communication that had been going on since September 1965. On a visit to London on 25th October, Prince Abdul Rahman, then Royalist Deputy Premier, confirmed that 'thousands of Egyptian troops' had been withdrawn. On the 30th, the Cairo newspaper *Al Ahram* stated that 10,000 soldiers would be brought home from the Yemen each month for seven months, beginning on 1st December, and that only one small contingent would remain to be part of the joint UAR-Saudi Arabian peace commission force. This tended to confirm that there had been well over 70,000 UAR troops in the Yemen during the summer of 1965.

It was suspected that Nasser was on the point of withdrawing from the Yemen altogether, so that he could concentrate upon his forthcoming confrontation with Israel. Certainly during the first two months of 1966 UAR troops evacuated many parts of northern and eastern Yemen. Royalists and non-committed tribes harassed retiring Egyptian columns wherever they could and often caused casualties, but their exaggerated and often entirely false claims of battles fought and won rebounded on them and made no real impression on public opinion. Bombing by UAR aircraft was reduced and generally only used when tribal warriors hung on too close to the tails of withdrawing Egyptian units, or to give assistance to isolated Republican garrisons which still held out.

There was certainly fighting lasting for three or four weeks, during the latter part of January and into early February, in the Khawlan region to the east of Sana, in which the UAR High Command admitted suffering 'moderate' casualties, but claimed to have killed hundreds of tribesmen. Hashem bin Hashem, the Royalist Minister of Information, insisted that it was the 'fiercest fighting since the war began', and said that Royalist forces had killed over 2,000 Egyptians and had put 90 armoured vehicles out of action. The Republican Government said that the fighting was against a local tribe that had taken to banditry, and that although the sheikh was a Royalist, the majority of his tribesmen were Republicans. Fairly frequent reports of this conflicting nature made it hard to assess the true situation. There were skirmishes and ambushes, and jostling to get into the vacuum left by the withdrawing UAR units, but after minor eruptions things settled down again, much as they had been before.

In February 1966, Britain issued a White Paper on Defence which indicated that British troops would withdraw from Aden and the Federation of South Arabia by 1968. Until this moment Nasser never really believed that the British would ever pull out from this part of the Middle East. The White Paper caused him to pause, to re-think and to change his mind about leaving the Yemen. The prospect of moving into a power vacuum left by a British withdrawal was more than he could resist, and so he produced his famous 'Long Breath' strategy in which he withdrew all his troops from outlying parts of the Yemen and concentrated them within the triangle of Sana, Hodeida and Taiz. Nasser now looked southwards rather than northwards, and increased the facilities for arming and training dissidents at Taiz for the purpose of raids into the Federation of South Arabia. He intended to reduce the size of his force to about 20,000, but to equip and condition this remainder so that it could quickly move southwards into any territory vacated by the British. At this stage he was anticipating that some sort of a cease-fire and peace arrangement would evolve between the Yemenis themselves.

In defence of his Long Breath strategy, withdrawing all isolated detachments and concentrating them in a few easily-held places, Nasser declared that the Jedda Agreement had not had the results he expected, and so he could not abandon the Yemeni Revolution. He would support it until it could defend itself, even if, he announced, this entailed staying in the Yemen for another five years.[1] His Long Breath strategy would reduce both the cost and the size of the UAR Expeditionary Force. On 13th April, a UAR spokesman said that the evacuation of northern Yemen had been completed, and it was stated that some 30,000 troops had been withdrawn. It was also stated that another 15,000 had been pulled out from the Jauf, and by the end of May it was almost certain that the UAR Expeditionary Force in the Yemen had been reduced to about 20,000 men.

The Royalists made grandiose claims of sweeping into territory abandoned by the UAR forces, but with a very few exceptions they made hardly any advances at all. Practically the whole of the Egyptian evacuation of the north and east had been accomplished under secret safe-conduct agreements with the various Royalist commanders, and this enabled the UAR troops to get clear with almost no casualties, despite imaginative communiqués issued from the Royalist camps. Republican garrisons assisted by UAR air support, remained in many places and baulked the Royalist advances. Sada, for example, was evacuated by UAR troops on 6th April, but a Republican garrison remained. Royalist propaganda gave out that the Republicans had been overwhelmed and that the city was in Royalist hands, only to have to admit in May that it was still in Republican possession.

Once the UAR military presence had been withdrawn, many of the tribes had no desire to accept Royalist obligations, and remained obstructively neutral. The Republican Government claimed that the vacated areas were held for it by the resident tribes, but this also was far from the truth in most cases. In large sectors of the territory evacuated by the UAR forces it mattered little which side nominally was dominant, as they were totally devastated, with villages razed to the ground, wells

[1] It is often alleged that Nasser's reaction to the British Defence White Paper was to say that he would stay 'twenty years' in the Yemen. That expression was later used by Field Marshal Amer, and gained wide publicity.

destroyed, agriculture disrupted, livestock slaughtered and the people, those who were left, living in caves on the mountain sides. The years of 1964 and 1965 had been ones of partial drought and famine, and 1966 was little better. Most of the people did not get enough to eat.

On 13th April, Abdullah Iryani, Republican Minister for Local Government (brother of Abdul Rahman Iryani, then Deputy Premier), was shot dead by an assassin who afterwards committed suicide. Lieutenant-Colonel Ahmed al-Rohoumi, the Finance Minister, was wounded in the same incident. The assassin was Abdul Wahah al-Washali, a journalist, who had been influenced by Chinese propaganda and had written articles condemning the Soviet Union for its policy of peaceful co-existence. The Soviet Ambassador at Sana had protested, and al-Washali had been arrested on the orders of Abdul Rahman Iryani, who had been acting Premier while Hassan al-Amri had been away on a visit to Cairo. The Governor of the prison had allowed al-Washali parole to visit his family.

Hassan al-Amri had always been considered pro-Egyptian and pro-Nasser, but he became irked by UAR insistence on continuing to control the Yemen's internal finances and all foreign aid. He had ordered some armoured cars direct from East Germany, but the UAR would not let him have them. The assassination of Abdullah Iryani gave him an excuse to reshuffle his Government, which he did on the 18th, bringing in advocates of an independent Yemeni line, like Hassan Mekki, Hussein Dafai and Yehia Mansour. Hamoud al-Jaifi, now also with independent views, became Defence Minister.

The overbearing UAR attitude to Yemeni affairs continued to spread discontent, and in May, during Mr. Kosygin's visit to Cairo, the UAR Government tried to prevent Hassan al-Amri from seeing him. But the Soviet Premier insisted on meeting al-Amri, and offered to arm and equip a Yemeni army of 18,000 men, saying that East Germany would send the necessary equipment. This was firmly vetoed by Nasser, as was also a request by the Yemeni Premier for the release of Yemeni foreign exchange deposits retained in Cairo banks. Hassan al-Amri and his Ministers began visibly to bridle at the restrictions.

The cordial friendship established between Nasser and King

Faisal at the Jedda meeting of August 1965, began to wane, and as the failure of the Harad Conference became obvious, animosity again flared up openly. During his Long Breath strategy withdrawal phase, on 22nd March, Nasser warned that if any parties of Royalists moved over the border from Saudi Arabia into the Yemen, the bases of Qizan and Najran would be bombed. Such threats caused King Faisal to strengthen his air defences, and on 1st May it was announced that twelve Hawker Hunter jets had been ordered from Britain. It was also said that a contract had been signed with a British firm to construct an airfield[1] just north of the Yemeni frontier in the coastal region. On the same day, Nasser threatened to occupy both Qizan and Najran, alleging that they were centres of infiltration, and on the 4th, the Republican Government issued a statement laying claim to the south-western part of Asir province, including Qizan and Najran.

In July, a peace plan was proposed by the 'moderate' Republicans for a direct settlement between Royalists and Republicans, without reference to either the UAR or Saudi Arabia. It was suggested that there should be a Supreme State Council, to include Ahmed Numan, Abdul Rahman Iryani and Mohammed al-Shami, the Royalist Foreign Minister. A Consultative Assembly of ninety-nine members was to rule the country for a year, at the end of which there would be a referendum. This seemed to gain considerable support within Republican Yemen, and although formal contact with the Royalist was not made on this issue it was enough to alarm Nasser. He had no intention of being by-passed, and took measures to squash the proposals firmly by sending as-Sallal, who had virtually been his prisoner in Cairo for some months, back to the Yemen to take political control once again.

During his absence from the Yemen, as-Sallal had retained the empty title of President, although it was Hassan al-Amri who ruled the country. But now Nasser had become thoroughly dissatisfied with Hassan al-Amri's increasingly independent policy, which was bringing him into sympathy, and almost into alliance, with such 'moderate' Republicans as Ahmed Numan and Abdul Rahman Iryani. Hassan al-Amri was not at all keen on as-Sallal

[1] Although not explicitly stated, this was at Khamis Mushait, where an existing landing strip was to be enlarged and modernized.

returning to assume the powers of the Presidency, and protested to Nasser, but it was to no avail. So strongly did Hassan al-Amri feel about this that on his orders Republican soldiers mounted guard on the airports at Sana and Taiz on 11th and 12th August, to arrest the President on arrival. Guards were also mounted on the Yemeni radio stations and the Presidential Palace to prevent anything being done to arouse sympathy for as-Sallal.

Heavy pressure was placed on Hassan al-Amri by the UAR Ambassador, and he was forced to recall his troops and rescind his orders. As-Sallal, after almost a year of absence, was able to land in the Yemen and take up his quarters in the Presidential Palace. His presence at once precipitated a crisis between his supporters, who were mainly extremely pro-Nasser and pro-UAR, and the 'moderate' Republicans, now openly headed by Hassan al-Amri. On the 17th, a message was sent to Nasser by a group of Republican sheikhs, accusing him of interfering in Yemeni internal affairs and attempting to impose as-Sallal on the people by force. The message also demanded the withdrawal of the UAR Expeditionary Force.

The feeling against the return of President as-Sallal was such that a delegation of prominent Republicans, led by Hassan al-Amri, went to Cairo on 9th September to protest to Nasser, and to ask that as-Sallal should be permanently exiled from the Yemen. This delegation included Hassan Mekki, Hamoud al-Jaifi, Ahmed Numan, the Yemeni Chief of Staff and other senior Yemeni officers. On the 16th, UAR Security Police arrested the principal members of the delegation, and after questioning Abdul Rahman Iryani and Hamoud al-Jaifi were released. In short, twenty-four of the sixty-man mission were detained, in secret confinement, and the remainder were kept under strict surveillance.

This was a smart *fait accompli* by Nasser on as-Sallal's behalf, and it was almost superfluous for Radio Sana that day to announce that as-Sallal had accepted the resignation of Hassan al-Amri, his Government and the Republican Council. Two days later as-Sallal assumed the Premiership and formed a Government, Abdullah Jizailan, the Deputy Premier, and Mohammed al-Raini, the Minister for Tribal Affairs, both retained their positions as did two other lesser ministers, but the new men in the Government included Abdul Dhaifallah and

Kassem Ghaleb, both of whom were strong pro-Nasser men, and also Mohammed Ahnoumi, a pro-Sallal supporter, who surprisingly enough was also a Shafi from the Tihama.

On the same day, the 18th, as-Sallal made some senior army changes. He appointed Abdullah Jizailan to be Deputy Commander-in-Chief (as-Sallal had remained the nominal Commander-in-Chief throughout) and nominated a new Chief of Staff to replace the one detained in Cairo. On 7th October, a full army purge was put into effect. About one hundred senior officers were placed on the retired list, including Hussein Dafai, who had been a Minister in the Numan Government, the arrested Chief of Staff languishing somewhere in Cairo, and the commanders of the artillery, armoured corps, paratroop and infantry elements. The military commanders of Taiz, Ibb, Sada and Beida were also removed.

A sweeping purge of the civilian administration was also carried out by as-Sallal. On 19th September he had accused many prominent people of sowing seeds of dissention between the Yemen and the UAR, declaring he had proof of this and would bring them all to trial when enquiries were completed. He called them 'deviationists and profiteers'. On the 24th, he removed Mohammed al-Attar, who had been a minister in the Numan Government, from the Presidency of the Yemeni Reconstruction and Development Bank, alleging that he had supplied Hassan al-Amri with funds for illegal political purposes, and he dismissed Mohsin al-Aini, who had also been a minister in the Numan Government, from his post as Yemeni Representative at the UN.

Now in full cry after those who were not in complete sympathy with UAR aims, Sallal on 30th September said that some of the former ministers, now held in Cairo, in the al-Amri Government, had received money from both America and Saudi Arabia, and had collaborated with those two countries against the UAR. He declared that they would be tried for treason, but later, on 14th November, it was reported that the UAR Government had rejected his request to have the Yemeni ex-ministers extradited. Nasser was keeping them as aces up his sleeve for future schemes of his.

After the arbitrary execution of a sheikh, both the Hashid and Bakil tribal federations withdrew their support from the as-

Sallal Government. They began openly to favour a 'middle way' policy, and gave shelter to dissident Republicans, army deserters and other refugees from the as-Sallal regime of whom there were soon to be fairly large numbers. Meanwhile, however, the wily Sheikh Abdullah al-Ahmer, paramount chief of the Hashid federation, maintained secret contacts with the Commander of the UAR Expeditionary Force in the Yemen.

Meanwhile a peace plan, eventually known as the Kuwait Agreement, was being hammered out without any consultation with the Yemeni Republican leaders. Hassan al-Amri had complained to Nasser about this when he went to Cairo before being summarily imprisoned. In April 1966, dismayed that the Harad Conference had failed miserably and that peace in the Yemen was as far away as ever, the Ruler of Kuwait had instigated negotiations with both Nasser and King Faisal, with his own representatives as go-betweens, suggesting that they both meet in Kuwait to try and settle their differences on the Yemeni problem. Although on 28th May Nasser had rejected the idea, mediation by Kuwait continued throughout June and July, until eventually on 1st August, it was announced that representatives of both Nasser and King Faisal would meet in that country for peace talks on the Yemen.

This meeting took place in Kuwait on the 17th, with the Kuwaiti Foreign Minister present, and when the talks were concluded some three days later, it was announced that agreement had been reached on a peace plan based on proposals submitted by the Kuwaiti Government which were being referred to the UAR and Saudi Arabia for consideration. No details were published and there was a great deal of speculation and anxiety, especially among the al-Amri Government (then in power) which had not been consulted at all. Unofficial reports indicated that the proposals suggested a transitional government, formed from all Yemeni factions but with a Republican majority, from which members of the Imam's family would be excluded. There should be an interim period of ten months during which the country should be known as the 'State of Yemen', thus avoiding the use of the controversial words 'Republic' and 'Imamate'. In this period UAR forces would be withdrawn and replaced by a joint Arab force which would remain to supervise the plebiscite.

The Kuwait Agreement, whether or not these were its actual

conditions, was never implemented, partly because both the Republicans and the Royalists resented the fact they had not been represented and so were reluctant to co-operate, but mainly because Nasser would not withdraw his troops. This latter point was made clear on 5th September, when simultaneous statements that UAR troops would not be withdrawn from the Yemen were made by Field Marshal Amer in Cairo, by President as-Sallal in Sana, and by the Commander of the UAR Expeditionary Force in the Yemen. On the 27th, Hassan Kholi, Nasser's special representative in Sana, insisted that the Kuwait Agreement was still alive, but added ambiguously that the UAR was firmly resolved to defend the Republic at whatever cost. But by 2nd November, Abdullah Jizailan, the Deputy Premier, was openly repudiating the Kuwait Agreement, saying that it was impossible to envisage the sending of a mixed Arab force to replace that of the UAR, as no Arab country would seriously think of sending contingents for such a task. In any case, he asserted, the people of the Yemen would never renounce their defence pact with the UAR. So the Kuwait Agreement faded out completely.

To counteract the moderate and nationalistic trends many Republicans were developing, as-Sallal in an anniversary speech on 26th September announced that he would implement the July 1964 Agreement between himself and Nasser to co-ordinate the policies of the two countries as a step towards complete unity, which, he claimed, would legalize the presence of UAR troops in the Yemen. This Agreement, like so many others, had been an empty one so far. As-Sallal insisted that the Republic could not survive without UAR assistance and that those who said the country could defend itself were traitors who wanted to liquidate the Revolution.

On the same day, in Alexandria, Field Marshal Amer said that the essential aim was to prevent the Yemen from going back into the past, and that UAR troops would stay in the Yemen for twenty years if this proved necessary. He was merely repeating with emphasis what Nasser had said immediately after the publication of the British White Paper on Defence in February 1966. The Field Marshal added that only about £E¼ million a year was being spent on the UAR Expeditionary Force, and that this amount was being reduced now that the new strategy was being applied. This indicated that all foreign aid meant for the Yemen was being used to maintain Egyptian occupation troops, as the figure mentioned was absurdly small for the numbers involved. The Commander of the UAR Expeditionary Force also chimed in, on the same day, to confirm that his soldiers would remain in the Yemen just as long as the Yemeni Revolution was threatened by conspiracies.

A Royalist communiqué, dated 1st October, claimed that its commandoes had carried out in Sana the previous day, successful bazooka raids on as-Sallal's residence, which had been set on fire, and on the house of the Soviet Ambassador. This was true, although later Royalist allegations[1] were generally without foundation. Any subsequent bazooka firing and damage was invariably done by dissident Republicans who wanted as-Sallal out of the way. There was little doubt that as-Sallal was extremely unpopular with many Republicans. The antagonism showed itself in demonstrations, terrorist attacks and even spasms of armed insurrection, and only the heavy presence of UAR troops kept these subversive activities to a minimum. The Cairo newspaper *Al Ahram* alleged on 8th October that Hassan al-Amri and Ahmed Numan had headed a plot, organized by the American Central Intelligence Agency and financed by King Faisal, to overthrow the Republican regime at a moment coinciding with an invasion of Syria by Jordanian troops. This had only been foiled by as-Sallal's return to the Yemen just in time. The newspaper also reported that as-Sallal's Presidential Palace had been shelled by Hassan Amri's supporters, but that little damage had been done.

Feeling in the Yemen ran strongly against America at this time, mainly because it supported, and was so closely linked with, Saudi Arabia. The road from Taiz to Sana had been completed in November 1965, but al-Sallal disclaimed any obligation, declaring that the road had been a gift by America to the Imam and not to the Republic. The road was also unpopular because, unlike the one built by the Chinese from Hodeida to Sana which had a smooth tarmac surface, it was unpaved and trucks travelled in a continual dense cloud of dust which caused

[1] There were at least two other bazooka attacks about this time on as-Sallal's residence, but they were made by dissident Republicans. As-Sallal still retained his large personal bodyguard of UAR soldiers.

discomfort and many accidents. Nevertheless, it remained a valuable communications link for the Republicans. The Americans had also produced 'piped' water to the city of Taiz, making it the only one in the whole of the Yemen with this elementary facility, but again it did nothing to soften the harsh feeling towards America.

During October there was an underground struggle between extremist elements of the pro-as-Sallal and anti-as-Sallal Republicans, which erupted in grenade-throwing incidents, explosions and shootings, mainly in Sana but also, to a lesser extent, in Taiz and other cities. These incidents became so numerous, coinciding as they did with a series of political trials and executions, that the Government banned the carrying of arms and grenades, threatening the death penalty for those caught in possession of them. When an incident occurred, UAR armoured patrols would dash to the scene firing indiscriminately at all in sight. Inevitably people were killed or wounded, but it proved an effective way, perhaps the only practical one, of keeping some sort of order and stability amongst citizens whose political hatreds were running so high.

There was a wholesale wave of arrests, amounting to well over 2,000 in the last week of October, and Government buildings and barracks had to be taken over to house the prisoners. This brought the estimated total of arrests since the return of as-Sallal to the Yemen to over 5,000. The Egyptians had taken over the prison service, such as it was, which gave Nasser and as-Sallal a big advantage in curbing political opposition. At this stage Nasser could not trust the Yemeni soldiers to guard so many prisoners, who might contaminate their warders with subversive political ideas. A large number hastily left Sana for their own safety, including Sheikh Abdullah al-Ahmer, of the Hashid federation, who fled to avoid arrest.

As-Sallal now summarily dismissed two of his ministers, Mohammed al-Riani, who had been a minister in every single Government, including that of Ahmed Numan, since the Revolution, and Hussein Dafai, who had been appointed by as-Sallal on his return to the Yemen without his consent being obtained, and who had refused to take office. Hussein Dafai was subsequently arrested, and, it is believed, tortured.

On 19th October, as-Sallal announced that a State Security

Court had been established under the direction of Mohammed Ahouni, Minister of the Interior, to try cases of subversion, and on the 25th, Mohammed al-Riani and fourteen others were arraigned for treason. It was alleged that al-Riani had collaborated with American, British and Saudi Arabian intelligence services, and that he was the chief of a terrorist network in Sana responsible for recent explosions in the city. He and Colonel Hadi Issa, the recent Deputy Chief of Staff of the Yemeni Army, were accused of mounting a bazooka attack on the Presidential Palace. Al-Riani, Issa and five others were found guilty and condemned to death. They were publicly shot, immediately after the trial, and their bodies were exhibited outside the city gates in the old barbaric tradition. Others were sentenced to terms of imprisonment. As-Sallal also ordered the execution of the Police Chief for ordering his armed police to fire into a Yemeni mob that had attacked an Egyptian post at Sana.

In November, at Ibb, a man was publicly executed for carrying arms, and at Sana, on 3rd December, five men, one alleged to hold the rank of general in the Royalist forces, were shot in the city square for taking part in terrorist activities and for receiving arms and money from British and Saudi Arabian sources. Others were sent to prison. On the 10th, two Republican soldiers convicted of subversion were promptly shot in front of a large crowd, which brought the number of public executions officially announced since 25th October, up to fifteen. In fact, Mohammed al-Attar in a letter published in a French newspaper,[1] said that about thirty other people had also been shot without any announcement being made. This was probably an understatement. Meanwhile, several of those in detention 'died' in prison.

As-Sallal's repressive measures caused many of those out of sympathy with him to flee into territory that had been evacuated by the UAR forces earlier in the year. A number of former ministers and army officers of varying rank fled southwards to Aden to claim political asylum, most alleging that as-Sallal was merely an Egyptian puppet (which was close to the truth) and protesting piously that they were only anxious to liberate the Yemen from the UAR yoke. It was estimated that over 1,000

[1] *Le Monde*, 21st December 1966.

people had left Sana since as-Sallal's return, of whom all but a tiny minority had joined what virtually amounted to a dissident Republican resistance movement, now openly referred to as a Third Force. This force was led by Sheikh Abdullah al-Ahmer, who sheltered and supported a group of Hassan al-Amri's followers who were trying to establish a regime opposed both to the Royalists and to as-Sallal. Nasser became seriously concerned about this Third Force which was operating from Khamir, in Hashid country, over sixty miles north of Sana, and ordered his ground forces to hunt down as many of its prominent personalities as possible, while his air force bombed the region.

From his headquarters at Riyadh, in Saudi Arabia, Ibrahim al-Wazir, the leader of the so-called Federation of Popular Forces sponsored by King Faisal, claimed that the fighting in the Yemen was virtually between the UAR forces on one side and the Yemenis on the other, regardless of their former loyalties. He said that all that the Yemeni people wanted was the implementation of the Taif Agreement, of August 1965, which recommended a provisional Yemeni Government that was neither Republican nor Royalist, an opinion undoubtedly pushed on to him by King Faisal who would have liked to see such a Yemeni Government materialize. These statements were only partially true. The motives of Ibrahim al-Wazir were distrusted by the majority of dissident Republicans, who considered he had secret ambitions himself to become the Imam, and was merely using the situation and the Federation of Popular Forces as convenient cover for his plans.

In the Royalist camp there was indecision and some confusion, mostly as a result of the sickness of the Imam. After making a supreme effort just before the Harad Conference to stump the countryside to rouse the tribes to his cause, he had retired in April (1966) to Taif in Saudi Arabia for medical treatment, and here he remained. The Imam's personal appeal had not been really a success, and there was a falling off of support from the Zeidi tribes despite the withdrawals of UAR troops under Nasser's Long Breath strategy. In August, Royalist leaders met at Taif to consider the situation. The tribes were still reluctant to give wholehearted support to the Imam, there was jealousy and suspicion amongst the Royalist commanders and personalities, and inefficiency in organizing for the war. Saudi Arabian gold had bred instability in the Royalist ranks, as a goodly proportion seemed to find its way into individual pockets. Nasser's policy was changing, and UAR troops were creeping back into territory they had earlier evacuated. The problem was whether or not to resume the war with renewed vigour, and most of the Royalist commanders were in favour of starting an offensive. But King Faisal did not want hostilities to break out again, and threatened to stop his cash contribution when he realized that the Royalists were about to take to the field. Despite this it was agreed at Taif that an offensive should be launched, considering that the Republicans were so divided against themselves. The return of as-Sallal, and subsequent events at Sana, probably tipped the scales.

The Royalists were also upset by the fact that King Faisal had sent his agents with money and arms into territory evacuated by the UAR in an attempt to persuade them directly to support Ibrahim al-Wazir's Federation of Popular Forces. The Imam agreed to the formation of an Imamic Council of ten members, with himself as President, and announced that he agreed in principle to the Imamate becoming constitutional. The formation of the Council was largely a matter of necessity, due to Mohammed al-Badr's failing health. The personality who came to the fore was Prince Mohammed Hussein, who as Deputy President took charge of the Council in the frequent absences of the Imam. Prince Hassan retained the Premiership, but concentrated more on foreign affairs than the war. Prince Mohammed Hussein retained the overall command of the eastern part of the Yemen while Prince Hassan Hassan became the overall commander of the western sector. The decision to mount an offensive was forced through by Prince Mohammed Hussein, and Royalist preparations began.

Meanwhile, since the early summer, Nasser, who had completely changed his intentions, had begun to reinforce the UAR Expeditionary Force in the Yemen, until by November its strength had risen from about 20,000 to well over 60,000. In September, after a pause of several months, UAR bombing raids re-commenced, and night bombing with the use of flares was resumed in the Jauf region in October. Egyptian troops were sent to reinforce isolated positions such as Sada, tenuously held by elements of the ramshackle Yemeni Army. This marked the end of his Long Breath strategy and the start of a more aggressive one, which he anticipated as the prelude to stepping into the vacuum caused by British withdrawal from Aden. He intended to forestall any moves King Faisal might make in that direction.

On 1st October, the Royalists issued their first military communiqué for several months. Full of brave words, it said that it was anticipated that large-scale fighting might be expected to break out again soon, and that preliminary skirmishing was already in progress. In fact, other than a small concentration of Royalists near Sada, hardly anything at all came of this as a result of King Faisal's threats which destroyed all the efforts of the Royalist commanders to launch an offensive.

When Nasser announced that he would not pull his troops out from the Yemen, relations between the President of the UAR and King Faisal deteriorated further. King Faisal had hoped that the Kuwait Agreement would have provided some solution, and even when it was quite clear that Nasser would not accept its conditions, he hoped that the Third Force might emerge strongly in the Yemen to take over the Government and so prevent civil war from flaring up again. In October, he sponsored a meeting of Royalists and representatives of the Federation of South Arabia states at Taif. At this, Mohammed al-Shami, the Royalist Foreign Minister, proposed the establishment of a Council to consist of two Royalists, two representatives from the Federation of South Arabia and two Saudi Arabians, to form a common front against the UAR, the Egyptian-aided FLOSY[1] and the NLF.[2] Had the British remained in Aden, this plan might have met with success.

On 14th October, UAR aircraft raided Najran, causing some deaths, and also Qizan, where the bombs fell harmlessly into the sea. This was the first admitted UAR raid on these Saudi Arabian towns since June 1963, and it was claimed they were due to navigational errors. However, King Faisal now decided that it was no good continuing to keep the peace with Nasser, whose aggressive intentions and activities could no longer be concealed. The King may also have felt a little stronger and more confident, as the thirty-seven Thunderbird ground-to-air missiles, supplied by Britain, were now in position at Khamis

[1] FLOSY—Front for the Liberation of Occupied South Yemen.
[2] NLF—National Liberation Front.

Mushait, and some British aircraft had been delivered to the Saudi Arabian air force. On 2nd November he said that while peace negotiations had been in progress he had asked the Royalists to exercise restraint, but that they could not wait indefinitely. This was taken as a signal by the Royalists to resume military activity.

Whilst admitting that there was fighting in certain northern areas, especially those adjacent to Qizan and Najran, Abdullah Jizailan, the Republican Deputy Premier, stated that the military situation remained calm. He was correct in that there were no large-scale clashes, but after a long period of quiet the Royalists began to stir themselves, and a series of skirmishes were fought over large sectors of the Yemen in December. Apart from brushes between UAR troops and Royalist tribesmen, there were also occasional clashes between Egyptian forces and Republican tribes, in the search for dissident leaders.

The Royalists were still not having any great success in organizing themselves on a sound political basis, but on 5th December they had another try when they announced that the Imam had virtually handed over the majority of his powers to the Imamic Council, now reduced to six members although still presided over by himself. After consultation, the Imamic Council would be able to make senior appointments, subject only to the Imam's approval. This step was no doubt taken to give the outward appearance of a constitutional monarchy which would gain sympathy abroad, but in fact it was little more than a Regency Council acting for the Imam while he was sick. Although he tried to keep up the image of a leader living with his hard-pressed subjects in the mountains and sharing their dangers and hardships, the Imam remained at Taif in Saudi Arabia.

The year of 1966 drew to a close with the surprising Republican appointment of Abdul Rahman Baidani as the Yemeni Ambassador to the Lebanon. Baidani, the pro-Egyptian Vice-President and Deputy Premier in the first Republican Government, had fallen out with as-Sallal, and retired to exile in Cairo. The arrival of this well-known Egyptian sympathizer provoked two Yemeni members of the diplomatic staff to defect to the dissident Republicans, declaring that the newly-appointed Baidani was abusing his powers. Baidani retaliated by suspending the two men for currency frauds.

CHAPTER TEN

The Fall of as-Sallal

MAIN EVENTS

1967	
January 5th	Royalist HQ at Ketaf bombed out by UAR aircraft.
18th	As-Sallal forms Popular Revolutionary Union.
February 11th	Tunisia withdraws recognition of as-Sallal regime.
18th	Jordan withdraws recognition of as-Sallal regime.
March 3rd–8th	Republican Third Force—Yemen Revolutionary Front Conference.
17th	Seventeen Yemenis executed in Saudi Arabia.
April 10th	New Royalist Government announced.
24th	Ex-King Saud visits the Yemen with Field Marshal Amer.
25th	Bazooka shells fired in Taiz—two Americans accused.
28th	American AID programme terminated.
May	UAR Expeditionary Force reduced in size.
June 5th–10th	Arab war with Israel.
June	Royalist offensive in the Yemen.
July 1st	Royalist HQ at Ketaf again heavily bombed.
6th	UAR three-week offensive begins.
August 1st	Republican Deputy Premier visits Soviet Union.
2nd	Conference of Arab Foreign Ministers at Khartoum.
August 29th–September 1st	The Khartoum Conference.
October 3rd	As-Sallal refuses to meet the Tripartite Committee.
10th	Last UAR soldiers leave Taiz.
12th	Saudi Arabian aid to the Royalists ceases.
16th	Last UAR soldiers leave Sana.
November 3rd	As-Sallal leaves the Yemen *en route* for the Soviet Union and calls at Cairo.
5th	As-Sallal is deposed by army officers and seeks political asylum in Iraq.

During December 1966 a series of explosions took place in Saudi Arabia at military installations, government offices and Royal Palaces, and on 10th January 1967 the Saudi Arabian Government confirmed that a number of Yemenis[1] had been arrested and had confessed to carrying out acts of sabotage under the direction of the UAR command in the Yemen. The Saudi Arabian police also seized thousands of leaflets printed for an organization known as the 'Federation of the People of the Arabian Peninsula', and on the 24th this political body broadcast a statement over Radio Cairo in which it claimed that further explosions had taken place in Saudi Arabian Government offices. It said that it was prepared to launch a terrorist campaign against British and American advisers in Saudi Arabia, similar to that being waged against the British in the Federation of South Arabia.

On 17th March, the Saudi Arabian Minister of the Interior announced that seventeen Yemenis had been found guilty of sabotage at a secret trial at Riyadh, and had been publicly beheaded. Eleven of them were said to have confessed to causing bomb explosions. It was alleged that attempts at sabotage were committed in Najran, Khamis Mushait and Riyadh by men trained by UAR instructors in Cairo and Taiz and sent to Saudi Arabia with explosives to kill people and damage property. Radio Cairo boasted that the Federation of the People of the Arabian Peninsula was responsible for the attacks, but these executions nevertheless caused protests in other Arab countries. The UAR National Assembly denounced them, a stick of dynamite was thrown into the garden of the Saudi Arabian Embassy at Beirut, demonstrations took place in Aden, and the Yemeni Republican Government sent a note to the Arab League calling for an immediate enquiry. Mohammed al-Attar alleged on behalf of the dissident Republicans that thousands of immigrant Yemenis had been arrested in Saudi Arabia, where they worked, but he admitted that most of them had not concealed their Republican sympathies, and despite strong pressure had refused to collaborate with the Royalist group headed by Ibrahim al-Wazir.

Nasser's antagonism towards King Faisal had prompted him

[1] At least 200,000 Yemenis worked in Saudi Arabia.

in January to invite ex-King Saud to settle in Egypt. Saud still claimed the throne and had not really reconciled himself to being ousted by his brother, Faisal. Nasser obviously hoped to be able to split Saudi Arabian loyalties, and stir up dissidence within the country in order to distract attention from the Yemeni Royalist cause. In retaliation, King Faisal closed down the two Egyptian banks in Saudi Arabia. Nasser replied by again sequestering all Saudi Arabian property[1] in the UAR, except that belonging to ex-King Saud and other accepted Saudi Arabian political exiles. The sequestration order had only been lifted in August 1965, at a time when it seemed as though Nasser and King Faisal might be reconciled.

In a broadcast in March, ex-King Saud denounced the executions at Riyadh, and the next month visited the Yemen himself, accompanied by Field Marshal Amer. He was welcomed by as-Sallal, who greeted him as the legal king of Saudi Arabia. Saud replied that he recognized the Yemeni Republican Government on behalf of his subjects, and at a mass meeting on 24th April he expressed hopes for a Republican victory. Saud, who presented $1 million to the Republican Government, said that he had left his country to avoid bloodshed, but that the continued presence of British and American mercenaries was forcing him to reconsider the situation. Nasser now tried to set up a Liberation Front for Saudi Arabia, though without much success. As Saud was believed to retain a big tribal following in the deserts, Nasser's aim was to make King Faisal anxious about possible sabotage to Saudi Arabian oil pipelines and US-owned oil installations.

The Saudi Arabian members of the joint peace commission set up under the Jedda Agreement of August 1965, had returned to their own country in January, after being accused of instigating a plot against the as-Sallal Government. As-Sallal had forbidden them to leave Sana, refusing to guarantee their safety if they did so. Later, on 17th March, at Mecca, King Faisal called for the withdrawal of all foreign aid to the Yemen, declaring that he would accept Observers from other Arab states along the Saudi Arabian border regions, if UAR forces would withdraw, but nothing come of this and so his statement was never put to the test.

[1] Reputed to be worth about $47 million.

Now that Imam Mohammed al-Badr was having medical treatment in Jedda and Taif, the official headquarters of the Royalists gravitated to caves near Ketaf, about thirty miles north-east of Sada, just north of Wadi Amlah, where Prince Hassan the Premier held court. Here he was frequently joined by Prince Mohammed Hussein, who was now virtually the 'Deputy Imam', a designation that was often openly bestowed on him.[1] The caves near Qara, where the Imam had sheltered during the early years of the war, were practically deserted, and now that all the foreign journalists and visitors were channelled to Ketaf, it became a natural target for UAR bombers. On 5th January, a large air raid killed over a hundred people in the nearby village of Ketaf,[2] and further air raids on the 19th literally wiped out this Royalist headquarters, killing most of the staff. Prince Hassan and Prince Mohammed Hussein were both absent at the time and so escaped. The Royalists alleged that phosgene gas bombs had been used, and asked the Red Cross to investigate. In fact, this was only a tactical defeat, as none of the prominent Royalist leaders had been killed and there were plenty more similar sites for headquarters in that part of the Yemen. For a short time, Prince Hassan moved his headquarters back south into Wadi Amlah, about ten miles away. The bombing of Prince Hassan's headquarters and the subsequent Royalist allegation, aroused the controversy over the possible use of poison gas bombs, and journalists rushed off to investigate, arriving at Ketaf on the 27th. None, however, could find any definite proof. Pakistani doctors at the Najran hospital, some forty miles to the north in Saudi Arabia, stated they had treated over a hundred suspected cases of poison gas victims during the previous three weeks, but again Western journalists found nothing positive to convince them.

On the 31st, an International Red Cross spokesman at Geneva admitted that there was no clear proof that the UAR was using gas bombs, and simply appealed to the combatants to use humane methods of warfare. On the same day the UAR Minister of Information denied the allegation that UAR aircraft were

[1] He was in fact Deputy President of the Imamic Council and thus nominally senior to Prince Hassan, the Premier.

[2] The village of Ketaf had a total population of about 500 people at the time.

using such weapons in the Yemen, and said that his government intended to ignore the accusations. He added that the UAR would accept an immediate UN enquiry into this matter and that the Republican Government had agreed to provide it with facilities to prove the falsity of this anti-UAR propaganda. Two days later as-Sallal confirmed he would accept and help a UN enquiry team. But the UN still hesitated, as did the Red Cross, for reasons best known to themselves.

During January of this year UAR aircraft occasionally hit at targets just inside Saudi Arabia. On the 27th, Najran was hit, while a party of Western journalists was in the town. There was another raid the following day. In February, the Saudi Arabian Government protested to the UN, but on the 28th U Thant blandly replied that he was powerless to deal with the matter because the facts were sharply in dispute and he had no means of ascertaining them accurately.

King Hussein of Jordan was once again wavering in his friendships. After a visit to King Faisal on 18th February, he withdrew his recognition of the as-Sallal regime, saying that he had informed as-Sallal over three weeks earlier that unless the UAR forces withdrew from the Yemen and UAR aircraft ceased bombing the Yemeni people, he would take this action. As a reprisal, the UAR on the same day refused Jordan's request to permit British and American aircraft carrying consignments of arms to Jordan to land at UAR airfields or to overfly UAR air space. The reason given for this refusal was that the UAR had evidence that the arms would eventually be used to attack Yemeni Republican forces. A week previously, on the 11th, Tunisia had withdrawn its recognition of the as-Sallal Government on the grounds that it did not have effective authority. For several months prior to this the Tunisian Government had been denouncing the 'atrocities' committed by the UAR Expeditionary Force, but this had merely been prompted by a shift in Arab relationships that had enabled King Faisal briefly to form an anti-Nasser bloc which consisted of Saudi Arabia, Jordan, Iran and Tunisia, and to receive open sympathy from Morocco and Kuwait as well.

Within the Yemen, Nasser was having difficulty in countering Chinese influence. China had already contributed aid to the value of about $45 million, and as this had been made up of a mixture of labour and materials, it had largely circumvented Nasser's insistence that all outside aid for the Yemen be channelled through the UAR. Currently, for example, the Chinese, quite independently of the UAR, were constructing a centre for 800 students which they proposed to staff when completed.

In the Republican camp the new year of 1967 had begun with the execution of the former commander of the tiny Yemeni armoured corps,[1] at the UAR headquarters in Sana. He had been a close colleague of Mohammed al-Raini, and this tended further to deepen the Republican rift, especially in the military element. In February, the Yemeni chargé d'affaires in Czechoslovakia defected to the Royalists. In an effort to heal the rift and channel the loyalties of all Republicans behind his own policies and those of the UAR, as-Sallal formed the Popular Revolutionary Union, modelled closely on Nasser's Arab Socialist Union and planned as an improvement upon his abortive Popular Union. Addressing its first session on 18th January, he announced that he had formed the Union to protect the Revolution and ensure its progress, admitting that such revolutionary measures as he had carried into effect since his return were with full Egyptian help and co-operation. He accused various others of trying to stifle the Revolution. This opening session was attended by three representatives of the Egyptian-backed FLOSY, led by Abdul Qawee Mackawee, a former Aden Chief Minister. As-Sallal openly pledged his support for FLOSY's struggle against the British.[2]

But Republican divisions deepened, and in March a political organization which became known as the Yemen Revolutionary Front held a conference in the northern mountains, from the 3rd until the 8th, which was attended by representatives of the Hashid and Bakil tribal federations, and many refugee Republican politicians, officials and officers. A spokesman for this new splinter Front, Ali Ahmed al-Dhubah, said that the conference had adopted resolutions condemning both the UAR and Saudi Arabia as responsible for the war, and condemning too the

[1] Colonel Ali Hamid al Yemeni.

[2] On 30th April the Yemeni Republican Government formally extended its territorial waters from three to twelve miles, thus encompassing the British-protected islands of Kamaran and Perim, and also claimed air space to a height of 5,000 metres.

detention of Hassan al-Amri and other Yemeni Republicans in Cairo. It was intended to petition the UN to form a neutral committee to investigate UAR war crimes in the Yemen, and itself to try and form a 30,000-strong guerrilla-type army to fight against the UAR occupation forces.

By this time there was some cause for thinking that the majority of Yemenis were not keen to have Imamic rule back again, despite the semi-anarchy in parts of the country. Black, bitter memories of Imamic cruelties and repressions lingered on. The Yemenis were sincere Moslems, and the Zeidis amongst them acknowledged the Imam as their spiritual leader, but a great many were coming round to the view that religion and government should be separated. Only a small number of mountain tribesmen still insisted that the Imam should be re-invested with full temporal powers. The two most powerful tribal influences, the Hashid and Bakil federations, so often in the past called the Wings of the Imamate, no longer even partially subscribed to the reinvestment of the Imam as an absolute monarch. Since the *coup* of 1962 they had got used to a measure of political freedom. They did not relish the revival of the hostage system, which they thought would be inevitable if the Imam returned to power, although some of them did not particularly object to the Imam, or a member of his family, assuming the leadership, provided he renounced the Imamate and all claim to a hereditary throne.

Ibrahim al-Wazir, the nominal leader of the Saudi Arabian-backed Federation of Popular Forces, had been endeavouring since December to persuade Republican Third Force factions sheltering beyond the effective reach of as-Sallal, in Hashid territory, either to join his organization, or at least openly to co-operate with it. Despite the tempting financial attractions he offered, he had no success, partly because the Republican Third Force personnel lacked both political and military framework and were divided amongst themselves as to objectives and limitations, and partly because Ibrahim al-Wazir was personally distrusted. In February 1967, Ibrahim al-Wazir said at Geneva that the Federation of Popular Forces was about to call a conference that would proclaim an 'Islamic State of the Yemen' and would demand the withdrawal of UAR troops and the ending of Saudi Arabian aid to the Imam. After further efforts, he did manage to produce a vague statement on co-operation with the Republican Third Force, and issued it on 12th March. But the words were meaningless, and nothing really had been achieved.

King Faisal's policy was to woo the various groups of dissident Republicans with money and help, and encourage them either to form themselves into a patriotic front against the as-Sallal Government and the UAR, or to join Ibrahim al-Wazir's Federation of Popular Forces. Despite pressure the Royalists co-operated less than half-heartedly with this Federation, and many would have nothing to do with it at all. Apart from the Royalists, most dissident Republican factions, and indeed personalities, accepted Saudi Arabian money at one time or another, although they hesitated to admit this. In fact at this stage, the only truly independent group was the rather woolly Yemen Revolutionary Front, in which Mohammed al-Attar played a prominent part.

King Faisal's policy of rallying sections of the Yemeni people hostile to, or distrustful of, the Royalists and their ambitions, and of giving the Republican opposition to the as-Sallal Government a national rather than a purely ideological character, caused repercussions in the Imam's camp. Faisal had never been very favourably inclined towards the Imam, and had supported his cause more because it was a thorn in Nasser's side than because he was a fellow monarch in an increasingly Republican world. His policy caused an open split amongst the Royalists in March, when Prince Abdullah Hassan, the commander on the 'Khawlan Front',[1] and some other of the Royalist commanders announced they would immediately suspend all military activities as a protest against the inclusion of dissident Republicans in the Royalist Government. The Prince declared that the Saudi Arabians gave the Royalists less power and initiative than the UAR gave as-Sallal, and said that many Royalists felt they were merely taking part in a war the UAR and Saudi Arabia were fighting on Yemeni soil. He announced that he was tired of fighting for other people, and added that Sheikh Ali al-Gadr, the paramount chief of the Bakil federation, that stretched well into the Khawlan region, associated himself with these sentiments.

[1] The various Royalist army groups still retained the numbers that had been bestowed on them early in the war, but at this stage it is more convenient and accurate to refer to them by the name of their location.

He also stated that a degree of anarchy was beginning to spread in the Yemeni mountains, where the Imam's authority was frequently challenged.

On 10th April, a new Royalist Government was announced, with Prince Hassan, the Imam's uncle, retaining the Premiership, and Prince Abdul Rahman, another uncle, the Vice-Premiership. Mohammed al-Shami kept Foreign Affairs, and other ministers included Prince Mohammed Ibrahim (Finance) and Sheikh Sala Masri. Prince Abdullah Hassan, who had so recently voiced open criticism, was appointed Minister of the Interior. It was noticeable that no dissident Republicans were included, and that only under pressure did the Imam accept tiny, ineffectual constitutional limitations to his authority. Prince Mohammed Hussein, who appeared to be the real power behind the throne as Deputy President of the Imamic Council, remained the 'Deputy Imam'.

On 14th January, in a speech tailored for foreign consumption, Abdullah Jizailan had declared that there was no longer any need for mediation in the Yemen because peace and stability reigned throughout the country. While this was not, of course, accurate, most tribesmen had disappeared to their homes for the winter and were not a serious threat at that time. In fact there was little serious fighting during the first five months of the year, although there were numerous tiny incidents of ambushes, mined roads, small raids and UAR punitive actions. Egyptian aircraft carried out almost daily bombing during this period.

The UAR air force now seldom undertook saturation raids, such as the one that had been used to knock out Prince Hassan's Royalist headquarters at Ketaf in January, but instead attacked minor localities and small villages of no apparent strategic significance, rather than large centres of population. The aim was to inspire fear without alienating too considerable a section of the Yemeni population. Many casualties were inflicted in these raids, but not as many as the Royalists claimed, mostly because of the sparseness of the population. Imam Mohammed al-Badr's figure of 1·5 million casualties and homeless in four and a half years of war in Royalist-held territory, for example, was not acceptable. It amounted to about one-third of the population of the whole country, and certainly more than were under, or susceptible to, his influence. However, the selective UAR bombing made it dangerous to remain in the villages and soon practically everyone in the mountains was homeless.

A gradual change had taken place in relations between the tribes and the as-Sallal Government, and the former harsh treatment originally advocated by Nasser and objected to so much by Ahmed Numan, had been considerably softened. UAR force was now used with calculated restraint. Autonomy was restored to most of the tribes by the Republicans—what so many of them had fought for against Imams for centuries—and most were left to their own devices, provided they abstained from helping the Royalists. Those which did so were periodically bombed, and received no aid or money at all, while those which assisted the Republican Government in any way were rewarded with food, arms and money. Nothing was given or paid out by either the UAR or the Republican Government, unless for some service rendered. For example, the Hashid federation received money to 'guard' communications, especially between Sana and Sada, and any incident caused payment temporarily to cease.

This policy was quite successful and influenced a growing number of tribes to come over to the Republican side, to be rewarded and left alone instead of continually harried from the air. During April and May there was a considerable switching of loyalties from the Royalists to the Republicans, not only those within immediate reach of UAR guns and bombs, but in outlying areas as well. These changing loyalties enabled Republican detachments to re-occupy such cities as Barat, Marib and Harib. At the same time Royalist influence declined considerably, and in May Prince Abdullah Hassan, the Minister of the Interior who was also the commander of the Khawlan Front, admitted that over two-thirds of the Yemen was entirely outside Royalist control.

Anti-American feeling ran high in Republican Yemen, and when on the night of 25th April two bazooka shells were fired at an ammunition store in Taiz, killing a Yemeni and a UAR soldier, two officials of the US Agency for International Development, AID, were arrested and accused of intending to destroy the city. The Republican Government declared it would cancel this AID programme, arranged in 1959, and as anti-American hostility was whipped up, demonstrators broke into the AID buildings, damaging property and vehicles. On the 28th, an

American spokesman said that the charge was a complete fabrication, but that the USA had been compelled to terminate the AID programme, which had already given $5 million worth of goods and services to the country. In reply, the Republican Government confiscated all American equipment and assets in the Yemen, amounting to over $4 million. Thus, abruptly, ended one most valuable of all AID schemes, that of improving water supplies so vital to health, development and agriculture. The Americans had already improved the water supply situation in some 200 population centres, including Sana and Taiz.

On 13th May, the two Americans were committed for trial, and it was stated that if convicted they would be liable for a death sentence. Three days later, as it happened, they were released on bail, and after negotiations allowed to leave the country. About 130 other US personnel working in the Yemen were also hastily evacuated. Other countries nevertheless persevered with their individual aid programmes, and the Soviet Union began to construct an all-weather road from Taiz to Hodeida. The UAR, Iraq and Kuwait continued to help with staffing schools and hospitals, and for these activities personnel were also sent from Sweden and Hungary. The Chinese textile factory near Sana was now in full production.

Tension between Nasser and King Faisal remained high, and during May there were more allegations of UAR aircraft bombing Saudi Arabian territory, of hitting Najran on the 11th and Qizan on the 14th, and causing casualties. On the 16th the UAR Chief of Staff in the Yemen claimed that the Saudi Arabian rocket base at Khamis Mushait, where British Thunderbird missiles had been installed, had been attacked, but no confirmation of this was available from any other source.

Meanwhile, Nasser was working up to a confrontation with Israel, and his new strategy in the Yemen enabled him to thin out his forces there and bring more of them back to Egypt. His new policies effected a double economy, both of money, which was not paid out except for something positive achieved, and of men, as the growing popularity of the Republican cause meant that less were needed for punitive actions and garrison duties. As the Royalist leaders became more agitated, and the mountain tribesmen showed less and less inclination to be roused into activity, the strength of the UAR Expeditionary Force dropped to 30,000, and then by the end of May, to less than 20,000 men.

As is well known, the confrontation between the UAR and Israel, culminated in a short, sharp war, lasting from 5th to the 10th June, and ending with the ignominious defeat of Nasser and the Arab states involved. This war had the apparent effect of uniting all Arabs everywhere against the Israelis, but the Arab states were no more in unison with each other than they had ever been, as the boastful and empty propaganda utterances made clear to the world audience.

During the first days of June, apart from one spate of bombing, UAR aerial attacks on the Royalists in the Yemen ceased. More troops were withdrawn to Egypt until the Expeditionary Force numbered less than 15,000. UAR garrisons were brought in from outlying cities that had recently been re-occupied, such as Barat, Harad, Harib, Maidi and Marib, and Republican soldiers were left to hold them. Hundreds of guns and armoured vehicles were shipped back to the UAR. Soviet material was stockpiled for safety in the Yemen, which was out of range of Israeli aircraft, and it was estimated that there were at least a hundred Soviet aircraft in crates on the airfields at Hodeida and Sana.

The Republican Government seems to have made capital out of this brief, dramatic Middle East war, while the Royalists did not seem to be able to take the same advantage of the circumstances. When the war began, both the Hashid and Bakil federations pledged their loyalty to the Republican Government, thus formally deserting the Imam. Led personally by Sheikh Abdullah al-Ahmer, the paramount chief of the Hashid federation, about 25,000 armed tribesmen descended upon Sana, in a flush of enthusiasm, to declare their support for Nasser. They were warmly welcomed, and then quickly but tactfully sent back to the Hajja region and the north to replace withdrawing UAR troops. They were given a ceremonial send-off by both President as-Sallal and the UAR Commander in the Yemen.

The Royalist Government appealed to the UAR to send its Yemeni forces to fight against the Israelis instead of the Royalists, pledging that it would not attack the Republicans when they had gone. UAR aircraft answered with aerial bombing attacks on 5th and 6th June, as a warning for the Royalists to keep their distance. Piqued by this the Royalists mounted a June offensive, to which the absence of UAR aircraft activity, armour, guns and troops gave some success, and although they made hopelessly exaggerated claims to attract world attention, they did carry out several ambushes of withdrawing UAR columns. They also claimed the credit for a few raids made by other tribes hostile to the UAR forces. Elements of both the Hashid and Bakil federations took advantage of the situation to kill, plunder and pay off old scores as the opportunity arose, despite the pledge given by their paramount chiefs of loyalty to both Nasser and as-Sallal. The Royalists managed to occupy Harad and Maidi, and advance some way down the coastal plain towards Hodeida. The small coastal town of Loheira was besieged, and about 700 inhabitants were hastily evacuated to the nearby British-protected Kamaran Island. Tribes giving vague allegiance to the Imam took possession of both Harib and Marib, driving out the Republican soldiers.

On 1st July, UAR aircraft once again became active in the Yemeni skies, when there was a heavy bombing raid on the Royalist headquarters, now once more established in the caves near Ketaf. Other air raids followed, and daily bombing again became the rule as UAR aircraft, equipment and troops returned to the Yemen. The UAR Expeditionary Force soon rose to a strength of 25,000 men and higher. On the 6th, a new Egyptian commander was appointed, Major-General Abdul Kader Hassan, and he at once despatched punitive columns in all directions. In most places the Royalists were pushed backwards, although they had much better weapons than ever before. By the 20th, the Republicans had relieved Loheira and were in possession of both Harad and Maidi. But the UAR forces failed to re-take Hajja, falling back after a three-day battle, and were not quite so successful in the east and the south either, where both Marib and Harib remained under Royalist control. This three-week offensive had only partly restored what on 1st June had been a very favourable Republican position.

On 3rd July the Royalists lost an able supporter. Ali Salih Fidama, who for three years had been broadcasting anti-Republican propaganda on their behalf from the Aden radio station controlled by the Government of the Federation of South Arabia, was killed in ambush while on his way from Aden to Royalist-held territory. He was a colourful, swashbuckling figure who had served in the German Arab Legion in Russia in World War II, and been awarded an Iron Cross. Before the Yemeni *coup* he had been the Governor of a small Yemeni province. He was an outstanding personality and very much a thorn in the side of the Republicans. In February one of his sons had been kidnapped and taken into Republican Yemen. Fidama was threatened that if he did not stop broadcasting for the Royalists his son would be tortured to death. As he continued to broadcast, it must be assumed that his unfortunate son met this fate.

After the moderately successful three-week UAR offensive, fighting died down in the Yemen and a sort of stalemate set in, although UAR bombing, minor skirmishing and raiding continued almost as a matter of course. The reason for this rather unexpected halt in operations at a time when another similar offensive would have set the Royalists rocking back on their heels, was that Nasser, because of the adverse circumstances he found himself in after his disastrous war with Israel, had by now made the decision to cut his losses and responsibilities, and withdraw from the Yemen completely.

A suspicion of Nasser's decision must have dawned in as-Sallal's mind, causing him deep anxiety, because the still very ramshackle Republican army, which had a total strength of less than 7,000 men, had recently been deliberately starved by the UAR of arms and equipment. Its limitations had been sharply emphasized in the June Royalist offensive, and as-Sallal knew that should Nasser abandon him, he would be hard put to defend the Republic with such an ill-trained and ill-equipped force. His army had never really got over the wholesale purges of its senior officers, and its morale was not of the best, nor its loyalty to him too certain. On 1st August Abdullah Jizailan, the Deputy Premier, was sent off at the head of a large Republican delegation to Moscow to discuss Soviet military and economic aid to the Yemen. He was obviously instructed to do his best to persuade the Soviet Union to deliver any such aid direct, and not allow it to be channelled and diverted by the UAR. He was partially successful in this. A Soviet Military Mission was sent to the Yemen to assess what was required, and work out what could be done to improve the Yemeni Republican Army.

In August, the UAR forces had trouble with the Arabian

Liberation Army.[1] This was a small mercenary force of between 500 and 600 men, in camp outside Taiz, which had been recruited by the UAR especially for commando raids. It was ordered to prepare to attack some local anti-UAR tribesmen and had refused. Both UAR and Republican troops were rushed in to quell this mutiny, and during the turmoil, some of the Republican soldiers joined the rebels and turned on the Egyptians. A stalemate ensued. No further action was taken, but the Arabian Liberation Army was allowed to wither away.

Having made up his mind to withdraw from the Yemen, Nasser instigated peace talks by proxy, and at a conference of Arab Foreign Ministers held at Khartoum on 2nd August, he proposed that the Jedda Agreement of August 1965 should be put into operation, and that any difficulties should be referred to the arbitration of three Arab countries, one to be nominated by the UAR, one by Saudi Arabia and the other by the Conference. On the 8th, a Saudi Arabian spokesman said that King Faisal's conditions for a Yemeni settlement were the withdrawal of all UAR forces, and the ending of all military assistance to both Republicans and Royalists. It was also suggested that some sort of organization be set up to ensure these conditions were honoured. This response obviously suited Nasser, but not President as-Sallal, and on the 16th, as-Sallal said that the people of the Yemen would reject the Jedda Agreement, because they wanted a Republican regime and would have no other. On the 24th the Sudanese Premier, on a visit to Cairo, announced that Nasser had accepted the Sudanese proposals for ending the war in the Yemen, proposals which had already been approved by King Faisal. He added that Nasser and Faisal would meet in Khartoum to discuss details.

Prompted by the Israeli victory, the Khartoum Conference, held from 29th August to 1st September, was attended by Nasser, King Faisal, as-Sallal, other heads of Arab States and several ministers. At this conference Nasser virtually abandoned the Yemen, a course Field Marshal Amer (who committed 'suicide' on 15th September 1967) had been urging him to follow for years. UAR involvement in the Yemeni civil war had always been unpopular in Egypt, and at this critical period of his leader-

[1] Originally formed for the 'liberation' of South Arabia, it had since become more ambitious.

ship of his own country, Nasser wanted to cast off all drags and embarrassments that might add to his own unpopularity after the June defeat. He agreed to start withdrawing his remaining forces from the Yemen on 15th October, and to complete the evacuation by 15th December. King Faisal, for his part, said that he would stop military supplies to the Royalists. It has been suggested, and it may be true, that Nasser only intended to withdraw the bulk of his forces from the Yemen, retaining a foothold in the form of a small token force that could be reinforced when circumstances were more auspicious, but that King Faisal forced him to make a complete evacuation on pain of withholding a subsidy he and the Ruler of Kuwait had agreed to give Nasser to compensate for the loss of the Suez Canal dues. The Suez Canal had been blocked during the war with Israel, and had been made impassable to shipping.

On 31st August, the Sudanese Premier formally announced a UAR-Saudi Arabian agreement on the Yemen which would end direct aid and involvement. Since the breakdown of the Jedda agreement, King Faisal had been sending money, arms and supplies to the Royalists. Roundly denouncing what became known as the Khartoum Agreement, and insisting that it had been concluded over his head and without consultation, as-Sallal announced on 2nd September that his Government was not bound by it. He added that he had always been opposed to the Jedda Agreement, considering both Agreements to be an interference in Yemeni internal affairs. On the same day, in Beirut, Prince Hassan, the Royalist Premier, said that his Government would not be a party to any such proposals until all UAR Forces had withdrawn from the Yemen.

A Tripartite Committee was formed, consisting of Mohammed Ahmed Mahgoub the Sudanese Premier, Ismail Khairallah, Foreign Minister of Iraq, the country named by the UAR, and Ahmed Laraki, Foreign Minister of Morocco, the country named by Saudi Arabia. On 28th September the Tripartite Committee declared that its objective was to bring about a national coalition, and that it wanted a series of meetings with the various personalities concerned. It flew off to Beirut to see Mohammed al-Shami, the Royalist Foreign Minister, who insisted that when all UAR troops were withdrawn there should be a peace conference of at least two hundred Yemeni leaders of all denominations to choose a Council of Eight to govern the country until a plebiscite was held.

On 3rd October the Tripartite Committee went to Sana, but as-Sallal refused to meet its members although they lingered three days for this purpose. As-Sallal had tried to prevent the Committee from coming to the Yemen at all, but it had arrived in a UAR aircraft, under UAR protection. Its presence caused unrest in Sana. A wave of riots was instigated by Yemenis bitter at being deserted by the UAR, and about thirty Egyptians were killed. The Tripartite Committee reported the facts to Nasser and asked him to release his Yemeni detainees, most of whom favoured making peace with the Royalists. Hassan al-Amri was kept in Cairo, but most of his colleagues were released. Abdul Rahman Iryani flew straight to Sana, while Ahmed Numan went to Beirut, where the Royalist Foreign Minister was. The Committee went to Saudi Arabia where King Faisal endorsed the Royalist proposals, but it refused to visit either Imam Mohammed al-Badr or Prince Mohammed Hussein, the 'Deputy Imam'.

This time Nasser really meant what he said, and on 11th September the first large batch of UAR troops embarked at Hodeida for Egypt. On 6th October *Al Ahram*, the Cairo newspaper, reported that all civilian advisers and experts were being withdrawn as well. The last UAR soldiers pulled out of Taiz on the 10th and had completely evacuated Sana by the 16th. The last Egyptian troops, leaving from Hodeida, were clear of the Yemen by early December. On 12th October the Sudanese Premier confirmed that Saudi Arabian aid to the Royalists had ceased.

On 3rd October, the day the Tripartite Committee landed at Sana, a group of Yemeni army officers submitted a fifteen-point ultimatum to as-Sallal, demanding a new Cabinet, and condemning Government corruption and inefficiency. As-Sallal said he would accept it. The disturbances caused by the arrival of the Committee had been slow to subside, and there was pressure in the capital for Governmental changes to cope with the new situation. Worried about the future, and in particular about the loss of his cherished 3,000-strong UAR bodyguard, on 15th October as-Sallal reformed his Government, bringing in a few senior army officers in an effort to obtain the support of the

Yemeni armed forces. In addition to the offices of President and Premier, as-Sallal took on those of Foreign Affairs and Defence. A few supporters of Hassan al-Amri (who was still detained by Nasser in Cairo) were included in the Government, but Abdullah Jizailan, the former Deputy Premier, was dropped. It was said that by rejecting the demands for reconciliation put forward by the Yemeni politicians recently returned from Cairo detention, he lost what remaining support he had amongst the tribes, and because he would not listen to suggestions of peace talks with the Royalists many others turned away from him.

His Government reorganized, as-Sallal announced that he was about to visit Moscow, ostensibly to attend the fiftieth anniversary celebrations of the Soviet Union, but obviously to try and expedite any military aid Abdullah Jizailan had arranged. He left the Yemen on 3rd November, and on the way he stopped off at Cairo to see Nasser to enlist his support. Nasser was not pleased to see him, and bluntly refused to delay the evacuation of his Expeditionary Force, or to give any material assistance or encouragement. Nasser advised him to resign and go into exile. Stubbornly, as-Sallal rejected this advice and moved off towards the Soviet Union.

No sooner had as-Sallal left Cairo than Nasser sent an open message to his Commander-in-Chief in the Yemen, instructing him not to block any attempted *coup* should there be one. This was a more than sufficient hint for the discontented Yemeni army officers. On 5th November, tanks trundled into Liberation Square at Sana, and soldiers took over Government buildings and the radio station without a shot being fired. It seemed that as-Sallal did not have a single friend able or willing to stand up for him while he was abroad. The Yemeni High Command formally announced that as-Sallal was deposed, and in Iraq, where he had hoped to find support, as-Sallal sadly asked for and received political asylum.

CHAPTER ELEVEN

The Siege of Sana

MAIN EVENTS

1967	
November 5th	Presidential Council of Three formed. Moshin al-Aini becomes Premier.
13th	Cease-fire announced—not effective.
23rd	Ahmed Numan resigns from Presidential Council.
30th	British leave Aden.
December 1st	Siege of Sana begins.
18th	Hassan al-Amri appointed Premier.
23rd	Hassan al-Amri forms new Government.
1968	
January 12th	Beirut Conference.
22nd	Open support from South Yemen.
February 8th	Siege of Sana ends, after seventy days.
March 22nd	NLF plot against Hassan al-Amri discovered.
March	Saudi Arabian aid to Royalists ceased.
August	Fighting between Zeidi and Shafi army elements in Sana.
October	Royalist commander defects to Republicans.
December 15th	Hajja falls to the Republicans.
1969	
March	Prince Mohammed Hussein resigns as 'Deputy Imam'.
June and July	Secret Saudi Arabian contacts with the Republicans.
July 25th	Prince Abdullah Hassan murdered.
September 3rd	Sada falls to the Republicans.

As soon as as-Sallal's deposal had been announced on 5th November, Radio Sana announced that the country was to be governed by a three-man Presidential Council and a sixteen-man Cabinet. The Presidential Council was to consist of Abdul

Rahman Iryani, Ahmed Numan and Mohammed Othman, all three of whom had been detained in Cairo by Nasser at as-Sallal's behest, and all of whom were thought to be in favour of peace talks with the Royalists and the Saudi Arabians. Mohsin al-Aini became Premier, and the Government pledged itself to uphold the Republican constitution. The next day, Iryani said there would be discussions with Royalists and tribal leaders, and immediately called a conference of sheikhs, which, he promised, would be followed by negotiations with Royalists. He also released some 3,000 political prisoners. For the time being Ahmed Numan remained at Beirut instead of hurrying back to the Yemen as most of his colleagues had done.

King Faisal, who had officially stopped all aid to the Royalists,[1] persuaded Imam Mohammed al-Badr to agree in principle to negotiate with the Republican Government and to call a press conference to announce the fact. The Imam, now a sick man living almost permanently at Jedda and almost a stranger to his much-publicized mountain cave headquarters, went into Royalist-held territory in the Yemen to drum up support and to make his announcement in a dramatic setting. Once in the Yemen, however, he found that there was considerable opposition to this course, both from his commanders in the field and from the Zeidi tribesmen. The Royalist commanders felt that the time was just about ripe to close in for the kill. They pointed out that UAR troops were rapidly thinning out and would soon have been evacuated completely, taking with them their aircraft, tanks and guns, that several tribes and influential people, believing the Republican regime could not be maintained without Egyptian bayonets, were withdrawing support or changing sides, and that the so-called Third Force was disintegrating for the same opportunist reasons. Many of the Zeidi tribesmen in the mountains had come to look upon the war as a welcome source of arms and money. They neither wanted the war to end, nor the Imam to return with full authority to curb their brigandage.

Imam al-Badr found the field commanders in the Yemen, led and encouraged by Prince Mohammed Hussein, the 'Deputy

[1] According to many reports it seems doubtful whether Saudi Arabian aid to the Royalists ever did cease completely, although in November and December 1967 it was certainly severely cut down.

Imam', determined to mount an offensive against Sana as soon as they could. Depressed and alarmed, Mohammed al-Badr hurriedly returned to Saudi Arabia without holding his intended press conference. This incident perhaps marks more significantly than anything else the Imam's loss of direct influence over the course of the war, and the crucial weakening of his authority.

Although a cease-fire was announced on 13th November, when both sides paused and a number of Republican sheikhs met Royalist leaders near Sana, it was only the calm before the storm and an opportunity for some unofficial local agreements to be made between UAR detachment commanders and Yemenis to allow the Egyptians to withdraw unhindered. On 23rd November Ahmed Numan, still an absentee, resigned from the Presidential Council because he said the Republican Government had made no attempt to hold the promised peace talks but was in fact preparing to re-start hostilities. The Republican leaders, headed by Abdul Rahman Iryani and mostly of moderate persuasion, seemed at a loss to know what to do when the Royalist offensive suddenly hit them in the last days of the month.

Certain that this was the vital moment to strike the final blow, Prince Mohammed Hussein had mustered all the 'regulars' available and rallied several thousand tribesmen to march upon, encircle and crush Sana. He boasted that he had about 5,000 'trained' soldiers and some 50,000 tribal warriors and while these numbers may have been exaggerated, he certainly commanded the largest force the Royalists had ever succeeded in mustering for battle. Sana was a prestige prize for the Royalist commanders, while the prospect of sacking the capital was a magnet to attract the tribesmen. The Royalist forces had plenty of small arms and mortars, as well as a few guns, and the more complicated weapons were handled by mercenaries, reputed to number over 300, both European and Arab. As the UAR soldiers departed, so the Royalists closed in around Sana, until on 1st December they succeeded in blocking all the roads leading from the capital. Thus started what became an epic seventy-day siege.

During the early part of December, the Royalists ringing Sana crept nearer until they were ensconced on the mountains surrounding the city, from where they were able to lob mortar bombs and artillery shells down on to the defenders. In fact, this was not as serious as it might have been, in that every bomb and shell had to be carried by a mule or a man for many miles over extremely difficult terrain. This severely curtailed Prince Mohammed Hussein's ammunition supply, at a time when Saudi Arabian military aid had certainly slackened if not actually ceased altogether. Presumably most of the heavy ammunition that arrived outside Sana was held in reserve for a final offensive, but the bombardment did make the large Soviet-built airport, some twelve miles to the north of Sana, untenable for Republican aircraft, which had to use the smaller airstrip to the south-west of the city. Most foreigners hastily left the capital. They had little confidence in the ability of the Republican forces to hold it, and soon only a handful of Soviet and Chinese experts remained. Cut off by land, ringed by hostile tribesmen daily moving closer, and garrisoned by only about 3,000 Republican soldiers, the fate of Sana was beginning to look very precarious indeed, when on to this depressing scene came Hassan al-Amri, just released from detention in Cairo.

Hard-headed and ruthless, Hassan al-Amri was just the strong man required to deal with such a desperate situation, and he had immediately flown into Sana to take charge of its defences. Having already taken Ahmed Numan's place on the Presidential Council, on 18th December he was appointed Premier and Commander-in-Chief of the armed forces. Mohsin al-Aini, who had tried unsuccessfully to prevent tribes switching their allegiance to the Royalists, resigned. Hassan al-Amri set about improving the ill-trained and ill-equipped Yemeni army, which still only numbered about 7,000 soldiers, less than half of whom were in Sana. Nasser had vaguely promised to pay about £100,000 a month towards its upkeep until June 1968, but this was hardly enough and the source was unreliable, so al-Amri sought direct aid from the Soviet Union, sending Hassan Mekki, the Foreign Minister, off to Moscow. As the Soviet Union had no wish to see the Royalists in power again in the Yemen, or Sana to be snatched from Republican hands, it quickly arranged for a supply of arms to be sent, as well as a few aircraft. December was the month of Ramadan, when no food is eaten by Moslems during daylight. This tended to dampen down military ardour and restrict operations, and it prevented Prince Mohammed Hussein mounting an all-out assault on the city while its defences were weak and disorganized. By the time Ramadan was over, and the tribesmen spoiling for a fight, Hassan al-Amri had strengthened Sana, so that the one really big Royalist opportunity to seize the capital by force of arms was missed.

In Sana, Hassan al-Amri took on the powers of a military dictator. He ordered a curfew, regimented the citizens, destroyed buildings that obstructed fields of fire and inspired resolution in the defenders. Several 'traitors' were publicly shot and their bodies exhibited as an example. Having no illusions as to what their fate would be if the mountain warriors broke through the defences the citizens supported al-Amri and co-operated. They knew their very survival depended upon the success of his measures. Taking an unusual step, Hassan al-Amri mobilized most of the citizens into a sort of militia, issuing them with arms that began to arrive from the Soviet Union in late December. This militia became known as the Popular Resistance Force, the PRF, which spread to Ṭaiz and Hodeida and other parts of Republican territory. The populace was formed into small units, to supplement the tiny, scattered regular detachments, and given some elementary training in the use of the basic arms they were issued with, so that some effective resistance could be put up in the event of a Royalist attack. A few Soviet aircraft arrived in December, and these gave the Republican defenders a slight military advantage since the Royalists still had no air force. One MiG with a Soviet pilot was shot down by the Royalists, after which the Soviet aircraft were piloted by Arab mercenaries instead.

To press home this advantage, on 27th December Hassan al-Amri formed a new Government, including more military members, to step up the war against the Royalists and to stiffen the defences of besieged Sana. More Soviet arms arrived, enabling him to give rifles, grenades and explosives to the PRF, which soon numbered over 10,000 members in the capital alone. The elements of the regular army held the various positions outside the city walls, including the towering Jebel Nuqum, while the defence of Sana itself was completely entrusted to the PRF. Hassan al-Amri reckoned that it would put up desperate last-ditch resistance should the Royalist tribesmen ever break through.

Ramadan over, the real struggle for Sana began in January

1968, but although there was skirmishing on the outskirts of the city, the tribesmen did not often venture down from their mountains. Such forays as were made were carried out by the Royalist 'regulars', who invaded the complex of buildings that contained the Chinese textile factory, but were later driven out. On other occasions they assaulted and took outlying defensive positions, some of which changed hands more than once.

The roads leading from Sana remained firmly blocked, and during January the Republican defenders made three separate major attempts to break the restrictive ring. The first and largest such battle, in the first week of the month, dissolved in chaos, when a strong force of Republican soldiers, PRF militia and tribesmen loyal to the Republican Government, moved out to clear the road through to Taiz, only to run head-on into ambush a few miles from Sana. Confused fighting ensued in which soldiers, militia and tribesmen changed sides. Some 3,000 casualties were incurred by both sides in this prolonged struggle in mountain defiles where everyone seemed to be firing on everyone else. On the 9th, Hassan al-Amri appealed to his army officers who had defected to return to their units where all would be forgiven and forgotten, which confirmed the scale of the subsequent desertions from the Republican side. The other two big attempts to break the besieging circle were also in January, but both failed and resulted in more casualties and further defections.

Although the siege remained unbroken the defenders were able to hold out. The city was able to feed itself meagrely from nearby farms, fields and gardens, within the large valley in which Sana lay, and the Royalists were unable to prevent supplies being brought in by aircraft. As the first flush of enthusiasm faded, Prince Mohammed Hussein was beset by anxieties and doubts. His mountain followers clearly did not relish positional warfare, and had showed up poorly in such impromptu forays as they had engaged in against the defenders. They simply wanted to sit back on the heights around the capital, waiting like vultures for someone else to do the breaching of the defences, or else for starvation to take effect.

The Prince knew that even if he could persuade the tribesmen to assault across the wide open spaces between the base of the mountains and the city walls, which he doubted, such an advance would be halted by mass slaughter, as the defenders now had ample arms, ammunition and aircraft. The virtual destruction of their military organization and army, such as they were, would be an irremediable disaster for the Royalists. Even if the tribesmen got into the city, perhaps under cover of darkness or by treachery, they would have to face an armed citizenry that would fight desperately for their homes and lives, with the arms that Hassan al-Amri had issued out. It would no longer be the case, as in 1948, of killing and robbing unarmed defenceless people. As profitless days passed, dissensions arose between the tribes which worsened as each waited for the others to make the assault and take the casualties so that they could swiftly slip past them to plunder the city. Prince Mohammed Hussein was not able to produce enough money or arms to tempt the tribes to mount an attack, or even to persuade some of them to remain with his besieging force. Many slipped away to their homes, and by the end of January his numbers were considerably depleted.

The Royalist 'regulars' made several raids on outposts, set up ambushes and were involved in a certain amount of skirmishing, but these activities did not amount to much, although exaggerated and conflicting claims of victories achieved, casualties inflicted and booty captured, were issued by both sides. About thirty Soviet aircraft reached the Yemen in January, mostly flown by Yemeni pilots who had been training in the Soviet Union. These enabled Hassan al-Amri to hit back at the tribesmen exposed on the mountain ridges, who withdrew to more sheltered positions or melted away altogether. Soviet instructors were busy training more Yemeni pilots at airfields near Hodeida. Additionally, the Republicans were strengthened by support given by the National Liberation Front (the NLF) and a detachment of more than 600 NLF fighters arrived to take part in the defence of Sana.

While the battle for Sana was in progress, a new and powerful influence was appearing in Republican territory. The NLF had been formed in the Yemen sometime in the summer of 1963 under the leadership of Qahtan Mohammed al-Shaabi to fight against the British in the Federation of South Arabia. After stirring up unrest in the Radfan in 1964 and gaining considerable up-country influence, it moved as a terrorist organization into Aden, where it worked for a while with the Front for the Liberation of Occupied South Yemen, FLOSY, the UAR-sponsored organization which at one stage had three large training camps near Taiz. FLOSY was under Nasser's domination while the NLF was more nationalistic and independent, although it did not scorn to accept Egyptian aid. Differences soon arose, and in December 1966 the NLF severed its liaison and co-operation with FLOSY and formed its own fourteen-man executive. As the British occupation drew to a close in Aden, it embarked upon a deliberate campaign of assassination of key FLOSY personnel, which gave it ascendency and enabled it to become the *de facto* government when the last British troops left on 30th November 1967. Mohammed al-Shaabi became the President of what became known as South Yemen, FLOSY had been completely eclipsed and the former British-sponsored Federation leaders driven out to take refuge in Saudi Arabia.

On 22nd January 1968, President al-Shaabi of South Yemen, a country not recognized by King Faisal, came out openly in support of the Yemeni Republican Government, and despatched detachments of NLF fighters to help it in its fight against the Royalists. The NLF, considering itself to be an Arab movement not bound by artificial and 'temporary' boundaries, declared that it was against any negotiations with the Royalists at all, and only approved a separate, limited agreement with certain northern Zeidi tribes. The political aim of the NLF was eventual domination of all southern Arabia, including the oil-rich territories of the Persian Gulf. In training camps it had occupied near Hodeida and Taiz under UAR auspices, the NLF expanded and took a leading part in organizing the new PRF militia that was being formed in the Yemen for defence against possible Royalist attacks. President al-Shaabi's announcement that his country was fully in accord and sympathy with Republican Yemen was demonstrated in a practical way in February when two units of the South Yemen army, elements of the NLF militia, and a detachment of the Republican army, combined to attack Royalist tribesmen on the frontiers of Beihan State, and at other points along the joint border.

Meanwhile, at Hodeida, a strong Republican relief column had formed which included many armoured vehicles and guns. Under the cover of aircraft, it forced its way along the road towards the capital and fought a battle on the outskirts which broke the Royalist cordon. This breakthrough occurred on 8th February 1968, to end the seventy-day siege of Sana. The organization, conduct and efficiency of this relieving force had a lot to do with the assistance and planning of Soviet and other foreign supporters. For example, it was accompanied by Chinese personnel, who repaired the road as it moved forward and erected a vital bridge near the capital which allowed the armour to cross a ravine and take part in the fighting outside the city.

True, many tribesmen remained in the surrounding mountains, thwarted but hostile, and Prince Mohammed Hussein stayed at his field headquarters less than twelve miles from the capital, but with the aid of aircraft, armour and guns, the remaining roads from the city were opened one by one and Republican influence began to spread out around Sana once more. Clearly, the Royalists had missed their one big chance of seizing Sana, and once again the dreary, familiar stalemate that neither side could break settled between the combatants.

Meanwhile, the Tripartite Committee had met in Cairo on 30th December 1967, to arrange what became known as the Beirut Conference, which assembled on 12th January. This was a hopeless failure from the start, as not only did Republicans refuse to speak to Royalists but they quarrelled bitterly amongst themselves. Radio Sana declared that if Ahmed Numan, who was at the conference, did not stop indulging in anti-Republican propaganda, he would face trial for treason. Alarmed and worried about the extent of Soviet intervention in the Yemen, King Faisal threatened to renounce the Khartoum Agreement, and his $50 million subsidy for Suez Canal losses to the UAR hung in the balance for a while, as Nasser broke the propaganda truce by upholding the right of the Republican Government to seek outside aid.[1] Prince Abdul Rahman, leader of the Royalist Delegation to the Beirut Conference, said that his side would not stop fighting until Soviet aid ceased and Soviet technicians were withdrawn. Abdul Rahman Baidani, the Republican spokesman, accused King Faisal of bad faith, claiming that although the UAR troops had been withdrawn from the Yemen,

[1] It is believed that early in January 1968, Mr. Brezhnev, the Soviet Communist Party Secretary, postponed a visit to Cairo because he did not wish to be in the UAR when (as was then hourly expected) Sana fell to the Royalists.

the King was continuing to send military supplies to the Royalists. It seemed as though everything was back where it had been a few brief months before, with the same political divisions, the same conflicting arguments, the same factional squabbles, the same personal hatreds and total military stalemate.

Once it was seen that Sana was not going to fall and the Royalists were not going to sweep into Republican territory with fire and sword, Republican leaders and their supporters recovered some of their former confidence. They saw Soviet arms arriving, the Yemeni army expanding and becoming more efficient, and Soviet technicians taking the places of the departed Egyptians. Hassan al-Amri began to have suspicions about the loyalty of certain elements of the PRF militia, feeling that the independent-minded NLF was obtaining far too much control of it. To counterbalance this he encouraged the shattered FLOSY to become active again in the Yemen, a course that at once made him unpopular with the NLF.

Once the Sana situation had been stabilized, Hassan al-Amri made arrangements to visit both the UAR and China, and indeed he flew off to Cairo. But he must have been alerted to trouble at home as, without visiting Peking, he suddenly returned in time to foil a NLF plot to seize a large consignment of Soviet arms, including fifty tanks, that was being landed at Hodeida. There was a scuffle between al-Amri's Government troops and NLF elements of the PRF, which was won by the Yemeni regular soldiers. Many NLF and left-wing PRF members were arrested, but most were later released, as they were all Shafeis, to try and avoid exacerbating religious friction within the country. In South Yemen, President al-Shaabi was also having trouble with extremist NLF members, where differences between the army, which was British-trained, moderate and religious, and the NLF leaders, were widening. On 20th March, the army arrested many NLF members to forestall the extremists from seizing power, now that they had mustered several thousand active supporters. Government purges followed, and although President al-Shaabi seemed to emerge with greater authority than before, parts of South Yemen remained in extremist NLF hands, and there were revolts and dissidence throughout the year in that newly-emergent country. Hassan al-Amri's crackdown on the NLF in the Yemen and the permitted anti-NLF activities of

Abdullah Asnag, the leader of FLOSY, allowed to operate from Taiz, caused relations with South Yemen to cool off, and talks held between representatives of both countries did not seem to ease the situation although both professed that their ideals were in accord. The Russians also tried hard to bring about a reconciliation between the NLF and FLOSY, but animosity grew.[1]

By mid-1968, the Republicans, with Abdul Rahman Iryani as Provisional President and Chairman of the Presidential Council, and Hassan al-Amri as Premier and Commander-in-Chief of the armed forces, had again consolidated their hold on roughly half the country, including Sana, Taiz, Hodeida and most of the south and the coastal plain. Considerable material and technical assistance had been given by the Soviet Union, and the Yemeni regular army, which had risen to a strength of about 10,000 men, was better equipped and trained than it had ever been during UAR involvement. It seemed quite capable of holding Republican territory against anything the Royalists could muster to fight it. Hassan al-Amri was proving to be a firm but moderate ruler, who although single-minded and ruthless, did not generate such extremes of hatred and dislike as as-Sallal.

The apparent security of military stalemate provided a shield behind which factional differences bubbled to the surface again. Sheikh Abdullah al-Ahmer, paramount chief of the Hashid federation, and many other sheikhs, were either back in the Republican fold or on liaison terms with the Republican Government once more, but they all had cautious reservations, and signs of an emergent Third Force could again be seen. Religion again became an issue which could set Zeidis and Shafeis against each other. During the last week in August, for example, disturbances in Sana followed the appointment of a Zeidi officer as Chief of Staff, and the allegation that a *coup* organized by the commander of the Sana garrison, who was a Shafi, had been forestalled. Generally, the Shafeis complained that Zeidis were getting the top army jobs and the best government posts—the old pattern of disagreement was repeating itself on the Republi-

[1] In July 1968, FLOSY, which from its base at Taiz had been instigating trouble in the interior of South Yemen, formed a new Revolutionary Command, which did not include Abdullah Asnag, considered to be too much of a moderate.

can side. Politically, the rising influence of FLOSY neutralized that of the NLF to some extent, making them less potentially dangerous to the regime.

In March (1968) Saudi Arabian aid to the Royalists had finally stopped altogether, severely limiting the striking power of the Royalist commanders in the field. Without money, arms and ammunition to use as bribes and rewards, they were reduced to encouraging brigandage against Republican forces and sympathizers. Their 'armies' dwindled at an alarming rate until they were left with only a handful of armed retainers to act as their bodyguard. Their presence was often no more than tolerated by some of the tribes who gave spiritual allegiance to the Imam. With no illusions as to their fate should they be captured or give themselves up, the 'fighting princes' began to leave the Yemen one by one, while those who remained lived in distinctly straitened circumstances, and sometimes on the charity of the local inhabitants when they were not strong enough forcibly to collect taxes to maintain themselves and their bodyguard.

Soon the senior remaining Prince in the Yemen was Prince Abdullah Hassan, the Minister of the Interior and former commander of the Khawlan Front. He lived at Sada, which was still held by the Royalists who had gained that city by trickery earlier in the year when the Siege of Sana was at its height. Non-Royalist commanders did not have the same threat hanging over their heads, and a few were encouraged by the Republicans to change sides. A notable defection was that of Qassem bin Monasser in October, who also persuaded some Royalist tribes to change their allegiance. His example was followed at intervals by others of lesser rank.

By the end of 1968 all foreign mercenaries, Arab and Western, had left the Royalist camp, and the military framework they had helped to bring into existence began to fall apart. The commanders quarrelled amongst themselves, as money dried up and manpower faded away. The only fighting of any note that occurred in this year, apart from the Siege of Sana, happened in November and December when the Republicans sent a strong column to attack the Royalist-held city of Hajja, which fell to them on 15th December.

The Royalist leaders continued to quarrel bitterly, and in his struggle to retain power and their loyalty, the Imam came into direct conflict with Prince Mohammed Hussein, who had openly taken to styling himself the 'Deputy Imam'. Sick though he was, Imam Mohammed al-Badr won. In March 1969, Prince Mohammed Hussein resigned his position of the Imamic Council, and abruptly deserted the Royalist cause.

The façade of Royalist unity and optimism was now rapidly falling apart, and taking advantage of this, during June and July, Saudi Arabian officials made secret contacts with the Republican Government and Third Force personalities. On 25th July, Prince Abdullah Hassan, the senior remaining Royal Prince in the Yemen, was murdered at Sada. The assassin was never identified, but as the Prince was involved in quarrelling with other Royalist commanders, and intriguing with the Saudi Arabians, and was suspected of being about to come to terms with the Republican Government, the field of suspicion was a wide one. Following this incident, squabbling broke out in Sada. Hassan al-Amri took advantage of this and sent a strong force to attack the city, which fell to the Republicans on 3rd September, after which the fighting again subsided.

As the immediate Royalist military threat began to evaporate, Abdul Rahman Iryani, the President, and Hassan al-Amri, the Premier, consolidated their regime. Their policy was to avoid deliberately antagonizing Saudi Arabia, which noted the volume of Soviet arms and personnel pouring into the Yemen and accused it of becoming a Soviet satellite. In an effort to reduce dependence on Eastern Bloc countries, the Republican Government sought friendship and aid from the West to counterbalance this. It was moderately successful in its approaches to Western Germany, which resumed diplomatic relations with the Yemen and promised aid to the amount of £1·5 million, to be used for improving Sana airport, for road-building and irrigation schemes, and for setting up a national telephone system. In August, a start was made on constructing a new, motorable road from Sana to Sada. However, efforts to obtain British and American recognition continued to be unsuccessful, as were overtures to several other Western countries.

After eight years of civil war in the Yemen the situation remains uneasy. The military stalemate remains, with the Republicans holding just over half the country, and those with anti-Republican or Royalist inclinations the rest. Both have the capability to hold on to their territory for a long time to come. The Republicans do not have the military means to conquer the Zeidi tribes to the north and east of Sana, and these tribes in their turn do not have the facilities for carrying out more than nuisance tactics. The civil war in the Yemen has apparently subsided and spent itself, but in fact the antagonism is endemic and will continue. It is the heritage of centuries of violence, prejudice and hate.

APPENDIX I

Personalities

Of the several prominent characters involved in the war in the Yemen perhaps the best known and most disliked in the West is Gamel Abdul Nasser, President of the United Arab Republic, whose ambitions, evolving from his grandiose dream of the 'Three Circles', centred on Cairo, of pan-Arab, pan-Islamic and pan-African empires, led him to try and swallow up the Yemen as soon as he could. His diplomatic ability and his military failures are well known, and there is little need to enlarge upon them. Briefly, his dominant ambitions are ruthlessly pushed forward all the time, and in the Yemen his promises were never meant to be kept, as he anticipated that his bad faith would bring him advantages.

Nasser went into the Yemen without any clear idea of what was involved. He embarked on a strategy that was not based upon reasoned fact, and he became impatient when the fighting bogged down in 1963. Visiting the country for the first time in April 1964, he re-organized its government and instigated military operations, and it was only when he realized that there was no quick military solution that he switched to negotiation. He was about to cut his military losses and pull out of the Yemen, but changed his mind when the British Government announced its intention of early withdrawal from the Federation of South Arabia. The temptation to step into and exploit the power vacuum was too great, so he retained his Expeditionary Force in the Yemen but streamlined it and re-orientated it to face southwards. Had he not suffered a crushing defeat by the Israelis, the UAR military presence would no doubt still be in the Yemen.

Nasser intended the Yemen to be his puppet state and kept as firm a grip over its governments as he could, supporting, removing or forcibly detaining Yemeni politicians to this end. He seized all foreign aid meant for the Yemen and used it largely to defray the costs of his Expeditionary Force, merely doling out a little now and then to the Yemenis as a bait or minor reward for subservience. The small, ill-armed and ill-trained Yemeni army was deliberately starved. He had no intention of allowing it to develop into a competent force with high morale, in case it became nationalistically independent and a danger to his plans. Nasser has only reluctantly removed himself from Yemeni affairs and there can be little doubt that he will return to them as soon as he can, assuming that he is able to settle some of his other urgent troubles. Certainly it cannot be concluded that the Yemen, or Arabia, has seen the last of him.

The other rather sinister protagonist in recent Yemeni affairs is Colonel Abdullah as-Sallal, founder and recently President of the Yemeni Arab Republic, who kept returning to the fore regardless of unpopularity, set-backs and periodical dismissals by Nasser. Unloved and unlovable, as-Sallal's inability to bend even slightly with the wind, to be human at times, to charm individuals and to assess the swing of public opinion, cost him many friends and admirers he may have had, and, ultimately, his position. For a long time he was the focal point of the Revolution and the Republic, and many rallied to him for this reason, believing him to be sincere and honest in his purpose, and prepared to overlook his less attractive traits. That he was cruel and merciless and an accomplished intriguer, all traditional Yemeni characteristics, did not worry his supporters. It was his sheep-like acceptance of Nasser's domination, despite its adverse effect on the country and the people, his failure to get on with moderate Republicans, his implacable refusal to talk peace with the Royalists or the Saudi Arabians, his huge UAR bodyguard, and his lack of success in persuading Nasser to allow foreign aid to reach the Yemen direct, that caused his glamour to fade and be gradually replaced with disillusionment, dislike, contempt and finally hatred.

When Nasser no longer had any use for him, as-Sallal was ruthlessly discarded, and when he would not accept Nasser's advice to resign and go into exile, Nasser caused him to be overthrown. Now just another exiled Arab revolutionary figure, as-Sallal sits in Iraq, watching and waiting. His chances of again taking a prominent part in Yemeni affairs are slim. He has no strong personal following and many enemies, while his rigid revolutionary doctrines are unpalatable for the practical moderates now in power. But it should not be forgotten that he has been out of office before and has made come-backs, although of course always with Nasser's support, so he cannot be dismissed completely from the Yemeni scene, especially while Nasser is capable of probing into the Yemen once more and requiring a compliant stooge. As the revolutionary leader who initially established the Republic his place in its history books is assured, whatever his enemies may say, but meanwhile he is a live, brooding figure, potentially dangerous to many in the Yemen.

Perhaps the only Republican personality who has tended to be constantly underrated is Hassan al-Amri, who emerged as the 'strong man' and victor of the seventy-day Siege of Sana. A Yemeni army officer, who accompanied Mohammed al-Badr, then crown Prince, on his trip to London in November 1957, al-Amri was one of the original plotters of the Republic. He became a senior minister in the first as-Sallal Government, and then stepped quickly up to become Vice-President, when Abdul Rahman Baidani was dropped early in 1963, in which capacity he acted on several occasions as Head of State during as-Sallal's absences abroad. Al-Amri formed a Government after Ahmed Numan resigned in July 1965, and remained in control while as-Sallal was detained in Cairo for a year. He too, in turn, was arrested by Nasser in September 1966, and kept in detention until released in December 1967, just in time to take charge and pull the Yemen through a very critical period. Hassan al-Amri is now regarded as a moderate. He seems to get on with most of his colleagues, and as an experienced army general and administrator, by Yemeni standards, he will have a stabilizing effect on the Republic if he remains in power, or near the seat of power.

Initially pro-Nasser and pro-Egyptian, Hassan al-Amri gradually changed his views. The turning-point came in 1966, when Nasser refused to release Yemeni deposits and credits held in UAR banks, tried to prevent him from seeing Mr. Kosygin in Cairo, and would not allow him to take up the Soviet offer to arm and equip a Yemeni army of 18,000 men or let him take a delivery of armoured cars which al-Amri had ordered direct from East Germany. With firm Republican principles, al-Amri is dedicated to supporting the Republic and is opposed to the restoration of the Imamate in any form. He has welcomed Soviet assistance to replace that formerly provided by Nasser. Once his friend and supporter, Hassan al-Amri turned against as-Sallal and indeed tried to prevent as-Sallal's return by force in August 1966, so it is unlikely that there would be any future collaboration between the two.

The other personalities on the Republican side, such as Abdul Rahman Iryani, Ahmed Numan, Mohsin al-Aini, Mohammed Othman, Hassan Mekki, Hamoud al-Jaifi, Abdullah Jizailan and many others mentioned in this account have been mellowed by the experience of being in and out of government since 1962, an experience which has brought caution and a developing sense of nationalism. While all most probably would co-operate with the Soviet Union, or even the UAR again, to obtain material assistance, it is doubtful whether any would willingly revert to the former subservient position under Nasser's domination. This means that the chances of a responsible, moderate, Republican Government continuing to hold office are good, and this is something which will obviously make for stability and perhaps even prosperity in the Yemen.

APPENDIX II

Forces

Despite an infusion of modern Soviet weapons and the presence of a Soviet military training mission, the Yemeni regular army, now with a probable strength of about 11,000, is still relatively untrained, and its officer corps needs building up. Moreover, the army is rent by the Shafi-Zeidi dispute, which erupted in open fighting between the two factions in Sana in August 1968. Its composition is not exactly known, but there is now a large ratio of Shafeis in the ranks, although the officer corps is still predominantly Zeidi. The army possesses at least 100 armoured vehicles, over 200 guns and about 40 Soviet aircraft. A military committee, with Hassan al-Amri as Chairman, has been working on a plan to reorganize the armed forces. They will now have to be given technical training to enable them to handle the more sophisticated weapons that are being received from the Soviet Union. Soviet instructors will make a far better job of developing the Yemeni army than did the Egyptians. The successful defence of Sana raised morale considerably and gave younger officers confidence in themselves—so much so, in fact, that they may band together to force the pace in the Yemen, and may even try and overthrow or override the more cautious Republican leaders.

The Popular Resistance Force militia, hastily formed in the desperate days after the UAR withdrawal, now has a reported strength of over 40,000. Given some political instruction, in an attempt to model it on the militia of Mao Tse-tung, it is armed at a very elementary level with whatever can be spared, and possesses a mixture of old rifles, grenades and explosives. Its primary purpose is to defend Republican territory against the Royalists. A few 'commando' units have been raised, and some fought at the Siege of Sana, but this emphasis has been slackened as there are doubts as to the political reliability of certain elements of the PRF.

Expanding from Taiz, once Britain pulled out from the Federation of South Arabia, the NLF raised and motivated a large section of the PRF. At one stage it was thought that the NLF might sponsor a 'break-away' Shafi federation, as its leaders fell out of sympathy with Hassan al-Amri and his predominantly Zeidi Government. To counteract this, Hassan al-Amri encouraged the re-emergence of FLOSY, which was also working to gain control over as much of the PRF as it could. However, FLOSY is entirely Shafi and so may not be keen fully to support al-Amri and his Zeidi colleagues unless their attitude towards the Shafeis is modified considerably. One can perhaps forecast that there will be more schisms within the PRF as the Government, the NLF and FLOSY struggle for domination. The counter-balance, upon which the Republican Government must rely heavily, is a strong, well-armed, well-trained and disciplined regular army which is loyal to it. There is still some way to go before this becomes an accomplished fact.

It should be remembered that the Yemen is still basically a backward tribal society, although the impact of the war has brought about certain changes. The main one is that the strict authority formerly wielded by the sheikh and the tribal elders over their tribesmen has been weakened. The appearance of roads and vehicles in Republican territory has given the younger men a mobility they never had before, which has enabled them to leave their tribes and visit the cities and towns. Previously, even to wander into another tribal area was to invite capture or death. In the cities the tribesmen saw bright lights, cafés, cinemas and shops full of transistors and luxury goods, and they were able to listen to startling revolutionary concepts. Many did not return home, and the cities became overcrowded, but those who did go back took with them new, unsettling attitudes, and were no longer meekly acquiescent to the demands of their sheikhs. Also, the power of the Seiyids, those who claimed descent from the Prophet, demanded special privileges, and under the Imams had developed into a rapacious class of petty government officials, had been broken completely.

There is greater freedom of thought in the country and a general questioning of tradition. While the Egyptians were not liked, their ideas were listened to and their way of life examined. 'The Voice of the Arabs' from Cairo led many to become discontented with conventional restrictions. This was especially so in Shafi territory, where Shafeis were anxious to cast off Zeidi domination. Under the cloak of UAR occupation, the Shafeis developed politically much faster than did the Zeidis, and soon began to feel themselves to be as good as, and then better than, backward Zeidis. The Shafeis, who form at least half the population of the Yemen, are fully committed to some form of Republican regime, and would not tolerate the return of the Imam under any circumstances. Even now they are agitating for a larger share in the Government and for greater representation in the senior ranks of the civil service and the army. The possibility of a wholesale national movement arising to encompass all the southern part of the Yemen cannot be overlooked.

While the war brought a certain amount of mobility to the Zeidi tribesmen also, it has not affected them nearly so much as it has the Shafeis, although many Zeidis and Zeidi tribes have come over to the Republican side and absorbed as a result a measure of relaxation from primitive tradition. Those who assumed that all Zeidis would automatically rally to the Imam, who was their acknowledged religious head, overlooked the fact that the Zeidi tribes are a disunited, restless assembly of small groups, riddled with suspicions and hatreds. Intrigue and treachery have been endemic for centuries, and each continues to play the other at its own game. Until firm government is imposed, these tendencies will no doubt remain—certainly as long as each tribe is autonomous in its own valley. It was because of this that the Royalists had a distinct lack of success in forming a standing army, or persuading the tribesmen to come under orders and fight to a set, operational plan.

Soviet policy of seeking to penetrate into the Middle East to thwart American and Western interests there, means that the Russians have now replaced the Egyptians in the Yemen. This clearly marks a new phase of events in Arabia. Soviet economic and material aid is being given to the country, Soviet arms and equipment are being supplied to the Yemeni army, a large Soviet Military Mission is now back at Sana, and Soviet instructors and technicians are busily at work. The ultimate Soviet aim is to instigate revolt in Saudi Arabia, to reinforce its toe-hold in

South Yemen and to wield paramount influence in the Persian Gulf area when Britain withdraws. It cannot be overlooked that the Soviet Union wants naval bases and naval facilities at both Hodeida and Aden, and is working hard to obtain them. The Soviet Union is desperately anxious to have the Suez Canal reopened and may provoke another UAR-Israel war, in which the final outcome may well differ from that of June 1967.

The influence of the NLF should not be underrated, and although Hassan al-Amri has temporarily checked its growth in the Yemen, the Republican Government may yet have to come to terms with it. Having once defeated its UAR-sponsored rival, FLOSY, in the Federation of South Arabia (now South Yemen), the NLF may be tempted to try and seize power in the Yemen in a similar way. Hassan al-Amri had a dispute with his newly-emergent neighbour to the south, whose President, Qahtan al-Shaabi, rode to power on the NLF organization. He is still the nominal head of the NLF, and must have considerable influence within it. Although President Qahtan al-Shaabi has his own internal problems, he will be prepared to look eastwards and northwards, as the NLF visualizes a united Arabia under its domination.

A final reflection must be that the Middle East remains inherently unstable and that it comes as no great shock to wake up any morning and hear that this or that Arab state has had a revolution or a violent change of government. It cannot be ruled out, for example, that King Faisal may fall, in which case there might be widespread repercussions, or that Nasser's troops have once more entered the Yemen, or that as-Sallal has returned to power, or that the NLF has usurped the Republican Government at Sana, or that a Shafi confederation has declared its independence. In any of these eventualities the smouldering civil war would be given a new twist and be fought with temporarily renewed vigour.

Index

Index

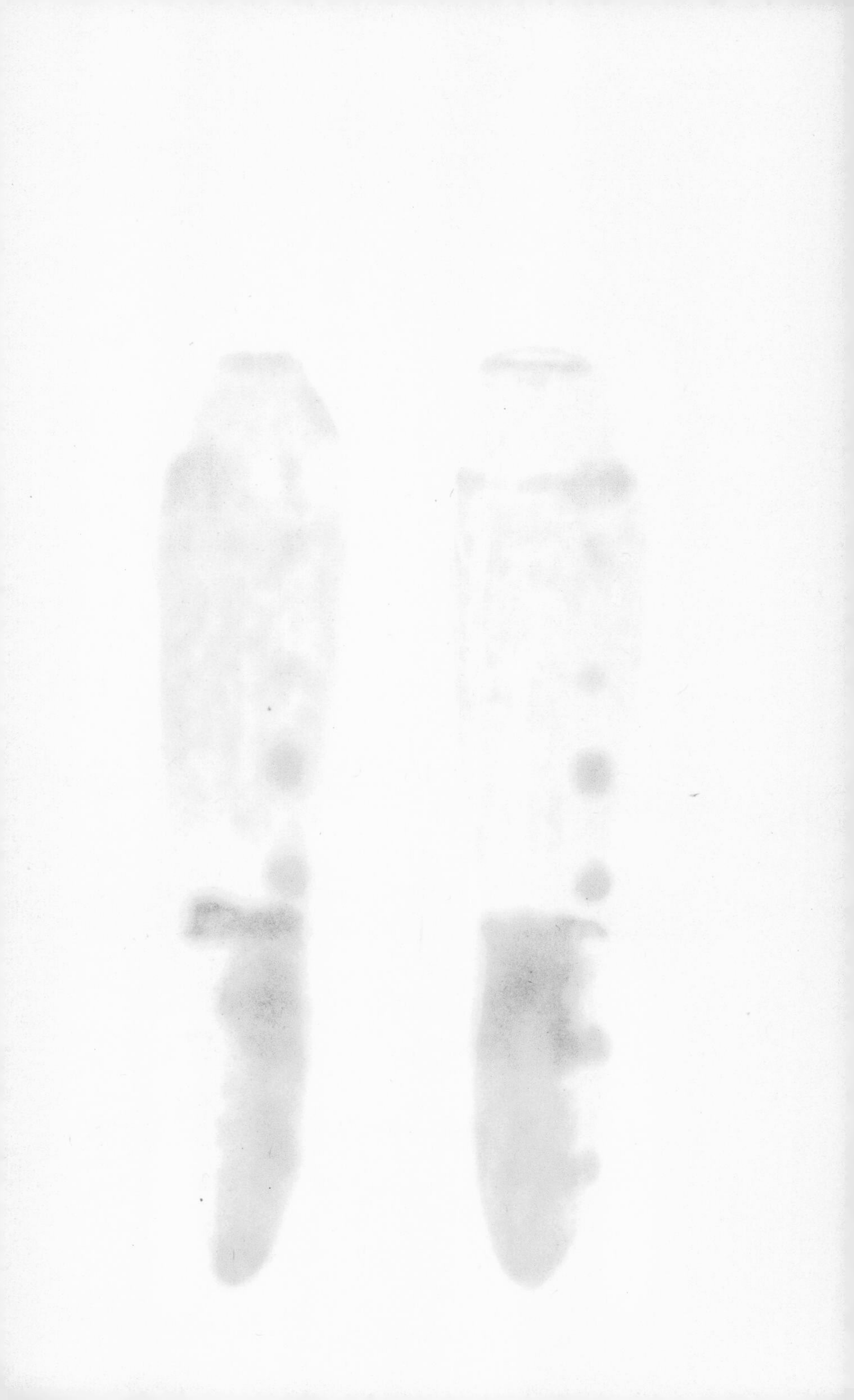